SUCCESS IN GRADUATE SCHOOL AND BEYOND

T0366543

SUCCESS

IN GRADUATE SCHOOL AND BEYOND

A Guide for STEM Students and Postdoctoral Fellows

Nana Lee and Reinhart Reithmeier • Illustrated by Nikko Torres

UNIVERSITY OF TORONTO PRESS

Toronto Buffalo London

© University of Toronto Press 2024
Toronto Buffalo London
utorontopress.com
Printed and bound by CPI Group (UK) Ltd, Croydon, CR0 4YY

ISBN 978-1-4875-2651-1 (cloth)   ISBN 978-1-4875-3964-1 (EPUB)
ISBN 978-1-4875-2650-4 (paper)   ISBN 978-1-4875-3963-4 (PDF)

Library and Archives Canada Cataloguing in Publication

Title: Success in graduate school and beyond : a guide for STEM students and
    postdoctoral fellows / by Nana Lee and Reinhart Reithmeier ; illustrated
    by Nikko Torres.
Names: Lee, Nana, author. | Reithmeier, Reinhart, author.
Description: Includes bibliographical references and index.
Identifiers: Canadiana (print) 20230579280 | Canadiana (ebook) 20230579337 |
    ISBN 9781487526511 (cloth) | ISBN 9781487526504 (paper) |
    ISBN 9781487539641 (EPUB) | ISBN 9781487539634 (PDF)
Subjects: LCSH: Graduate students in science – Life skills guides. | LCSH: Graduate
    students in science – Employment. | LCSH: Science – Vocational guidance.
Classification: LCC LB2371.L44 2024 | DDC 378.1/98–dc23

Cover design: Alexa Love
Cover illustrations: Nikko Torres
Interior illustrations: Nikko Torres

We welcome comments and suggestions regarding any aspect of our publications – please
feel free to contact us at news@utorontopress.com or visit us at utorontopress.com.

Every effort has been made to contact copyright holders; in the event of an error or
omission, please notify the publisher.

We wish to acknowledge the land on which the University of Toronto Press operates.
This land is the traditional territory of the Wendat, the Anishnaabeg, the
Haudenosaunee, the Métis, and the Mississaugas of the Credit First Nation.

University of Toronto Press acknowledges the financial support of the Government of
Canada and the Ontario Arts Council, an agency of the Government of Ontario, for its
publishing activities.

ONTARIO ARTS COUNCIL
CONSEIL DES ARTS DE L'ONTARIO
an Ontario government agency
un organisme du gouvernement de l'Ontario

Funded by the   Financé par le
Government   gouvernement
of Canada   du Canada | **Canadä**

Dedicated to all of our previous, present, and future students.
May you all create your own successes in life.

Contents

Preface

The primary goal of our book is to serve as a guide for current graduate students and postdoctoral scholars in Science, Technology, Engineering, and Math (STEM) to optimize their training experience. This guide book is also relevant to STEM undergraduates considering or preparing for graduate school. Graduate students in the Humanities and Social Sciences may also benefit from many of the tools provided in this book, particularly with respect to the development of their transferable skills. The book can be used as a resource for faculty members to teach courses or run workshops on graduate professional development. It may also assist career educators, graduate program officers, and student affairs professionals with their programming.

Many science students enroll in graduate school to pursue a PhD and follow the well-trodden academic pathway towards becoming a professor who conducts research and teaches in their discipline. The reality is that the majority of today's PhD graduates will work in a wide range of careers outside of academia; those graduating with an MSc often go on to professional school or enter the workforce after gaining valuable research experience. Importantly, many students find the transition from school to work difficult to navigate because they may lack the necessary skills and professional network. The challenges of career transitions of PhD graduates were highlighted in a 2021 report from the Council of Canadian Academies.[1] The report concludes: "The evidence is clear that many more people are graduating with PhDs from Canadian institutions than there are available academic positions – the role for which they are primarily trained in most disciplines. It also appears

---

1 The Expert Panel on the Labour Market Transition of PhD Graduates, *Degrees of Success* (Ottawa: Council of Canadian Academies, 2021), https://cca-reports.ca/reports/the-labour-market-transition-of-phd-graduates/.

that the supply of meaningful jobs outside of the academy has not kept up with the growing numbers of PhD graduates in Canada." This book is written to give guidance to trainees as they prepare for careers across multiple trajectories.

This book is designed to help graduate students and postdoctoral fellows *during* their training in the sciences to better prepare them for the transition from school to work. It is written in a conversational style, often with a series of questions posed to you, the reader. The questions are designed to encourage self-reflection, such as in prompting you to answer "Where am I now, where am I going, and how do I get there?" We'll cover questions such as (1) Do you know that you strengthen your technical abilities *and* transferable skills during your advanced scientific training? (2) How do you enhance these essential skills even more? (3) How do you market yourself with these strengths? The book emphasizes the importance of dedicating time, personal resources, and self-reflection to your professional development and career goals. This guidebook will help you to become more self-aware, to develop your set of essential skills, and to build your professional network. A key message we reiterate is that your professional development is essential through graduate school and beyond.

This guidebook outlines the skills and activities that lead to success. What do we mean by success? We define it as the life and career path you designed by maintaining your genuine self, knowing and applying your values, interests, and skills in a purposeful, meaningful way. True success is not defined by others. It is defined by you and may change throughout your life. It is not solely recognized as a university degree, awards, job acquisitions, promotions, and accolades. Some of the projects you are pursuing may ultimately grant you these, but true success is the process; the deep, inner mindful work; how you apply what you learn; and how you give back and contribute to your community and the world. This does not mean you must develop core competency skills and achieve your goals right away or all at once. You do not need to start your own company, write and edit for the student science journal, volunteer for the World Health Organization, compete for speech awards, and initiate a new student movement all in one year, or even during the course of your PhD studies – or life for that matter. These are all external accomplishments, and we appreciate that some people are motivated by these. Inner success is the process of maintaining your authentic voice in your beliefs, values, and, as a consequence, your actions that could lead to these accomplishments. True success is not just about the "winning" but, more importantly, learning and growing from the "failures" throughout your life journey. Perhaps the ultimate measure of success is happiness[2] or fulfillment.

This book is based on a curriculum-embedded graduate professional development (GPD) course for life sciences students that was developed by the authors at the University of Toronto in 2012.[3] As such, this is an ideal textbook for such a course. The book is written in a Canadian context, but will have value for trainees in the United States and other countries around the world as well. The book is organized into major sections that follow the trajectory of a graduate student (or postdoctoral scholar): self-reflection, wellness, skills, networking, and planning for future success. While GPD should be part of every graduate curriculum, this book applies more broadly to enhancing the graduate experience. This book is also designed to serve as a resource where GPD is not part of the graduate curriculum. It is a call to action for graduate students but also for supervisors, departments, or institutions who have not yet embraced GPD as essential to a successful graduate experience.

The ideas and concepts in this book are the opinions of the authors and not the University of Toronto. All readers and students are invited to read, contemplate, and put into effect the actions they find helpful. The ideas in the book are not to be considered a consultation. Students are encouraged to seek professional advice if they are having difficulties in navigating their graduate studies. This book is written from the perspective of two university professors through their own lived experiences. We hope it can serve as a useful guide in developing each reader's unique pathway to success.

Note for the Second Edition

A Note to Instructors: Designing a Course in Graduate Professional Development

The course[4] in graduate professional development created by the authors in the fall of 2012 in the Department of Biochemistry has been

---

2 R.A.F. Reithmeier, "How to Become a Successful Scientist: The 2022 CSMB Arthur Wynne Gold Medal Lecture," Canadian Science, https://cdnsciencepub.com/doi /full/10.1139/bcb-2022-0206.
3 N. Lee and R. Reithmeier, "A Graduate Course in Professional Development," Science, 2013, https://www.science.org/content/article/graduate-course -professional-development.
4 See the appendix to this book for a course syllabus.

replicated by other departments at the University of Toronto and other institutions. The course (BCH2021H) has been highlighted by the Council of Graduate Schools (CGS) as an example of best practices in graduate professional development in their 2017 publication *Professional Development: Shaping Effective Programs for STEM Graduate Students.*[5] The course consists of six two-hour classes that include interactive discussions about various professional development topics and networking sessions with professionals. Guest panelists, who are chosen largely from the department's graduate alumni, talk about their career pathways and the skills they developed during their graduate education that they found especially valuable in their careers. Networking time between guests and students is planned so that students may pose questions to the panelists and exchange contact information for follow-up chats. In addition, experts are brought in from the university community to complement the expertise of the instructors, teaching topics on conflict management or equity, diversity, and inclusion. The class is limited to 20 students to promote interaction and discussion. Students complete many exercises during the course, including career planning, informational interviews, writing cover letters and résumés, and presenting short pitches.

Through the years, the GPD course has been modified and updated based on feedback from students and best practices and resources from other universities. This guidebook is an update of our original book, *Success after Graduate School,*[6] that was based on our professional development course and was designed for graduate students, postdoctoral students, and faculty members interested in designing such a course. This edition is also an updated version for learners across the country so it includes resources not limited to just the University of Toronto. We have updated most sections, especially topics on life integration and equity, diversity, and inclusion, as we have grown as a society and as authors since 2015.

Instructors of GPD find optimal community-building if they are embedded in the department to teach the course and also advise students

---

5 D. Denecke, K. Feaster, and K. Stone, "Professional Development: Shaping Effective Programs for STEM Graduate Students" (Council of Graduate Schools, 2017), https://legacy.cgsnet.org/ckfinder/userfiles/files/CGS_ProfDev_STEMGrads16_web.pdf.

6 N. Lee and R.A.F. Reithmeier, *Success after Graduate School* (University of Toronto Bookstore, n.d.), https://www.uoftbookstore.com/product/9861.

GPD courses modelled after BCH2021 in the Department of Biochemistry, University of Toronto (course instructor)

1. Department of Immunology (Nana Lee)
2. Department of Physiology (Helen Miliotis)
3. Department of Pharmacology and Toxicology (Rebecca Laposa)
4. Department of Ecology and Evolutionary Biology (Helen Rodd)
5. University of Manitoba, Children's Hospital Research Institute of Manitoba (CHRIM) (Andrew Tse, Sarah Turner)
6. Immunopaedia GPD Course in Africa (Michelle LeTarte)
7. Institute of Medical Sciences (Yoojin Choi, Pamela Plant)
8. Department of Molecular Genetics (Bruce Seet)
9. Science to Business Academy (Nana Lee)

in leading initiatives driven by their own interests. For example, Nana instructs GPD courses for MSc, PhD, and Applied MSc students and advises new student groups such as the peer communications mentorship team, the student departmental blog, the Wellness and EDI committee, and the teaching in higher education workshop series. She also liaises with existing student career planning groups to enhance their programming. GPD is not just a course, but a place where students are empowered with skills to create ideas and implement them into realities.

Acknowledgments

The writing of this book was made possible by our own lived experiences. To our leaders, mentors, colleagues, and students, thank you for believing in and supporting our vision to make professional development an integral part of graduate education. Special appreciation and thanks go to Andrew Zhai, Yoojin Choi, Angela Zhou, Lazar Jovanovic, Ashton Trotman-Grant, and Stephanie Tran for providing editorial and content feedback. Thank you to Anita Balakrishna, Equity, Diversity and Inclusion (EDI) Strategist, and Shannon Giannitsopoulou, Office of Inclusion and Diversity Program Coordinator, both at the Temerty Faculty of Medicine, University of Toronto, for their feedback on the EDI chapter. We would also like to thank the expert reviewers for their insights and suggestions for an early version of this manuscript. Kathy Halievski is thanked for her expert editing of the manuscript.

Thank you to our families – Nana's partner Mike and three daughters, Hanna, Ellie, and Miran, and Reinhart's partner in life Kathleen – for supporting this writing project, mostly written during early mornings, late evenings, and weekends. I (Nana) also thank my close circle of friends (you know who you are!) who have inspired different aspects of my intellectual and emotional growth through the many years of life and especially during the time of writing this book. Special thanks to our parents, peers, teachers, and mentors, who believed in us and helped shape our successes.

We wish to acknowledge the land on which all of our North American universities operate, as for thousands of years it has been the land of many Indigenous peoples (native-lands.org). In particular, the land on which the University of Toronto operates has been the traditional land of the Huron-Wendat, the Seneca, and the Mississaugas of the Credit First Nation. Today, this meeting place is still the home to many Indigenous people from across Turtle Island and we are grateful to have the opportunity to work on this land. A guide to land acknowledgment across Canada can be found at the Canadian Association of University Teachers.[7]

---

7 *Guide to Acknowledging First Peoples and Traditional Territory* (n.d.), retrieved March 30, 2023, from https://www.caut.ca/content/guide-acknowledging-first-peoples-traditional -territory.

PART I

Introduction

1 Why Graduate Professional Development?

Key Messages

- Graduate Professional Development (GPD) is (1) learning the core competency skills required to succeed as a working professional during and after graduate school, (2) a reflection of one's own journey in strengthening these skills, and (3) creating a meaningful career pathway through goal-setting and actions.
- Supervisors and universities are recognizing professional development as an integral part of graduate education.
- Career outcome data on PhD graduates are limited, but indicate that PhDs are gainfully employed in various sectors with most having the potential to create their own career pathways.
- Building your professional network begins in graduate school.

Students who enter graduate school are interested in continuing their education and training as a stepping stone to a rewarding career. Master's (MSc) students are often interested in gaining valuable research experience. Those with an MSc may go on to further education in a professional or PhD program, or enter the workforce. PhD students are interested in becoming experts in their discipline and making a significant contribution of new knowledge through research. Many of those who complete a PhD aspire to become a professor – this is a career goal that is often reinforced by their research supervisor who may serve as a role model. "I'm a successful scientist – just do what I did and you will be successful too" is a common refrain from supervisors. Accordingly, graduate students in science focus on developing relevant technical skills and knowledge in their discipline. However, the reality today is that the majority of science PhDs do not become professors, but do gain positions in public or private sectors.

Graduate school is not just about research, finishing your degree, and graduating. Graduate school is also the time to develop your transferable skills and build your professional network as outlined in an article in *Academic Matters*.[1] Transferable skills such as communication, critical thinking, teamwork, and leadership are abilities that can be applied to various tasks and professions. Developing these skills will lead to success in graduate school and beyond.

> The goal of graduate professional development is to ensure that graduates are prepared to take advantage of diverse job opportunities in the global market.

Most PhDs Do Not Become Professors

Where do PhD and MSc graduates work? Career outcome data are limited, though this is currently under active investigation. Several universities in Canada have completed PhD career outcomes data collection. The 10,000 PhDs Project at the University of Toronto (U of T) determined the employment positions in 2016 of 10,886 individuals who graduated with a PhD across all disciplines from 2000 to 2015 as reported in *PLoS ONE*, a peer-reviewed publication.[2] These data are available in a searchable format using an interactive dashboard at the University of Toronto School of Graduate Studies website.[3] Overall, 26 per cent of the U of T PhD graduates were employed as tenure-track professors, with variations across disciplines. In the physical sciences, 22 per cent of PhD graduates were employed as professors. In the life sciences, 18 per cent of PhD graduates were tenure-track professors, and an additional 9 per cent were working as research professors in university-affiliated, hospital-based research institutes. This compares

---

1 R. Reithmeier and C. Kelleher, "Mentorship Matters: The Case for Graduate Professional Development," *Academic Matters*, 2016, https://academicmatters.ca/mentorship-matters-the-case-for-graduate-professional-development.

2 R. Reithmeier et al., "The 10,000 PhDs Project at the University of Toronto: Using Employment Outcome Data to Inform Graduate Education," 2019, https://journals.plos.org/plosone/article?id=10.1371/journal.pone.0209898.

3 See "Employed and Engaged: Career Outcomes of Our PhD Graduates," School of Graduate Studies, University of Toronto, n.d., https://www.sgs.utoronto.ca/about/explore-our-data/10000-phds-project/.

to 53 per cent of humanities and 63 per cent of social sciences PhD graduates being employed as professors. About one third of physical sciences PhDs (e.g., engineers) worked in the private sector, and about a quarter of life science graduates did also, mostly in biotechnology and pharma. Very similar numbers were found in PhD career outcomes data from the University of British Columbia[4] and the University of Alberta,[5] suggesting that these career outcomes likely apply to PhD graduates of the U15 Group of Canadian Research Universities.[6]

In the US, the Council of Graduate Schools is working to help universities collect data on the career pathways of STEM graduates as outlined in their document "Understanding PhD Career Pathways for Program Improvement."[7] Similarly, the Coalition for Next Generation Life Science has posted PhD data on admissions, completion rates, and times to completion, which can be viewed by gender and citizenship from various universities, but robust career outcome data are yet to be accumulated.[8] Using online searches, the Stanford PhD Alumni Employment Project found in 2013 that 44 per cent of graduates were initially employed in the academic sector, including as faculty, academic staff, and postdoctoral fellows, while 31 per cent worked in the business, government, and not-for-profit sectors.[9] Further, a US career outcome study found that two thirds of MD/PhD graduates stay in academia, while 15 per cent transition into private practice.[10] In all, while more data are needed, it is clear that a large portion of graduate students and postdocs from the US go on to have careers outside of academia.

---

4 See "UBC PhD Outcome Survey 2016," Graduate and Postdoctoral Studies, University of British Columbia, n.d., https://outcomes.grad.ubc.ca/.
5 See "Results: The University of Alberta's PhD Alumni Researchers, Innovators and Leaders," Faculty of Graduate Studies and Research, University of Alberta, n.d., https://www.ualberta.ca/graduate-studies/professional-development/phd-alumni-study/results/.
6 See the U15 Group of Canadian Research Universities website: http://u15.ca/.
7 See Council of Graduate Schools, "Understanding PhD Career Pathways for Program Improvement," n.d., https://cgsnet.org/project/understanding-phd-career-pathways-for-program-improvement/.
8 See Coalition for Next Generation Life Science, "Answering the Call for Transparency," n.d., https://nglscoalition.org.
9 See Stanford University, Institutional Research and Decision Support, "Stanford PhD Alumni Employment," n.d., https://irds.stanford.edu/data-findings/phd-jobs.
10 L.F. Brass and M.H. Akabas, "The National MD-PhD Program Outcomes Study: Relationships between Medical Specialty, Training Duration, Research Effort, and Career Paths," JCI Insight, 2019, https://insight.jci.org/articles/view/133009.

With these statistics in mind, try not to think of your future career as one specific title. Instead of labelling your future career as "professor" or "industry scientist," ask yourself if you want to pursue scientific thought leadership, especially if you want to stay within research and development. Many students who have consulted us have said "I want to go into industry," thinking that perhaps research in industry might be different from academia. As an industry scientist, Nana wrote grants, troubleshot technical issues in the lab, trained mentees, and wrote reports and publications, while continuously working to integrate her work with life. Sound familiar? The only differences were that in industry you also had to consider business development and working with business clients. However, if you are interested in scientific research and the art of discovery – whether in academia or industry – then keep your research trajectory, publish papers, present at conferences, and network with academic and industry scientists. At the end of your PhD or postdoctoral fellowship, you will be known for your scientific thought leadership in the field of your expertise and accepted for that excellence by academia, industry, government, or a nonprofit organization. You will be able to take that research leadership you have developed during your training to any organization. So try not to think that you need to make the big decision of "academia or not" early on in your career.[11]

Supervisor as a Role Model?

The supervisor–student relationship is not a simple one, and it can have a powerful effect on your career path. A major role of professors in research-intensive universities, particularly in the sciences, is to act as a hands-on supervisor of graduate students and postdoctoral scholars. Your supervisor is a key person in your career development journey,[12] so finding a good match is important.[13] Your supervisor may serve as a role model, particularly if you plan to follow their pathway to an

11 N. Lee, "Developing Your Thought Leadership for Any Career," *Inside Higher Ed*, 2021, https://www.insidehighered.com/advice/2021/05/17/advice -grad-students-determining-whether-they-should-pursue-career-academe-or.

12 V. Galt, "The All-Important Graduate Student-Supervisor Relationship," *University Affairs*, 2013, https://www.universityaffairs.ca/features/feature-article /the-all-important-graduate-student-supervisor-relationship.

13 N. Lee, "Finding the Right Student-Supervisor Match," *University Affairs*, 2019, https://www.universityaffairs.ca/career-advice/graduate-matters/finding -the-right-supervisor-student-match.

academic position. Your supervisor can also be a mentor, but not all supervisors are role models or mentors. It is essential that you are able to have an open dialogue with your supervisor not only about your research, but also about your career goals. Even if your supervisor is very supportive of you working outside academia, you may still need additional mentors with diverse experiences to guide you along those paths. Supervisors are experts in training students to perform cutting-edge research, and many of them mentor their students through an academic career similar to the one they followed. Such an apprenticeship model worked well when universities were expanding and plenty of faculty positions were available. Today, universities have limited openings for the many highly qualified graduates, as the number of North American PhD graduates (in STEM) has doubled since the 1980s while the number of faculty positions has remained the same.[14] Fortunately, many career opportunities exist elsewhere.

It is vital that supervisors support their students with respect to their career development.[15] The 10,000 PhDs Project found that from 2000 to 2015, the number of U of T PhD graduates in physical sciences tripled and in life sciences doubled. The increase in graduates was absorbed by employment in the private and public sectors. Many supervisors are supportive, but unfortunately might not have the knowledge or network in other sectors to help. At a minimum, supervisors need to stay open to the likely possibility that their PhD graduates will attain employment outside academia.[16] There has been a call within universities to reimagine graduate education and supervision with better training of faculty members in mentorship and lab management, perhaps as an institutional responsibility.[17] Though many universities are making efforts to normalize and create supports for graduate students, you should try to take ownership of your future through graduate professional development activities to make more informed career choices to succeed in and beyond graduate school.

---

14 J. Gould, "How to Build a Better PhD: There Are Too Many PhD Students for Too Few Academic Jobs – But with Imagination, the Problem Could Be Solved," *Nature* 528, (2015): 22–5, https://www.nature.com/articles/528022a.

15 M. Wood, "How Supervisors Can Prepare Graduate Students for Diverse Careers," *University Affairs*, 2019, https://www.universityaffairs.ca/career-advice/from-phd-to-life/how-graduate-supervisors-can-prepare-graduate-students-for-diverse-careers/.

16 M. Wood, "Redefining Success After a PhD," *University Affairs*, 2019, https://www.universityaffairs.ca/career-advice/from-phd-to-life/redefining-success-after-a-phd/.

17 M.J. Greene, M. Vander Kloet, and M. Kasprzak, "Reimagining Graduate Student Supervision," *University Affairs*, 2018, https://www.universityaffairs.ca/career-advice/career-advice-article/reimagining-graduate-student-supervision/.

In addition to having various mentors, graduate students also need space and curricular time to develop their own interests and skills to help create their own path, whether that be in academia or not, as opposed to following what is "expected" of them. You can also start thinking about possible careers outside academia and recruit people from those fields to be your mentors. Students may look for career opportunities in a number of different sectors based on their experiences and goals – professional development provides support to get there. With the increasing number of graduates every year, career options outside of academia need to be embraced.

> The supervisor–student relationship can impact the student's drive and ability to participate in professional development activities during their degree and thereby influence the student's career choices following graduation.

University Support for Professional Development and Career Exploration

The transition from school to work can be challenging. Universities have developed various professional development and career supports for graduate students through career centres, libraries, graduate schools, faculties, and departments.[18] Be sure to make contact with experts in these supports early (i.e., once you have settled into your project), but know it's never too late in your program to seek expert career advice. University career centres have the expertise and contacts to help you develop your career path and explore possibilities. Need to write a cover letter and a résumé for a job application? Improve your writing and presentation skills? Figure out how your interests and talents can guide your career choices? Interested in a course/program outside academia? These resources can help you with all of these things. Be sure to let them know that you are a graduate student, as most career centres focus on undergraduates, but they are nonetheless aware of graduate student–specific issues and they are there to help you!

---

18 V. Galt, "Professional Development for Graduate Students," *University Affairs*, 2011, https://www.universityaffairs.ca/features/feature-article/professional-development-for-grad-students/.

Beyond Technical Skills

Graduate school in the sciences typically provides high-level training in a variety of techniques. In the biomedical sciences, these techniques range from quite sophisticated or specialized techniques like NMR or X-ray crystallography to common techniques like immunoblotting, PCR, or confocal microscopy, which are routinely used and widely applied. Graduate students become experts in a set of techniques and often see these as their skillset, but this is far too limited a view. Techniques change quickly and some become obsolete over time, so you must learn to adapt your technical toolbox and stay nimble enough to continuously incorporate new methods into your research. It is important to note, however, that techniques are only part of the hard skills that you need for a successful career. Hard skills such as writing papers and grant applications, analyzing data, and presenting your work are relevant beyond academia.[19] Through graduate professional development, you will become aware of your unique skillset and learn how to highlight your range of skills, which include technical skills and other "soft" skills, which may not be assessed in detail in the classroom. In the marketplace, these "soft skills" are also termed core competency or transferable skills, as these are essential to succeed and be promoted in any career. Below is a short list of some of these skills, with more details in chapter 9, "Developing Core Competency Skills."

Your unique skillset – Thought questions about how these skills may show up in your life

Technical skills – What laboratory or computer skills have you developed and how can they be applied broadly to different problems and in other venues?

Oral communication – How clearly and effectively can you communicate your ideas to scientific and non-scientific individuals, teams, large groups, and the public?

Teaching – What are your in-person and online teaching methods and are they effective to all learners?

---

19 J. McGuire and S. Baggott, "Hard Skills beyond Your PhD Remain Relevant beyond Academia," *Nature*, 2021, https://www.nature.com/articles/d41586-021-03756-0.

Writing – How can you present your ideas more easily, clearly, and persuasively on paper to get published and to win awards, contracts, grants, and business proposals?

Presentation – Can you create clear figures and slides that relay information and your ideas effectively to all audiences? Do you speak in an engaging and confident manner?

Project and time management – Time is valuable – how can you use it more wisely? Do you have a good sense of prioritization and keeping to the schedules you set for yourself?

Organization – Are you able to effectively plan and organize your day, research, or mentorship goals? Are you skilled at putting on activities or events for others?

Multitasking – Are you able to effortlessly move forward on your research project while taking or teaching classes?

Teamwork – Do you work well in groups? How can you ensure that you are an empathetic member of your research or teaching team? Do you take performance feedback as a welcome opportunity to grow? Do you know the basics of conflict management and equity, diversity, inclusion practices?

Problem solving – Are you able to get "unstuck" and think of alternatives on your own and with a team?

Leadership – Are you the go-to person who shows initiative and serves as inspiration to others?

Mentoring – Do you enjoy being helpful to others? Do people often come to you for advice? Do you provide a medium in which your mentees can provide feedback on your mentorship?

Data analysis – Can you dissect out the meaningful bits of information from complex figures and tables and draw your own conclusions?

Critical thinking – Are you able to analyze a project or publication and find questions or provide another perspective for the researchers? Are you able to provide helpful, constructive feedback for others?

Information handling – How do you sift through mountains of publications and pick out the pertinent ones?

Hypothesis testing – Have you come up with a novel idea and formulated a plan to test it?

Ethics – Are you true in the way you represent yourself and your work? How do you handle "grey" areas?

Strategic planning – Do you have an idea (with alternatives) of where you want to be in 5 or even 10 years? What is your multi-step, timelined plan of how to get there?

> *Work-life integration* – Do you spend enough quality time with friends and family, and on hobbies and your own wellness?
> *Business awareness* – Do you know how to assess if a product stemming from scientific research is marketable? Are you familiar with the pathway to innovation?
> *Global awareness* – How well-informed are you of society's needs and the global picture of scientific research?
> *Creativity* – Do you possess the imagination, supportive network, and entrepreneurial skills to combine your skillset, scientific background, and passions/curiosity to create a niche within a career or a new career entirely?

Your Professional Network

Now that you are aware that jobs in academia are not the majority and that participating in professional development activities can help you hone your core competencies, which are important in any future career, let's talk briefly about a skill that is critical for success in any field – networking. A professional network is a group of people connected to one another in your discipline and related career fields. A network builds your community and can help you find a mentor, in your job search and in crucial career moves.

It is essential to start developing your professional network as a graduate student. Your network for life begins with the other students in graduate school. Your first professional network is your supervisory committee and the professors you encounter in classes, seminars, and meetings and through your teaching activities. However, too many students graduate with little or no contacts outside their home department. Try to cast your net widely. By presenting your research and publishing papers, you build your professional network in your discipline across institutions. In addition, try to develop collaborations with other students and fellows and with other labs not directly related to your discipline. Your network can also include people in your university who provide professional development support for graduate students, as well as other graduate students that are participating in these professional development programs. In chapter 15, "Building Your Professional Network," you will learn how to carry out informational interviews as a tool to explore career options and build your network.

Finally, you likely participate in activities beyond your research, such as clubs, sports, and the arts. The people in these organizations share your interests and can be an important part of your network. By forming these diverse networks, your work, skills, interests, and abilities can become widely known.

Developing your skills and building your professional network will lead to success both in and beyond graduate school.

Information on graduate professional development at Canadian universities:

https://www.mun.ca/sgs/current/personalprofessionaldev.php (*Personal and Professional Development – School of Graduate Studies – Memorial University of Newfoundland*, n.d.)

https://www.dal.ca/faculty/gradstudies/currentstudents/professionaldevel.html (*Grad Student Professional Development – Faculty of Graduate Studies – Dalhousie University*, n.d.)

https://www.usherbrooke.ca/ssdp/fr/ (*Service Des Stages et Du Développement Professionnel – Université de Sherbrooke*, n.d.)

https://www.concordia.ca/students/gradproskills.html (*GradProSkills*, n.d.)

https://www.mcgill.ca/skillsets/offerings (*Offerings | SKILLSETS – McGill University*, n.d.)

https://www.uottawa.ca/graduate-studies/content-groups/student-hub-resources-professional-development (*Student Hub – Resources – Professional Development | Graduate and Postdoctoral Studies | University of Ottawa*, n.d.)

https://carleton.ca/gradpd/ (*Graduate Professional Development – Carleton University*, n.d.)

http://www.sgs.utoronto.ca/currentstudents/Pages/Professional-Development.aspx (*Graduate Professional Development [GPD] – School of Graduate Studies, University of Toronto*, n.d.)

https://grad.uwo.ca/career_development/competitive_edge/professional_development.html (*Western University*, n.d.)

https://uwaterloo.ca/graduate-studies-postdoctoral-affairs/current-students/academic-and-professional-development (*Academic and Professional Development – Graduate Studies and Postdoctoral Affairs – University of Waterloo*, n.d.)

https://graduatestudies.uoguelph.ca/postdoctoral/current/professional_development (*Professional Development – Graduate & Postdoctoral Studies, University of Guelph*, n.d.)

https://www.queensu.ca/exph/ (*Home – Expanding Horizons, Queen's University*, n.d.)

https://gs.mcmaster.ca/events/categories/professional-development/ (*Professional Development – School of Graduate Studies, McMaster University*, n.d.)

http://www.uwindsor.ca/graduate-profdev/ (*Graduate Professional Development, University of Windsor*, n.d.)

https://umanitoba.ca/faculties/graduate_studies/workshops/gradsteps.html (*Graduate Student Workshops – Faculty of Graduate Studies – University of Manitoba*, n.d.)

https://teaching.usask.ca/events/graduate/grad-pro-skills.php#About (*Graduate Professional Skills Certificate Program – Teaching and Learning – University of Saskatchewan*, n.d.)

https://www.ualberta.ca/graduate-studies/professional-development (*Professional Development – Faculty of Graduate Studies and Research, University of Alberta*, n.d.)

https://grad.ucalgary.ca/my-gradskills (*My GradSkills, University of Calgary*, n.d.)

https://ucalgary.ca/research/postdoc/current-postdocs/professional development/professional-skill-development (*Postdoc – Research – University of Calgary*, n.d.)

http://www.sfu.ca/dean-gradstudies/professional-development.html (*Professional Development – Graduate and Postdoctoral Studies – Simon Fraser University*, n.d.)

https://www.grad.ubc.ca/current-students/professional-development (*Professional Development – Graduate School at The University of British Columbia (UBC)*, n.d.)

Conclusion

We hope that after you have read this book, you will have acquired some knowledge and potential action items in moving your career and life forward. We hope that this guidebook will serve as just that: directions or a "GPS" in your travels as a graduate student and beyond. With any career-planning guide, much of the work is reflecting on yourself – your own values and interests. What inspired you to become a scientist? What will inspire you to move forward? What gap in this world will you serve? Your career journey will be strengthened by an interwoven tapestry of your technical and core competency skills, interests, and values – what you are good at, love to do, and care about in this world. As a graduate student, you have a privileged and unique lens on the world – you will be venturing onto the cusp of knowledge and innovation, where creativity, knowledge, and societal need collide. You will have the potential to find a gap in the world and create something to make it better for future generations. Some of you may become entrepreneurs or intrapreneurs. Some of you will become leaders for your projects, education programs, or within your community. All of you will become leaders of your own destiny. We encourage you to combine your scientific training and your curious passions for life to create a meaningful career path.

FURTHER DISCUSSION

1. What are your current career goals?
2. What skills do you feel need developing?
3. Describe your professional network.

TAKING ACTION

1. Research the career outcomes in your discipline using the 10,000 PhDs site: https://www.sgs.utoronto.ca/about/explore-our -data/10000-phds-project/.
2. Research professional development and career exploration resources available at your university.
3. Read this book.

PART II

Self-Reflection: Ready, Set, Go

2 Getting the Most Out of Graduate School

Key Messages

- Research remains the focus of graduate education and allows you to develop specific technical skills.
- Graduate courses, reading papers, and attending conferences provide you with knowledge about your discipline and help to develop your professional skills.
- Writing papers and a thesis will help you develop academic writing skills, and presenting your research will help you develop communication skills.
- Graduate school provides an opportunity to explore career options.

It takes more than just qualifying for the minimal degree requirements to graduate to get the most out of graduate school. In the sciences, a good graduate education is much more than performing experiments and publishing papers. A graduate education will provide you with the opportunity to become an expert in your discipline. But more importantly, it is a time to develop your skillset and build your professional network. An ideal graduate education prepares you for a meaningful life in academia and beyond. And remember, your degree does not define you.

Success in Graduate School

The focus of graduate studies, especially at the PhD level, is to conduct cutting-edge research that will make a significant advance in an area of study, usually accomplished through the publication of peer-reviewed papers and the writing and defence of a thesis.[1] Conducting research during graduate school starts with you becoming familiar with a body of literature, then coming up with an interesting question or hypothesis and, eventually, testing your ideas through well-designed experiments. The best projects aim to fill a gap in knowledge or address a pressing need. Through your graduate training, you will become competent in the application of various techniques, both simple and complex, and may even develop new methods yourself. You will work in a lab under the supervision of an experienced professor who is often a leader in their field. You will learn a great deal from your supervisor, your fellow lab members, and your supervisory committee members. Besides working at the bench, you will be engaged in many activities related to your research. You will present your work to your supervisor at one-on-one meetings, at lab group meetings, at committee meetings, and more formally at student seminars and scientific conferences. You will build your communication skills every time you have an opportunity to present your work. In addition, you will attend others' presentations, which will allow you to expand your knowledge base and improve your listening skills. Participating in course work and workshops will also help you to improve your knowledge base, as well as your technical, communication, and critical thinking skills.

The keys to being a successful graduate student are self-motivation, a strong work ethic, and a dedication to

1. Understanding your field in depth and big-picture science
2. Developing excellent technical and critical analysis skills
3. Generating significant new knowledge based on independent research worthy of publication in peer-reviewed journals
4. Effectively communicating your findings

You can increase your expertise in your field by taking formal courses, reading papers, and attending conferences, but you can do this even more effectively by teaching courses, presenting papers, and speaking at conferences, so be sure to look for these opportunities as well. You will be trained to use the latest technologies but may

---

1   A.I. Gotlieb, *Planning for a Career in Biomedical and Life Sciences: Learn to Navigate a Tough Research Culture by Harnessing the Power of Career Building*, 2nd ed. (Academic Press, 2018), https://www.elsevier.com/books/planning-for-a-career-in-biomedical-and-life-sciences/gotlieb/978-0-12-814978-2.

also develop new methods yourself. Carefully designed experiments to test a hypothesis will provide new insights and advance the field. Think about the big questions in your field and the gaps in knowledge that your research can fill. You will present your findings to your supervisor, your research group, and your department, as well as at meetings and through writing reports, papers, and your thesis. In addition to your own field, a thoughtful scientist is also aware of the big picture of various human endeavours including science, society, the arts, and culture so that the research is put into a human and global perspective. The meaningful question of "why" you do the research becomes clearer with such perspectives and can be strengthened when you present your research to diverse audiences, including the public through local organizations such as Let's Talk Science. Not only will you gain communication skills and a big-picture perspective on your work, but as a scientific ambassador of Canada being trained on the country's research funding, you should be able to describe to the taxpayer how you are using their hard-earned dollars. Grant agencies request research summaries for a general audience, so the skill to communicate complex science to the public is also relevant to your grant applications.

> It is important to engage in meaningful activities beyond research to get the most out of your graduate experience, for your own professional development and to distinguish you from other graduates.

Experiments, committee meetings, student seminars, courses, thesis writing, and publications are just some of the activities required to succeed in graduate school. Nonetheless, essential qualities for entering the academic or non-academic job market are not developed through graduate requirements alone. Both the hard skills of lab techniques and core competency skills such as verbal and oral communication, project management, problem-solving, knowing yourself, and working with others are crucial for the job search, and this development can begin before finishing your degree.

Getting the Most Out of Graduate School

How do you develop skills during graduate school that will give you an edge when entering the job market? As indicated in chapter 1, multiple resources and opportunities are available at universities that could suit your needs and help you to build your skillset. But nothing beats real projects, real people, and real life. This means that during graduate school try to seize opportunities to build your skills and professional network through your activities. While you are a student, also volunteer or take workshops or courses outside of your specific discipline, or engage in projects in additional areas of interest to develop your skills. Through these experiences you will also meet new people, thereby expanding your network. All in all, you will find a positive effect on your graduate studies. The first step of gaining "real life" experience is self-assessment – what are your values, interests, skills, and personal style? What do you care about? What are you good at? Check out chapter 3, "Knowing Yourself," for self-assessment tools.

When a company is given several résumés from candidates with equally excellent research backgrounds, those showing a wide range of core competency skills will be given the interview, during which time their people skills will shine, providing them with an even greater chance at landing the job.

Finding Your Way

Graduate students often grapple with finding their "passion" and vocation. Passion is described as "a strong liking or devotion to an activity, object, or concept." Nana has a passion for song writing, but some days are more creative than others. And she may have lulls in the process. Simon, a graduate student, has a passion for performing experiments but he may not even like it some days. Perhaps a more accurate term than "following your passion" would be heading towards your curiosities, as mentioned by Elizabeth Gilbert in *Big Magic: Creative Living Beyond Fear*.[2] What piques your interest? And does it keep going that way? Are you curious about all of its intricate details? Are you curious about its challenges even when it does not feel as comfortable

2 E. Gilbert, *Big Magic: Living Beyond Fear* (Riverhead Books, 2016), https://www.elizabethgilbert.com/books/big-magic/.

or familiar? Yes, follow your "passions" knowing that you will have days when those passions may feel less than passionate. Follow what you are curious about and you will grow. In addition, a "job" is the work you do for one organization, a "career" is a collection of jobs that takes time to build, and a "vocation" is what you strive to do in your life, something that may seem to be calling you.

Some students are navigators who have a clear goal in mind. Some are explorers who are adventuresome and open to options. Many are drifters who go with the flow, hoping to find something along the way. Which one are you? As a navigator, you may have known since grade school that you wanted to be a scientist and you chose your current lab through careful research and aimed to study a particular subject under a particular professor. As an explorer, perhaps you decided to go to graduate school to see what it had to offer and were not set on a specific research topic. Or maybe you are a drifter who did well in school and coasted along the academic route – maybe graduate school seemed like the choice many of your peers were choosing, so you followed. All of these paths are good – and remember, whether you are a drifter, navigator, or explorer can fluctuate throughout your life. Perhaps recently your research stopped inspiring you like it used to. So now you become an explorer who would like to take your training to another setting, perhaps working for a project funded by the World Health Organization that you read about in the newspaper. Perhaps you drifted into graduate school and got inspired by your research project and decided to explore an academic path. What are the skills and network you need to become an explorer and give yourself new choices and options? How do you make career transitions and get to where you want to be? Becoming a career explorer is the focus of this book.

Professional development for graduate students helps them explore a wide range of career options and develop skills that are transferable to careers in academia and beyond.

Example: Non-academic career exploration
Regardless of what brought you to your current training field, plan for success, develop your skills, and explore several career paths using your professional network. Here is an example:

Corey is in the second year of a PhD program and not certain of whether to continue PhD studies or quickly complete an MSc and get a job. To reach a decision, Corey spends months thinking about it and speaks to their supervisor and alumni who are MSc and PhD graduates. The opportunity to collaborate with a scientist in Europe who developed a new technique reignites a passion for research. Corey decides to continue with a PhD, to develop as a leader in science, perhaps in science communications or policy. During third year, Corey takes a graduate professional development class, strengthens communication skills, and finds alumni who speak about their current work and the exciting world of science policy. While writing up their PhD thesis, Corey interns once a week for a science policy maker and writes ideas on international research collaboration for the campus paper and a science policy blog. Just before graduation, the director of the science policy agency offers Corey a full-time job. During three interim months, Corey takes a trip across the ocean to Europe to meet collaborators and, through LinkedIn, finds science policy makers in Paris and Barcelona to share ideas on international policies. Corey returns home to start the job, but keeps in mind the experiences from Europe while planning the next few years of career development, which will include a new-found interest in global scientific policy.

As illustrated, the career exploration process never stops – it merely shifts from school to job to the next job. The key factor is planning a path to the career you want to strive towards and experiencing it through real life, real projects, and real people.

Example: Academic career exploration
Another example is illustrated for the academic route:
Mirae has always aspired to become a professor, and the graduate professional development course provided the encouragement to speak to postdocs and younger faculty in other departments and other universities.

Mirae spends most of the PhD at the bench, writing papers, setting up collaborations, presenting at conferences, writing grants, proofing others' grants and papers, and finding granting agencies that might fund a postdoc fellowship. Mirae also becomes involved in leadership roles with the Graduate Student Council, and experiences teaching as a teaching assistant, attends a number of conferences on topics that are applicable to future postdoc work, and grows a network.

A year to 18 months before finishing the PhD, Mirae applies to three top labs for a postdoc and then decides among them with a few priorities in mind: (1) the principal investigator (PI) must have a great reputation as a scientist and mentor, according to their alumni; (2) the lab must be in a top-tier institution with many opportunities for collaboration across research groups; (3) the lab must be in a city where Mirae's partner could find a job as well; and (4) the research must use the state-of-the-art technique Mirae already learned as a PhD student applied to a different model.

Mirae receives postdoctoral fellowship funding through a research foundation to which an application was submitted in the last year of graduate studies. Upon starting the postdoctoral fellowship, other mentors advise on applying for grants to guarantee a position as an early investigator and other collaborators to support stellar research. Mirae (1) maintains a network for career advice and opportunities, (2) works effectively to develop a unique research focus, (3) publishes significant findings in the area, (4) attends the top meetings in the field to get the word out, (5) teaches at workshops on some of the newly developed techniques, (6) proposes ideas and collaborates with lab mates and other labs, (7) supervises undergraduate and graduate students and works closely with technical staff, and (8) continues to develop writing and critical analysis skills by reviewing papers and writing sections of grant applications. Mirae is already developing their own ideas and has written up a draft grant proposal for the work to continue as an independent investigator. Once the work completed during the postdoctoral fellowship has been published, Mirae starts to give job seminars, is excited to tell others about the research and future plans, and continues working on developing skills and building a professional network even after landing a job as an Assistant Professor.

A PhD Is More Than a Credential

A PhD is a credential, but ideally, it's more than just a nice piece of parchment you frame and hang proudly on your wall. It can represent your adventures in exploring the graduate world, which include talking to professors outside of your own lab, finding alumni or other scientists outside of academia to answer questions and have discussions with, starting projects that inspire you, collaborating, discovering your passions, and living a life beyond your research. Keep in mind that with the considerable time and effort required to complete a PhD, the "passion" for it may fluctuate over time – do not think that you have be passionate about a topic 24/7 to make it a career. Be sure to speak to other graduate students outside your field of study. Or better yet, set up your own network and community of scholars. Most universities have organizations and activities for a diverse graduate student population. It is amazing the types of ideas that are exchanged when a biochemistry graduate student chats with a physics graduate student. Read – not just scientific journals but everything and anything that interests you. What is happening in the world? How can your science serve the world? Globally, real-life problems are solved not just by one discipline, but by many disciplines intertwined. Interdisciplinary research and working in teams are highly effective strategies for helping solve today's challenges. Can you communicate with scientists outside your domain of expertise? Real-life problems require hard skills, soft skills, and collaborative efforts. These skills need to be strengthened during graduate school for you to succeed as a scientist in the real world, whether you work inside or outside academia.

A PhD is a necessary credential to assume a faculty position, but the skills you develop also prepare you for other jobs in academia and in other sectors of the economy where the majority of PhDs are employed.

Messing Up in Graduate School

It's easy to "mess up" in graduate school or not get the most out of your experience. Be sure to follow best practices and high ethical standards in all that you do.

---

10 easy ways to mess up in graduate school[3]
1. Disregard policies and regulations.
2. Ignore deadlines until the last minute.

---

3 Adapted from K.D. Haggerty and A. Doyle, *57 Ways to Screw Up in Grad School* (University of Chicago Press, 2015), https://press.uchicago.edu/ucp/books/book/chicago/Other/bo20832370.html.

3. Don't bother with timelines for your program.
4. Remain entirely focused on your own work.
5. Select an "easy" supervisory committee.
6. Have supervisory meetings only when your research is going well.
7. Meet with your supervisor only when necessary.
8. Keep your supervisor in the dark about your activities and responsibilities.
9. Ignore conflicts until they become a crisis.
10. Take unethical measures to ensure success.

If you maintain a genuine, authentic vision of yourself while growing as a scientist and as a human being and finding ways to serve the world around you, then you will avoid "messing up" in the ways listed above. All the right actions necessary to succeed in graduate school will follow as long as you maintain this course.

Working hard and publishing papers in top journals may not be enough to land your dream job. Why? Because others have also achieved a graduate degree and published good papers. Some graduate students focus on the impact factor of the journals or the number of publications as their ticket to success, but this is too narrow a view. What sets you apart? What experiences or skills have you also acquired that make you the best fit for the job? Start thinking about this early on, and develop your core competency skills and a broad professional network. Strengthening the intersection through experiences of what you love to do, what you are good at, and what you care about will set you up to be a better fit for the job. Demonstrate initiative and leadership by getting involved with a club or organization that interests you. Start a project. Better yet, find a shortcoming in your student or community life and make a change to benefit others.

On the other hand, if you feel that you are just working on your supervisor's project, it may be time to reframe your thoughts and beliefs and change your actions, behaviours, and habits. You may discover that the track you are on – the one that seemed so right for you in the past – is not the one for you anymore. If this is the case, you need to know how to make the change and have the skills and connections to do so. Self-assessment tools described in chapter 3 provide an opportunity to evaluate how well aligned your values, interests, skills, and personal characteristics are with each other and with your supervisor.

Or have your interests changed since you started graduate school? If so, you may need to change course and become an explorer.

FURTHER DISCUSSION

1. Identify and discuss one reason you decided to go to graduate school.
2. Identify and discuss one person who influenced your decision to go to graduate school.
3. Identify and discuss one possible outcome of a graduate education.

TAKING ACTION

1. Create your academic curriculum vitae. Here are a couple of sources to get you started:
- https://www.elsevier.com/connect/writing-an-effective-academic-cv
- https://www.nserc-crsng.gc.ca/researchportal-portailderecherche /instructions-instructions/ccv-cvc_eng.asp
2. Research professional development and career exploration resources at your university and enroll in a course or workshop that interests you, not merely to "pad" your CV or résumé.
3. Develop a one-minute elevator pitch describing why you are interested in your research.

3 Knowing Yourself

Key Messages

- Reflecting on your beliefs, values, and interests will guide your daily actions towards success.
- Identifying the skills you need to develop will provide opportunities for growth.
- Personality and emotional intelligence play a major role in success.
- A growth mindset allows you to overcome challenges and be resilient.

We dedicate this chapter to knowing yourself. It's about self-awareness. It's about mindfulness and reflection. Something as simple as asking yourself What do I like and not like? Or as complex as What do I want or not want to be? To answer these questions in an explicit and intentional way, it is essential to closely examine your values, interests, skills, and personality. What are your core values? What are your interests? Are your interests aligned with your values? Have you made a list of your skills and know why core competency skills are important? What skills could you strengthen? You may have an interest, but can you develop the skills to pursue the interest? Do you have the motivation and patience to develop your weak skills? Many people focus on skills that they are already good at and neglect developing new skills. Are you willing to learn, even if it might take multiple iterations? Plans may need to be adjusted. What is your personality? Are you an extrovert or introvert? Do you thrive as an independent thinker or as a team brain stormer? Do you thrive as both? Your personality will inform how you work. Do you have a growth mindset? Do you practice mindfulness? Many of us have not thought very deeply about who we are, where we

are going, and why we do what we do. It's time to get to know yourself
a little better.

Self-reflection can promote confidence, action, and meaningful engagement,
but obsessive self-reflection can lead to doubt, inaction, isolation, and
even depression.

Individual Development Plans

A good place to start your self-reflection is with an Individual Development Plan (IDP). An IDP is a powerful self-assessment tool that iden-
tifies the skills needed to develop a pathway to success. MyIDP is an
interactive, web-based career-planning tool based on the Federation of
American Societies for Experimental Biology's 2003 *Individual Development Plan for Postdoctoral Fellows.*[1] MyIDP provides a list of 20 possible
scientific career paths that align with your interests and skills for you
to explore. The Canadian Institutes of Health Research (CIHR) has also
designed an IDP portal that comes with an IDP form to complete and
training modules.[2]
    IDPs consist of five steps:

1. Self-assessment
2. Career exploration
3. Goal setting
4. Plan development
5. Plan implementation

    The first step involves examining your values, interests, skills, and
personality. This then leads to career exploration using tools like informational interviews, networking, and experiential learning opportunities. Step three involves identifying and developing the skills necessary
to achieve your career goals. Step four involves developing a plan using
SMART goals (see chapter 9, "Developing Core Competency Skills").
At this stage it is important to discuss your career goals and plan with

---

1 *MyIDP Science Careers Individual Development Plan* (n.d.), https://myidp.sciencecareers
   .org/.
2 Canadian Institutes of Health Research, "Individual Development Plans" (n.d.),
   https://cihr-irsc.gc.ca/e/50516.html.

your supervisor and mentors. Finally, you need to take the necessary steps to implement your plan, which will require good time management and networking skills.

As detailed on the CIHR IDP site, there are many benefits to creating an IDP. IDPs lead to better career outcomes and job satisfaction. Trainees who can develop written career plans are more productive in their research and journal publications. Self-assessment allows you to identify careers that align with your values, interests, skills, and personality. IDPs allow you to focus on developing the skills required for your career.

It is important that you get meaningful feedback on your IDP. This could take the form of a workshop led by someone experienced in IDPs. An effective process is to discuss your IDP with peers. Nana and Reinhart have included classroom IDP discussions and private consultations as integral parts of their GDP courses. Importantly, IDPs are a powerful communication tool that can facilitate meaningful discussions with your supervisor and mentors about your career goals. This is key to managing expectations and avoiding conflicts. An IDP is best utilized as a "living" document that is reviewed and updated at least once a year to determine the progress you have made. Indeed, your career goals may change over the course of your degree, and an IDP will help you plan and transition from one path to another.

Values and Beliefs

What are your values? What do you care about? For researchers, common values are achievement, challenge, competition, innovation, productivity, recognition, teamwork, and truth. But what about values like creativity, diversity, empathy, health, and trust? The first group of values is related to the research enterprise, which is challenging and competitive and relies on innovation, productivity, and teamwork in the quest for knowledge and truth. The second group of values includes those related to dealing with others and required for high emotional intelligence. Reflecting on your core values will guide you in making purposeful decisions on your pathway to success. Your values will guide you not only in school and work but in all aspects of your life. To identify your values, you can sort them into three groups using a set of value cards: very important, important, and not as important.[3] You can

---

3 N. Nikolic, "Values Cards Exercise to Identify Values," n.d., https://neshnikolic.com /values-cards-exercise-to-identify-values.

then go further to identify your top three values and think about why they are so important to you. To get you started, you can find a list of values in the Science Careers Individual Development Plan[4] or in the My Career Skills Toolkit from the University of Calgary.[5]

Besides health and family, Reinhart values knowledge, which aligns with his interest in research and his desire to develop the skills to become a capable scientist. As an introvert, he had to work hard to develop the skills to be comfortable presenting on stage and teaching in the classroom. Over time his personality changed to that of an extrovert who enjoys interacting with others. Values that are essential to Nana are connecting with others, community building, creativity, and work-life integration. Whether as an industry research scientist or faculty member, Nana discovered that she gravitates towards and creates work environments in which she experiences these values. If a working environment does not have these values, then Nana creates meaningful engagements with others to foster the growth of these values in her workplace, a pursuit that in and of itself builds communities of people who share these values.

The term "meaningful engagement" will be used frequently in this book. We define meaningful engagement as an authentic involvement in an experience that deepens your understanding of the activity and contributes to your growth.

You have now created a priority list of your values. You need to be able to clearly articulate why your values are important to you. Your values may have been important in your decision to go to graduate school. For example, if helping society is one of your values you may decide to study environmental sciences. On the other hand, learning new things may be an important value to you and that is one reason you would like to earn a PhD: to be at the cusp of knowledge and innovation. You need to be authentic to yourself and your values, keeping in mind that some of these values may shift over time.

---

4 See "MyIDP Science Careers Individual Development Plan," 2016, https://myidp
   .sciencecareers.org/.
5 See Faculty of Graduate Studies, University of Calgary, "My Careers Toolkit for
   Graduate Students," n.d., mycareerskill-toolkit _dec2016.pdf.

Values stem from beliefs. To peel back another layer would be to think about what you believe in and why. Beliefs are what we assume to be true, sometimes with or without scientific facts or observation. Beliefs all have sources, whether from family tradition, religion, information, or a perception. Beliefs affect what we value, which then affect our behaviours towards the outside world. For example, the behaviour of procrastination is what the outside world sees, as the report arrives late. The behaviour of procrastinating may be due to the student finding the value of "competition" unimportant. The student's value here may stem from the belief that they are "not good enough." The source of this belief could be the perception that the student has a fear of failing.[6] Sources of beliefs and the actual beliefs affect values, which in turn affect interests and behaviours. It's good practice to check in with your beliefs and ask yourself if they still fit with your personal growth. Chances are some may change over time based on new information or knowledge.

How well do your values align with those of your supervisor? To determine this, you need to understand the values of your supervisor. Clear communication between supervisor and student is key, and this should start before you even decide to join the research group. Some simple questions you can ask during an interview are helpful to gain insight into your potential supervisor's values: Why did you go into science? What do you like about research? What are your career goals? What are your expectations of your graduate students? Do not make assumptions that the values of your supervisor are the same as yours. Some will not be, and that is fine. Everyone has different motivations that drive them. Your values, however, are what inform your interests. So, let's move onto interests.

Interests

While values are the core principles that guide your life and tend to remain relatively constant over time, interests and activities that you enjoy or are curious about are more likely to change. What do you love to do? With what actions do you fill your day? These interests can span all aspects of your life – at work, at play, and with family and friends. These various interests are all informed by your underlying values. As a graduate student or postdoctoral fellow, your interest in research is

---

6 These concepts are taken from N. Diercks, Professor at the Berklee School of Music, in a personal communication to Nana Lee.

usually based on your values. But you will also have other interests, perhaps sports, a hobby, or a cause. For example, if you believe that exercise can maintain long-term fitness, one of your values is health and you might have an interest in running and following a training schedule for an upcoming race. Finding time for your interests involves developing time management skills.

Allocating time for what you love to do and pursuing your interests, especially if they develop your skills, is very satisfying and fulfilling. Happiness is not about having it all, but about letting go of things you do not need. Everyone is "busy," whether they are a dean at a university, a CEO of a company, a parent, a postdoc or graduate student, a high school youth, or a toddler learning to walk or talk. Find time in your busy schedule to pursue your interests. These pursuits tell the world and potential employers that you can find an interest and follow it over the long term, while building your skills and participating in a community of like-minded enthusiasts. Such a pursuit may be the reason why you are hired over others in a competition for a career position. For example, a science postdoc believed in the importance of communicating research to the public, valued the craft of writing, and had an interest in starting the first departmental student magazine. She took writing and editing courses and took the initiative to start the magazine. By the time she applied for science communication roles, she already had an impressive writing portfolio that helped her land her first job. Henceforth, reflect on your beliefs and values, nurture your interests, and build your skills.

Skills

You already have developed a number of skills. What are you good at? What are your strengths? Think about the skills you use currently. Ask someone who knows you well what skills they think you have – get an outside perspective. There will also be skills you need to develop. Write down a list of your existing skills and the ones you would like to improve using the science careers IDP as a guide. What are your weaknesses? What do you need to work on? How can you make skills development a priority?

During your graduate program or your postdoc training, you will develop many skills. As a scientist you will develop technical skills and learn to apply them to a research problem. You may even develop new methods. The ability to learn new techniques that are vital to success in graduate school is an example of a transferable skill. Other transferable, or core competency, skills such as effective communication, empowering others, conflict management, and an awareness of concepts in equity, diversity, and inclusion are some examples of skills that you need to develop over many years.

Transferable skills are skills that can be applied in and beyond graduate school. The most important transferable skill is effective communication. You will learn to communicate your science through your publications and presentations. How good are you at scientific writing? Can you communicate your science to diverse scientific audiences? What about to the public? Persuasive communication is key to success in getting scholarships and research grants and in getting papers published. Pitches are key in business. Can you make convincing arguments in a clear and concise manner? Do others find it easy to follow your arguments? Getting feedback on your communications, whether written or oral, will enhance this key skill.

One method to assess your current skill level and to determine which skills you need to work on is a skills wheel.[7] There, you list the skills you need to develop around the wheel and score each one based on your current ability. You then rank each skill in order of importance. Once you identify the high-priority skills, you can set an action plan to develop them. Many skills can be developed through formal instruction such as in a course. Almost all skills can be developed through practice. You could revisit the wheel to show the progress you have made. Remember to focus on the skills that need work, not the ones you are already good at. You'll find more on skills in chapter 9, "Developing Core Competency Skills."

Personality

What kind of a person are you? Do you see yourself as an extrovert, an introvert, or a combination, depending on the situation? For example, some introverts are great on stage and love performing to an audience. How do others see you? Do you like to stand out or blend in? As a scientist, do you like thinking about problems or are you keen to perform experiments? Do you like to carefully plan everything or are you spontaneous? Do you like to gather information or do you go with your gut when making decisions? Do you quickly get a sense of other people or find it hard to read them? These are questions that you can try to answer by yourself, although it may be difficult without a bit of help.

---

7 See *The Skills Wheel* (New College Durham, 2016), https://tlateam.wordpress.com/2016/03/18/the-skills-wheel/.

Myers-Briggs Type Indicator

The Myers-Briggs Type Indicator (MBTI) is a useful method for determining your personality type that should be used with the assistance of an expert.[8] Am I an extrovert that likes to interact with others (focused on the outer world) or am I an introvert that prefers to work alone (focused on my inner world)? Do I use my senses to gather information or do I use intuition? Do I make decisions based on logic and thinking or based on feelings and empathy? Do I like structure or do I like to keep my options open? These four questions form the basis of the MBTI:

1. Extraversion (E) versus introversion (I)
2. Sensing (S) versus intuition (N)
3. Thinking (T) versus feeling (F)
4. Judging (J) versus perceiving (P)

You can see that the first group is more objective (ESTJ types) and the second is more subjective (INFP types). There can be various combinations of these 4 traits, resulting in 16 types overall. For example, ENTJ types tend to be leaders with innate abilities to understand and motivate others, INFJ types are driven by meaning and self-motivation, while ISTJ types are practical and task-oriented. Which type are you? The MBTI can be done online for a fee[9] but better yet with an MBTI Certified Practitioner working at your university. The MBTI is one tool you can use to get to know yourself better.

REINHART'S MBTI

As a part of a self-reflection exercise Reinhart completed the MBTI (indicated in **bold** in the grid, MBTI Step II), which revealed he has the ESTJ personality, consistent with his own view of himself as an efficient organizer. Upon reflection, these traits align with Reinhart's ability to organize a productive lab group and act as an effective departmental chair and in other leadership positions.

ESTJ is known as "The Efficient Organizer. People with ESTJ preferences are incredibly motivated, often organizing themselves, other people, and resources to achieve their goals. They value order and structure, and like to get things done. They're outspoken and prefer

---

8 Myers and Briggs Foundation, "My MBTI Personality Type," n.d., https://www .myersbriggs.org/my-mbti-personality-type/.
9 MBTI Online, "A New Perspective on You," n.d., https://www.mbtionline.com/.

MBTI Step II (*Myers and Briggs Foundation – MBTI® Step II™ Instrument*, n.d., https://www
.myersbriggs.org/using-type-as-a-professional/mbti-step-ii-instrument/home.htm?bhcp=1)

Extraverting	Introverting	Sensing	Intuiting	Thinking	Feeling	Judging	Perceiving
Initiating	Receiving	Concrete	Abstract	Logical	Empathetic	Systematic	Casual
Expressive	Contained	Realistic	Imaginative	Reasonable	Compassionate	Planful	Open-ended
Gregarious	Intimate	**Practical**	Conceptual	**Questioning**	Accommodating	**Early Starting**	Prompted
Active	Reflective	Experiential	Theoretical	Critical	Accepting	Scheduled	Spontaneous
Enthusiastic	Quiet	Traditional	Original	Tough	Tender	Methodical	Emergent

proven processes to new ways of doing things. They're also great at seeing potential problems that others may have missed. They make decisions easily – even tough ones – and move quickly to get a decision put into action."[10]

> Self-assessment involves linking what matters to you (values), what you enjoy (interests), what you're good at (skills), and what your characteristics or traits are (personality).

Emotional Intelligence

Emotional Intelligence or Emotional Quotient (EQ) is the ability to recognize and manage your own emotions and, more importantly, the emotions of others. This ability helps to guide behaviour, manage others, and adapt to and achieve goals. People with a high EQ have the ability to recognize how their emotions and the resulting behaviours can affect others. According to Peter Salovey, John Mayer, and David Caruso in their article "Emotional Intelligence: Theory, Findings, and Implications," there are four layers of emotional intelligence: perceiving emotions, understanding emotions, managing emotions, and using emotions.[11] These layers all involve emotions: your emotions and the emotions of others. According to Daniel Goleman, author of the influential book

---

10 MBTI Online, "ESTJ The Efficient Organizer," n.d., https://www.mbtionline.com/en-US/MBTI-Types/ESTJ.
11 J. Mayer, P. Salovey, and D. Caruso, "Emotional Intelligence: Theory, Findings, and Implications," *Psychological Inquiry* 15, no. 3 (2004): 197–215.

Emotional Intelligence,[12] there are five main elements to emotional intelligence:

1. Self-awareness
2. Self-regulation
3. Motivation
4. Empathy
5. Social skills

This list begins with understanding your emotions and then the emotions of others. (This concept will come up again when we discuss core competencies, which have three layers: dealing with self, dealing with others, and dealing with organizations.) Self-awareness is knowing the values that guide you and the interests that you have. You also need to know your skills, strengths, and weaknesses.

Self-regulation begins with an awareness that your behaviour can affect others. Can you control your emotions? Do you get angry easily? How do you speak to others? For instance, being direct may sound aggressive to others. Being soft may sound indecisive.

Next, what are your motivations? Motivation is linked to interests – if you lose interest, you lose motivation. This also gets back to your values and beliefs. Are you in research because you value knowledge, achievement, or recognition? During your graduate studies or postdoctoral fellowship, you may lose interest, and therefore motivation, in research. Examine why this is so. Is it because you don't value research anymore? Do you believe you are no longer suited for the research path due to imposter syndrome (which we all most likely had, by the way)? Do you believe you don't have the skills yet? Is it because the questions you are trying to answer don't seem as valuable as you once thought? Perhaps your motivation was linked to success (one of your values), and your experiments are no longer "working." Emotional intelligence is also about your ability to motivate others. This is particularly important when you assume leadership positions.

Empathy is the ability to put yourself in someone else's shoes and possibly feel what they might be feeling. It is not the same as compassion. Empathy involves being a good listener and being aware of not only the words that someone is saying, but how they are said, connecting at that particular moment. Body language provides strong clues. Supervisors were graduate students once, so they may have a good

---

12 D. Goleman, *Emotional Intelligence: Why It Can Matter More Than IQ,* 10th anniversary ed. (Bantam Books, 2005).

understanding of your concerns. But your experience may not be the same as theirs. Why? Because your beliefs, values, interests, skills, and personality are different. The times are different. If you are a teaching assistant, you might demonstrate empathy for an undergraduate student through mentoring, identifying, assisting, and referring students to wellness resources and acknowledging that you will address any accessibility concerns.

Finally, social skills refer to the ability to handle other people's emotions effectively. If you know that your supervisor is not a "morning person" and needs their 9 a.m. coffee before a discussion, then you might request a later morning meeting. Being mindful of others is a social skill exhibited by people with a high level of emotional intelligence. Once you have a better idea of your personality type, you may use the information to interact better with others. For example, instead of wondering why your colleague down the hall does not respond well to your "Hey, did you have a good weekend?" as you pop by his office, consider the possibility that you being an extrovert does not mix well with him being an introvert. Perhaps when you asked him, he was in the middle of working on a report and did not want to be interrupted with a long discussion about how his weekend went because it was not a particularly good one. If you do want to chat, you might email "Good morning! Would you want to go for a coffee break at 10 a.m.?" Such a suggestion gives introverted Tom a moment to think about it in private and then you can ask about his weekend during the break. We often hear about a clash of personalities in the workplace, but this need not be the case, especially if you develop a high level of emotional intelligence.

In summary, one may continue to grow and develop the emotional self with all relationships in work and life by (1) asking questions with empathy and curiosity to understand how the environment or system issue affected the other person's behaviour, (2) being aware of your own emotions and regulating them before responding to someone who might be upset, and (3) regulating your response so you are not responding negatively, as that would drive them further away. As a leader, think about how you can defer judgement and provide an environment of emotional and psychological safety for them and your team for next time and the future. (You'll find more on EQ and conflict management in chapter 6, "Negotiation and Conflict Management.") A number of tools are available to measure your emotional intelligence as outlined in the article cited here.[13] Your institution may offer professional advice

---

13 P.J. O'Connor et al., "The Measurement of Emotional Intelligence: A Critical Review of the Literature and Recommendations for Researchers and Practitioners," *Frontiers in Psychology* 10 (2019): 1116, https://www.ncbi.nlm.nih.gov/pmc/articles/PMC6546921/.

on assessing your emotional intelligence and what to do with the information in terms of skills development. Check it out.

Develop a Growth Mindset

A growth mindset ignites a passion for learning rather than a fixation on seeking approval and rewards. In her famous book called *Mindset: The New Psychology of Success*, Carol Dweck argued that personal, deeply rooted attributes like intelligence, personality, and even beliefs can change if you develop a growth mindset.[14] In a growth mindset, the effort and process matter more than results. Those with a growth mindset tend to value challenges and become optimistic with every success, big or small. It is the success of the process rather than the final results that promotes a growth mindset.

People with a fixed mindset don't like taking risks because they have a fear of "failure," which is usually identified in our traditional academic culture as not getting that "A" or a high GPA. Students are usually not rewarded on the process of learning, but they should be, as that is what is rewarded in the job market. Students are taught to "learn and repeat the information" on the test to achieve their A+. Thus, they tend to stick to what they are good at, which might manifest as them picking "safe" courses rather than courses that they might be more interested in or that would expand their knowledge base. Those students who have been continually rewarded by grades alone usually have a fixed mindset and may, as a result, become pessimistic when success eludes them. On the other hand, people with a growth mindset love to learn. They take risks, even if it makes them uncomfortable. They don't fear failure. They see setbacks as a learning experience and problems as challenges. So, challenge yourself. Learn a new skill, develop a new interest, think about your values. Even your personality is not fixed. With a growth mindset you can enhance your skills and become a more valued person to yourself, to others, and to your organization.

Moving Forward

Knowing yourself is a life-long journey. Your sources of beliefs, values, interests, and subsequent actions, habits, and behaviours are all affected by knowing your genuine true voice. You are constantly growing and, hence, some beliefs may change. Some beliefs may stay constant over your whole lifetime. When a core belief shifts, your values may

---

14   C. Dweck, *Mindset: The New Psychology of Success* (Ballantine Books, 2006).

shift too – which will result in varying interests. Embrace the changes. Most likely, you have not had to confront any changes in beliefs up until now, perhaps when you are trying to figure out the "why" behind your actions and life goals. You may view it as overwhelming or even frightening, but try to reframe the feeling to that of excitement and delightful anticipation to embrace the horizon, your own horizon.

FURTHER DISCUSSION

1. Sort Value Cards to identify the three values that are most important to you and discuss why. Write down your three core values on one coloured set of sticky notes, your interests on another colour, and your skills on a third set. Arrange the values, skills, and interests into trios and brainstorm with your classmates about how these three elements relate to one another. Four rules exist for brainstorming, which can be found in detail in design thinking references: (1) think of wild and crazy ideas, (2) generate as many ideas as possible within one minute, (3) defer judgement, and (4) think of generative ideas (build on those ideas already posted). After these ideas have been generated, you want to "tame" them down so the wild idea forms the foundation, and the actual engagement is a more realistic one (https://d1r3w4d5z5a88i.cloud -front.net/assets/guide/Field%20Guide per cent20to per cent20Human -Centered%20Design_IDEOorg_English-0f60d33bce6b870e7d80f9cc1642c8e7 .pdf). For example, a wild idea can be one where you "become the Prime Minister," which can be tamed down to "have an informational interview with a local politician." This would align with your value of public service, your interest in politics, and your skill as a communicator.

2. In a peer group, discuss how your beliefs and their sources may be affecting your values and subsequent actions. How do you hope to change these beliefs or values if you are limited by them in your life journey? These discussions are to remain confidential to the group and only positive support comments from peers are welcome.

3. With a partner, use eye contact and body language to express different emotions. See if they can guess your emotion.

TAKING ACTION

1. Try the MBTI® Step II™ Profile and reflect on what it says about your personality.

2. Take a workshop, course, or activity to enhance a skill you would like to develop, not one you are already good at.

3. Watch Nana's video on "Reflection": https://youtu.be/OoZKnm2er_U (Lee, n.d.-g). Set up clear goals with your peers for accountability.

4 Choosing Your Supervisor and Project

Key Messages

- Consider the areas of science that fascinate you and what topics you'd like to be immersed in during the several years you will spend in graduate school.
- Start early with your research into potential supervisors and their lab organization and culture to make an informed choice.
- Recognize that a supervisor–student relationship is a two-way street – consider expectations that go both ways.
- Engage with diverse advisors/mentors to prepare for your future and anticipate unexpected situations during the course of graduate school.

Choosing a supervisor is one of the most important decisions you will make during your graduate school journey. This choice will define your research project, which very often will become your area of research for the rest of your career. This choice is critical, not only for your future success but also for your current and future happiness.[1] In the sciences, graduate students typically work as trainees under the supervision of a professor. In the traditional apprenticeship model, the student is expected to continue along a career path similar to the supervisor, pursuing a postdoctoral fellowship with the anticipation of a future position as a research scientist at a university or an affiliated research institution. In this case, the supervisor may serve as a valued role model for this career path. However, as noted in the section on career outcomes in chapter

---

1 N. Lee, "Finding the Right Student-Supervisor Match," *University Affairs*, 2019, https://www.universityaffairs.ca/career-advice/graduate-matters/finding-the-right-supervisor-student-match/.

1, the majority of PhD graduates do not become professors, but rather work in the public or private sectors. Thus, while your choice of supervisor will certainly guide your career, especially in academia, engaging with diverse advisors and mentors will be a benefit for most students.

Start with the Science

One of the first points to consider in choosing a supervisor is which area of science you want to be in. Start with some questions you can reflect upon to help guide your awareness of the topic area you'd like to pursue during graduate school. Why do you value science? Why is it of deep interest to you? Do you have research skills you would like to develop? How adventuresome are you? Perhaps a subject in a course you took or a science paper you read got your attention. Or perhaps as an undergraduate student you worked on a research project that captured your interest. You may have a role model you admire and whose footsteps you want to follow. Some students have developed a strong interest in a subject because of a deep personal interest and are keen to make a meaningful contribution. For example, you may be an environmentalist and decide to go into "green" chemistry. Maybe you received a telescope for your eighth birthday and became fascinated with astronomy. One of the authors of this book, Reinhart, was drawn into research by a single red squirrel he encountered while working on a high school biology project.[2] The other author, Nana, found science through her fascination with the topic of space biology, which she learned about in the eighth grade from an enthusiastic science teacher. So think about what area of science you're interested in and what you hope to gain by pursuing this area.

Most graduate students select a discipline based on their undergraduate experience. Some follow a conventional pathway and drift into graduate school. You may carry out a research project as an undergraduate and then decide to stay in the same lab as a graduate student. This is an informed choice – a cautious, yet common one. You may be a navigator and carefully select a supervisor at another university within your discipline based on their reputation and apply to a particular graduate program through their university department. You may even contact the supervisor directly – in fact, this approach is the usual one for postdoctoral positions. Alternatively, you may be an explorer and wish to

---

2 R.A.F. Reithmeier, "Lesson from a Red Squirrel, Mentors and the Pathway to Success," *Biochemistry and Cell Biology* 92, no. 6 (2014), https://www.nrcresearchpress.com/doi/full/10.1139/bcb-2014-0058#.XqWHYi2ZORs.

look more broadly. Though few students are able to jump dramatically from one discipline to another, say from computing science to genomics, it's been done before. Noted molecular biologist and Nobel Prize winner Walter Gilbert actually did his PhD in physics at Cambridge where he met James Watson and developed an interest in molecular biology.[3] Some explorers even take a break between undergraduate and graduate school to travel, volunteer, intern, or work to get to know themselves better and to get some experience outside academia. As you can see, there are different ways of reaching a decision about which discipline to pursue in graduate school, and it's often based on your interests, skills, and personality.

Making an Informed Choice

Once you have narrowed in on a discipline, it's time to select a supervisor. If you are not yet sure of your choice of a supervisor, you could apply to programs of interest at several institutions. Except for some elite universities in the United States and the United Kingdom, the university where you carry out your research is of less consequence than your choice of supervisor and research project. Once you have been accepted into a graduate program, you can then do some research to make an informed choice in selecting a supervisor working in your area of interest. Up-to-date websites and recent publications are valuable sources of information. One way to learn about a supervisor's research environment and style is through a rotation system (discussed below) that some graduate programs have, where you spend a few weeks in a number of labs. In contrast, at some universities you may need to select a supervisor to be accepted, and there are no rotations. In this case we recommend that you visit the lab in person or at least have remote meetings with the supervisor and also with lab members. Also reach out to lab alumni (often listed on lab websites or as authors on publications) to get feedback on their graduate experience. A face-to-face meeting with your potential supervisor is invaluable so you can gauge if this is someone with whom you could build an open and productive relationship.

Once you have decided on a number of potential supervisors, reach out to them 9 to 12 months in advance with a short email message

---

3 Read this article from The Nobel Prize website: "The Nobel Prize in Chemistry, Walter Gilbert Biographical" (1980), https://www.nobelprize.org/prizes/chemistry/1980/gilbert/biographical/.

containing the following key points. (1) Why I am contacting you: "I am interested in pursuing a PhD in the area of signal transduction and Dr. X suggested I contact you." (2) Who I am: "I am a 4th-year undergraduate in Biochemistry and am completing an honours project in the lab of Dr. X on ABCD." (3) What I want: "I have read your recent paper in *Cell* and would like to discuss possible projects with you regarding ABCD. Please let me know when you might be available in the next two weeks for a Zoom meeting. Happy to provide any additional information." Don't hesitate to contact multiple potential supervisors, but do not send the same generic message to every member of the department!

It takes time to make an informed choice of who you would like your graduate supervisor to be, as well as what the topic of your project will be, so start early. While you are an undergraduate, talk to your current professors and get their advice, especially with regard to potential supervisors in your area of interest. Read their research papers and pay attention to what fascinates you. Talk to graduate students you know about their experiences. Talk to graduate alumni about what they took away from their experience and what they enjoyed and found valuable. Think deeply about your personal values and how they align with your interest in research. Think about your skillset and how you want to deepen and broaden it. Think about your personality and the kind of environment where you would thrive. Other personal considerations may include the following: Are you free to move to another city? Do you want to live away from your family and friends? Would living in another country appeal to you? These are all important considerations that only you can answer. Perhaps the most important question of all: Is graduate school for me? After all, you may spend the next five years or more in graduate school and, again, it is important that you are productive and happy. The key is to make an informed choice.

Not my first choice

Sometimes your first choice doesn't work out, so be sure to be flexible and have a Plan B. In 1972, Reinhart worked on histone proteins as a summer student in the National Research Council Laboratories in Ottawa. With encouragement from his supervisors, he decided to go to graduate school and continue to work in this field with a leading researcher at the University of British Columbia. Reinhart wrote a letter (remember this was 1972!) to the scientist and applied to graduate studies. A few weeks later, he got a reply from a different faculty member, who informed Reinhart that his top choice had moved to England, but that this other faculty member had an opening in his lab, which worked on membrane proteins, a totally different field from histones. Reinhart had learned a bit about membrane proteins in a biochemistry class and knew that they were a challenge to study, but were an emerging area in biochemistry. He read papers the scientist had sent and decided to accept the offer to work on membrane proteins. Reinhart continues to work on membrane proteins in human health and disease to this day. Not his first choice, but a good one nonetheless!

Consider the Lab Organization

Labs have different organizational structures, with the faculty member acting in a supervisory role. Some labs are hierarchical and others are flatter, being more collegial and interactive. Some supervisors give their graduate students and postdoctoral fellows freedom to pursue their own lines of inquiry, while others have very defined research projects for each lab member. Some supervisors run big labs that offer their students multiple opportunities for collaboration and teamwork within the lab. Other supervisors run small labs, meaning that students in these labs will often have daily interaction with the supervisor. Another point to consider when choosing a supervisor is how often they'll be around. A new faculty member often spends more time in the lab on experiments and working directly with trainees, while more senior faculty members may have demanding administrative duties that keep them away from the lab. Scientists travel the world to present their latest findings, so your supervisor may not always be available in person, especially if they are a high-profile scientist. Perhaps working with a senior scientist may not necessarily be the best choice for you. The choice depends on your personality. Do you like to work independently or do you prefer close supervision? Regardless of your choice, your degree of independence will likely increase as you develop a successful research project.

Supervisors may have little formal training in lab management, mentoring, and conflict resolution, but this is changing through workshops and courses that often start at the postdoctoral and early career stage (https://www.sciencema.com/).

So, there are a number of general questions that need to be addressed when choosing a lab. Is the lab a large one where you might be managed by a postdoc? Is it a small lab where you will have frequent contact with your supervisor? How much time does the supervisor spend with trainees? Is the lab well-equipped? Is there opportunity for collaborations and teaching? There are also many seemingly small considerations that contribute significantly to a healthy lab environment. Do lab members work cooperatively and are they willing to share expertise, or is the lab environment competitive? Do lab members help edit manuscripts and applications for each other? Is there a leader in the lab and can you work with them? Do all lab members attend meetings to present their work? Do some lab members seem isolated? What are lab meetings and journal clubs like? Are there positive interactions with other labs? Is there a common space to gather over coffee and lunch? How are the achievements of lab members celebrated? Do lab members socialize with each other? Are there fun lab outings? Do people seem happy and do you get a positive vibe? Getting answers to these questions will allow you to make a more informed choice.

Some departments allow new students to rotate through a limited number of labs before a supervisor is selected. Be aware that supervisors are also selective in their choice of student. So, you may not land a position with your top choice. Rotations will give you a feel for the lab, but don't expect to spend much time with the supervisor. You will probably be supervised by a senior graduate student or postdoc and indeed may be recruited to continue their project. Take the opportunity to talk to those working in the lab. After all, they are the people that you would interact with on a daily basis for the next few years. Talk science in the lab but also talk informally about lab culture over lunch, coffee, or drinks. These casual conversations are often more informative than discussions of the latest publication from the lab, no matter how important this might be.

Building a Healthy Student–Supervisor Relationship

A healthy relationship with your supervisor is key to your success as a graduate student. Both the supervisor and student have many obligations to each other. You need to be aware of these before you start your graduate program. The supervisor will outline the general features of the research project; provide training in the theory and applications of techniques; monitor student progress with regular meetings; participate in supervisor committee meetings; discuss published works relevant to the project; review documents including scholarship applications, progress reports, and draft manuscripts; and, most importantly, supervise the writing of the thesis. In turn, the student will learn new techniques; keep the supervisor up-to-date on progress; read relevant papers; prepare applications; and write drafts of papers, reports, and a thesis for the supervisor to review.

> Research is a competitive team sport where you will work closely with your supervisor and others towards achieving common goals based on shared interests.

Publications are essential to the success of the supervisor and their students. In the sciences, PhD studies typically take five years and may result in multiple publications. An MSc project may be achievable within a two-year timeline with a clear outcome that perhaps includes a publication. Publications remain the currency of success in graduate school. They establish a record of accomplishment for a graduate student. For the supervisor, publications are positive outcomes of a research project and are the most important component to the successful renewal of a grant. Thus, publications appear in the curriculum vitae of both the student and the supervisor and are a shared interest.

Graduate student work is typically funded by research grants obtained by the supervisor, which may also cover funding for technicians and postdoctoral fellows. In this way, graduate students often work as part of a team on an ongoing or new research project. A graduate student's stipend (a salary) may also be provided by the supervisor and come from funding on a specific project. This places the student into an employer-employee dynamic, which makes it important for a student and their supervisor to have a good working relationship. So you are both an employee and a student. Graduate students may also obtain funding through an independent salary award or scholarship, which provides the student with a certain amount of independence and recognition. As a graduate student, you could definitely apply for your own awards, adding your supervisor's support to ensure that you submit a competitive application with outstanding letters of support.

An important feature in a good student-supervisor relationship is that feedback is provided in a timely manner. As a student, you are expected to meet deadlines, and your supervisor should also be clear on when you can expect to have their comments back on applications, presentations, posters, reports, and thesis chapters. Of course, you need to be mindful of other duties your supervisor may have such as teaching, meetings, and grant deadlines. More on "Managing Expectations" is provided in chapter 5.

> Success in graduate school depends critically on a productive relationship with one's supervisor or thesis advisor that is based on shared interests and open and honest communication.

A key to a healthy student-supervisor relationship is clear and open communication with mutual respect, moving beyond discussions of your research progress and the writing of papers. These discussions could include your evolving career goals. Regular meetings with your supervisor are essential, whether formal and scheduled on a regular basis or via an "open door" policy where meetings can be more casual. And not all discussions need to take place in the lab or in your supervisor's office. Invite them for a coffee for a more casual conversation, especially if you are seeking career advice – and be sure to show your supervisor gratitude when deserved. Many supervisors interact with their students on a daily basis, especially in the laboratory environment. The frequency and duration of meetings need to be clearly defined early in the relationship.

Setting Clear Expectations

Choosing a lab is about finding a mutual fit for both you and your supervisor. As stated above, science is the top consideration in making a good choice. But there are other things to keep in mind when deciding to work with a particular supervisor. Some supervisors have lab member expectations on their lab website. Check out the social contract on the website of Dr. Pat Schloss at the University of Michigan.[4] If your prospective supervisor does not have one, or if their posted guidelines do not address your questions, then be sure to ask before joining the lab. Some sample questions for your potential supervisor or their lab members are listed below and are grouped into three categories: expectations around the research project, expectations around professional development support, and expectations from the department.

---

4 Read "Lab Social Contract" from the website of Pat Schloss, University of Michigan (2019): https://www.schlosslab.org/lab_business/social_contract.html.

A Expectations around the research project

1. What is the overall goal of your research?
2. Do you have a particular project in mind for me or do you expect me to come up with a project?
3. Will I be working alone on this project or collaborating as part of a team?
4. Will I have the freedom to develop my own research project?
5. Is there a translational/industrial aspect to the project?
6. What research grants do you currently have to support this project and when are they up for renewal? Do you have any support from industry?
7. Where will my funding come from?
8. What equipment do you have for my project and who will train me to use it safely?
9. What are my hours of work? May I work from home?
10. What is the format of your lab meetings? How are they documented? How often do they occur?
11. How long do your students typically take to complete their research and thesis?
12. How many papers do they typically publish? How many do you expect from me?
13. How is authorship on papers decided?

B Expectations around professional development support

1. Where do most of your students go after they graduate? Where are they now?
2. Do any of your alumni work in industry? Perhaps you can suggest some that I could contact?
3. I'm interested in working in industry and would like to do an internship during my program – could I take a one-term leave of absence to do this?
4. What professional development courses or workshops could I take?
5. I'd like to develop my leadership skills – do you have any suggestions? Are there any in-lab initiatives/activities I could volunteer for?

6. How much funding is available to send me to a meeting every year to present my research or to attend a workshop or course to develop my skills?
7. What graduate courses do you suggest I take?
8. What teaching assistant positions are available? Am I required to be a teaching assistant?
9. I'm interested in medical school and plan to do a Master's degree – do you have a suitable project that I can complete and publish within two years?
10. How often do you meet individually with your students? Do I need an appointment?
11. If I have an issue or concern about my professional development, how do you want me to address it?
12. Where do I go if I have a health issue?

C **Expectations from the department**
1. How many courses do I need to take?
2. Can I take courses in areas outside of my discipline?
3. What is the vacation policy?
4. What is the sick leave policy?
5. Can I choose my supervisory committee members?
6. Does your department participate in the EDI (equity, diversity, inclusion) Dimensions Charter program? (*NSERC – Dimensions – Charter*, n.d., https://www.nserc-crsng.gc.ca/NSERC-CRSNG /EDI-EDI/Dimensions-Charter_Dimensions-Charte_eng.asp)
7. How do you feel about EDI policies?
8. Is there a graduate student association and how do I get involved in student activities?
9. Who may I contact if I have an issue or concern about changing expectations?
10. What support can I expect from the Departmental Chair and Graduate Coordinator?
11. What is the role of the School of Graduate Studies?
12. Where can I find the regulations and policies that govern graduate education?

The *Oxford English Dictionary* defines a mentor as "an experienced and trusted advisor."

The Importance of Having Diverse Mentors

Your supervisor is a key to your success as a graduate student, but it is also vital to recruit others to serve as your mentors. A mentor may share information with a mentee about their own career path, as well as provide guidance, motivation, and emotional support. Your supervisor may play a role as a mentor, providing guidance and advice on your long-term career goals. But not all supervisors are good mentors, and many are not aware of career paths outside of their own. Indeed, the journal *Nature* has argued that supervisors need to be better mentors.[5] Supervisors can provide good advice on the career path they followed and may encourage you to follow the same path. In this way, they can serve as a valued role model, someone who is an admired example that you would like to emulate. Other members of the department, including professors and senior postdocs, can serve as mentors. To ensure diversity, it is useful to have mentors outside academia, especially if you are considering a career in the private or public sectors. It is also essential that graduate students have mentors outside the line of authority, such as another academic in the same or different department in order to obtain different perspectives.

Characteristics of a good mentor

- Accessible with an open-door policy
- Experienced and seasoned
- Enthusiastic and optimistic
- Empathetic and respectful
- Open-minded and appreciates differences
- Patient and good listener
- Honest and consistent
- Savvy and realistic
- Trusted and sensitive in confidential matters

---

5 D. Mehta and K. Vavitsas, "PhD Supervisors: Be Better Mentors," *Nature* 545 (2017): 158, https://doi.org/10.1038/545158a.

Anticipating Change

No matter how well informed your decision is, keep in mind that things can change. Your project may not go well and you may need to change course. You may be working on a collaborative project and need to work effectively with others. People will come and go, and you may develop personal issues with some lab members. Your own motivation may change over the years. Your initial intention of becoming a professor may wane and you may become more interested in working outside of academia. The key is to be adaptable to change, especially in your career goals as you progress through your graduate studies.

Dealing with conflict during your graduate program may be very difficult to navigate because the student-supervisor relationship is not a level playing field. The student often works on a project that is funded by the supervisor's grant. Pressure can be applied to the student to produce results needed to publish papers to renew grants. If the student's funding is paid directly by the supervisor's grant, this puts further pressure for getting the grant renewed on both the supervisor and the student – a shared interest. The student needs good letters of reference for awards and the next phase of their career, so they need to stay on good terms with their supervisor. All of these aspects can place an additional burden on students, often leading to stress and anxiety. Having open and honest lines of communication from day one, where both supervisor and student can voice their interests and find common ground, is key.

What happens when the unexpected occurs? If you sense differences in interests between you and your supervisor, it is best to address them earlier than later. Three or four years into a research project is no time to make a major change. Assess your satisfaction at the six-month and one-year points. It is possible at these early stages to change supervisors or even departments. Talk to your graduate chair and be prepared to outline your concerns and possible solutions. If you realize at year two that your supervisor and you are not a great fit, it is possible to write up a Master's thesis and then transfer into a different PhD program. Often it is possible to discuss your concerns in a supervisory committee meeting, or privately with a committee member. Your graduate coordinator or departmental chair is the next level. More serious concerns can be brought to the attention of a graduate ombudsperson or the School of Graduate Studies. It would be helpful to know these pathways before you start your graduate program.

A few critical points may cause tension and anxiety as you move through your academic program: (1) choosing your supervisory committee, (2) selecting your courses, (3) transferring from a Master's to a PhD program, (4) publishing your first paper, and (5) writing and defending your thesis. Your supervisory committee will monitor your progress and provide advice. Committee members can often provide complementary expertise and in some cases be collaborators. Seek advice from other students and discuss your choices with your supervisor. Select graduate courses that will fill your knowledge and skill gaps, even those offered by other departments. Transferring from a Master's to a PhD program is a big step. Your supervisory committee will assess your potential to complete a PhD, which requires the ability to drive a project to a successful conclusion. If your project is going well and you are comfortable in the lab environment, continuing your studies may be an easy choice. On the other hand, if your project is not going well or the lab environment is not a good fit for you, consider writing up a Master's thesis and moving to another lab for your PhD. Many students are not interested in completing a PhD. It is essential that you make this clear to your supervisor before you join the lab. Many students who complete a Master's degree often continue their education in professional schools. If this is your intention, make sure it is clear to your supervisor so they can design a project that can be completed in a timely manner, usually one and a half to two years.

Writing your first paper is both exciting and challenging. You may be expected to write at least the first draft with feedback from your supervisor. Some supervisors are more hands on, especially if there are multiple authors. Authorship on papers is a common point of conflict. It is best to discuss this with your supervisor as your project develops. Be sure to seek help with your writing, especially if English is not your first language. A handy guide to improve your writing is the classic book *The Elements of Style* by William Strunk Jr. and E.B. White.[6] Many graduate schools offer workshops and courses in academic writing, including writing scholarship applications. Persuasive communication is a skill you may develop during graduate school.

Although you are just starting out, be aware that a common point of conflict occurs near the end of a graduate program, which is often poorly defined. A PhD involves a "significant contribution to new knowledge," but what is "significant" varies by university, field, department, and even supervisor. Clearly the research needs to be of high enough quality to be published. Typical PhD programs are completed in four to six years, but it is not the time or even effort spent, but rather the work accomplished, that counts. The graduate student may feel

---

6   W. Strunk and E.B. White, *The Elements of Style*, 4th ed. (Pearson Publishing, 1999).

they have spent enough time on a project and are ready to write their thesis and graduate, while the supervisor may recognize the student as an experienced member of the research team and would like them to continue the project and publish another paper or two. Indeed, an additional paper may benefit the student if they plan to continue on the academic track. Papers do form the basis of most theses in the sciences; thus, the interests of the supervisor and student may be aligned here. A thesis is the main requirement of research-intensive graduate programs, not papers. But what if the student is not interested in a postdoctoral fellowship and plans to enter the workforce? The student may not wish to continue to work on the project just to publish another paper. Be aware that this may create a conflict. The key is not to avoid differences but to develop the skills and tools to manage them *before* they become conflicts. "Negotiation and Conflict Management" is the topic of chapter 6.

Conclusion

The choosing of your supervisor and graduate school is a pivotal decision that will affect many formative years of your graduate education and life. The science, type of mentorship, lab culture, institutional support, alumni outreach, city, and sense of community and belonging will all affect your choice and subsequent journey. Collect all the information before you make this important decision and find what is best for you and your values and interests.

FURTHER DISCUSSION

1. In one sentence outline the reason for your choice of supervisor. Discuss how this will serve you and your work throughout your time in graduate school.
2. What word or phrase describes a healthy lab culture to you? Discuss why this is important to you.
3. Discuss the potential advantages/disadvantages of a lab rotation system.

TAKING ACTION

1. Prepare a list of three potential supervisors and consider the pros and cons of each based on your research interests and personal circumstances.
2. Read a paper from a lab you are considering applying to, and be prepared to discuss possible projects with the potential supervisor.
3. Reach out to a current or former member of a lab you are considering to learn about the organization and culture of the lab.

5 Managing Expectations

Key Messages

- Setting realistic and achievable expectations forms the basis of an action plan to move forward.
- Ensure that your expectations and your supervisor's expectations are aligned, and communicate your expectations regularly and in writing.
- Expectations will change throughout your graduate school journey – be ready to adapt.
- Outline your career expectations and discuss them with your supervisor.

This chapter provides guidance and some tools you can use to set and manage expectations. Your expectations for yourself in graduate school are high. Your supervisor's expectations of you are high. You also have high expectations of your training, graduate program, department, and university. But are they realistic and achievable? Clear lines of communication between you and your supervisor are essential to ensuring that expectations are met. It is vital that you have a good idea about what you expect to achieve in graduate school beyond getting a degree or further training.

Setting Expectations

During your graduate studies, you are expected to develop your knowledge and advance knowledge in your discipline by carrying out original research. You are expected to develop high-level technical skills. You are also expected to develop your communication, critical thinking, and problem-solving skills and be able to work as a productive member of a team. Getting regular assessment and feedback on your

During your training, your expectations of yourself may be to:		
Scientific	1.	Work closely with your supervisor in designing an exciting project that will make a significant advance to the field using the latest methods to produce results for publication in top journals and to include in your thesis.
	2.	Acquire technical and critical analysis skills.
	3.	Increase your knowledge base of your discipline by taking courses, reading papers, and attending seminars and meetings.
Professional Development	1.	Enhance your communication, problem-solving, and teamwork skills.
	2.	Develop teaching skills by presenting your research and by instructing and mentoring other students.
	3.	Develop your professional network so that you have a rich pool of connections to learn from and keep in touch with as you carry on in your career development.
Life	1.	Use your graduate or postdoctoral experience as a foundation to land a best-fit first job that will launch your lifetime career path.
	2.	Be content with your work-life integration.
	3.	Create a fulfilling, meaningful career path and life, honest to you.

skills development is essential. Work effectively and consistently on developing a complete skills toolbox so you can set and meet expectations during your graduate training.

These are probably some of your expectations. But are they clear to your supervisor and are your supervisor's expectations clear to you? Are all of these expectations aligned or are any of them in conflict? Too often, assumptions are made about the expectations of another person. The origin of confusion, conflict, and distress in any relationship can be assumed expectations. Open and honest communication is the key. Indeed, the first discussion of expectations should occur *before* you commit to a supervisor or project.

Expectations that are realistic and achievable come with a timeline. Some expectations are immediate, such as what experiment you expect to complete today. Others are longer term, such as publishing your research and writing and defending your thesis. It is also important to note that expectations will evolve and change over time. For example, your supervisor may expect you to assume more control over your project as your research progresses. You may be expected to work more independently and perhaps to help train and mentor others. You will expect your supervisor to help you complete your graduate program or postdoctoral fellowship in a timely manner and with the next step of your career in mind. The expectations you and your supervisor have of each other will evolve over your graduate program. This is normal, and expectations should be continually evaluated and modified as necessary.

It is also important to note that expectations may change and they may change quickly. Problems can emerge. For example, what if the equipment you were using has broken down and needs to be sent out for repair for three weeks? Or a family member needs your assistance with an unexpected issue? You need to be able to pivot quickly and find alternative solutions. You never want to remain "stuck." Finding yourself "stuck" is an opportunity to research, learn, and problem-solve with a team or on your own. One of the key skills you will learn in graduate school is problem-solving. The challenges you face will allow you to develop this skill. In fact, you will likely be asked about how you solved a challenge in a future job interview.

A key element to success in graduate school and beyond is setting realistic and achievable expectations for yourself and your supervisor.

Part of setting and meeting expectations is staying connected with your supervisor either through casual daily conversations in the lab or via scheduled video or face-to-face meetings. Email is to provide information, action items, and agendas or to follow up on a meeting, but is not the place to discuss personal problems or conflicts. When you meet your supervisor and/or committee, come prepared with an agenda or a written list of topics for discussion. Document the results of the meeting with an action plan focused on meeting expectations. Be sure to meet regularly, confirming with your supervisor what frequency works for both of you, be it weekly, monthly, or something in between. Use the negotiation skills that you will learn in chapter 6, "Negotiation and Conflict Management," to set these mutual expectations.

Here is some advice for arranging productive meetings. Book the meeting at a mutually agreeable time and send an agenda to your supervisor before the meeting so they know what you would like to discuss.

An example would be:

1. Summary from last meeting
2. Results of recent experiments

3. Figure updates for publication
4. Statistical question for dataset
5. Next steps

After the meeting, it is always good practice to document the results. For example, your supervisor may have discussed a new idea or direction with you. It's a good idea to follow up with an email summarizing the discussion, to be clear that you are on the same page. For example, after the meeting, you might send an email with the following: "I understand that you want me to work with our postdoc to develop a new high-throughput drug screening assay and that you have spoken to them about this arrangement." You can also go back to the agenda, type up action items for each point, and send them to your supervisor. This will give you a record of what was discussed to prevent miscommunication regarding your research progress.

CRAVE for Managing Expectations

The mnemonic CRAVE (see box below) is useful in assessing your expectations on an ongoing basis. Are expectations clearly articulated? Are they realistic? Are they achievable? Have they been validated? Setting expectations forms the basis of an action plan to move forward. You can also use CRAVE to assess your activities in a purposeful way. Writing down your expectations and discussing them with your supervisor is certainly a best practice.

CRAVE for your research expectations

Clear – Is the rationale for the project clearly articulated – the what and why?

Realistic – Is the timeline and workflow realistic – the where and when?

Achievable – Do you have the skills and support to achieve the goals – the who and how?

Validated – Is the research plan validated with feedback from your supervisor and committee – are you and your supervisor in agreement with the expectations and the timeline?

Expectations – Do you and your supervisor share a common interest in meeting the expectations of your project goals?

CRAVE for your professional development expectations

Clear – Is the rationale for professional development activities clearly articulated – the what and why?

Realistic – Is the timeline of the activity realistic – the where and when?

Achievable – Do you have the skills and support needed to achieve the goals – the who and how?

Validated – Is the activity validated with feedback from your mentors – are you and your mentors in agreement with your expectations and timeline?

Expectations – Do you and your supervisor share a common interest in meeting the expectations of your professional development and career exploration?

An example of the CRAVE method for a meaningful engagement may be your desire to have an experience as a teaching assistant (TA) to contribute to the education of undergraduate students and deepen your understanding of pedagogy. Are you clear about why you would like to teach? Perhaps you are interested in developing your communication skills or assuming a future teaching position. Is it realistic for you to take on this additional task? How much time would you have to invest in this activity outside the lab? If your TA work will take three hours a week, explain to your supervisor how you will make up for that time in the lab. Next, do you have the skills required for teaching? Perhaps the university provides training for TAs. How does this activity allow you to meet the expectations of your supervisor? You will have to articulate to your supervisor how teaching would improve your communication, writing, and mentoring skills, helping you to be more successful in your research and preparing you for an academic or non-academic career path. Finally, set expectations for your teaching activity that align with your and your supervisor's values and interests. For example, you might address their research interest by offering to help find potential future research students for their lab from your classes. After discussing all of these points, come to an agreement with your supervisor, which will validate your plan with mutual benefits. Coming to an agreement will require good negotiation skills, the topic of chapter 6.

My Great Expectations

What are your expectations of yourself? You have done well as an undergraduate student. You can learn material easily, have good study habits, and are good at writing exams; these are great academic skills.

But what about knowing yourself and the sources of your beliefs? What about the "why"? What major challenges have you faced? How good are you at facing failure? Graduate studies, especially at the PhD level, are traditionally about becoming an expert in your discipline and pushing forward the limits of our knowledge. These experiences often come with difficulties and roadblocks. This is where graduate studies differ from undergraduate education. Therefore, your expectations should change, too. Imagination and curiosity are more useful skills in research than book smarts and a perfect GPA. Indeed, some students who find school easy and enter graduate school with a high GPA often have a difficult time. This is not because they are suddenly not "smart," but rather because they have not developed problem-solving skills or have never needed to make a major change in direction or approach. Dealing with perfectionism is a common issue for graduate students.

A graduate degree in the sciences is all about exploration and pushing forward the boundaries of knowledge. So, even if you memorized the latest textbook in a discipline or your supervisor taught you everything they know about a subject, this alone will not advance the field. To paraphrase Captain Kirk, "To go where no one has gone before" – that's what research is all about, exploring the unknown and dealing with uncertainty. As mentioned previously, you need to have a strong work ethic to succeed in research. You also have to be able to deal with failure, or what can be better reframed as "growth opportunities." Expect these to arise, and learn from them. Thomas Edison took 1,000 attempts before he created a lightbulb that worked. These were not 1,000 failures, but 1,000 steps to success. Embrace these opportunities, as they will make you more enlightened, scientifically and professionally.

Indeed, many of the major breakthroughs in research are made quite by accident, not by clever design. How good are your skills of observation? Can you see what others may miss? Can you connect two seemingly unrelated concepts to find something new? Of course, many experiments fail because of technical mistakes, which is not what we are referring to here. Perhaps your results do not support your hypothesis or that of your supervisor. This can cause a great deal of stress and anxiety. Perhaps you need a more effective approach to answer the question. Or perhaps you are trying to answer too specific a question or too big a question. Think more broadly. What are the major questions in the field? How can you make an impact? What is the knowledge gap you are trying to fill? Are you resilient? Can you pivot quickly? These questions can be answered by being mindful, a skill that needs to be developed, especially by science students who by nature may not be very reflective. Review chapter 3 on "Knowing Yourself" for more on mindfulness.

My Supervisor's Expectations of Me

What are your supervisor's expectations of you? Were they clearly articulated to you, or have you made assumptions of what they are? In business, these expectations have strict timelines and are often called deliverables. There will be "deliverables" during your graduate education – i.e., anything with a deadline. The big one is, of course, your thesis. Other examples of deliverables include a report for a scheduled committee meeting, an application for a scholarship, an abstract for a meeting, data for a grant application, and a slide for a presentation. Write down the tasks you need to complete and be very mindful of their deadlines. Do you understand your supervisor's rationale for having you complete these deliverables? Their interests in the deliverables? Why these expectations are important to your supervisor? Perhaps your supervisor needs results quickly for a paper to submit by a grant deadline. If you feel that the expectations are unrealistic, say so, but give a reason why and provide an alternative. Be solution-oriented. Be authentic to yourself. Do not overpromise. If you need help, ask for it, with details. You need to clearly articulate your needs to your supervisor and come to an agreement or compromise on those matters. For example, you may need help with a new technique or data analysis. Perhaps you don't have enough mice available right now to produce a sufficient sample size for the desired results, so you discuss this with your supervisor and you both agree that you'll do a similar experiment but instead of using the transgenic model, you'll use a pharmacological inhibitor. As you work towards the mutually agreed goals, keep up regular communication, provide updates and look for feedback and acknowledgment. This will ensure that you are comfortable that your supervisor's expectations for the next meeting are realistic and achievable. Perhaps you could ask someone to help you with assays, do data analysis, or read a draft of your report before you hand it in. Make sure you give yourself enough time to do a good job. Your reputation is on the line.

It takes time to build a solid reputation, but it can be lost very quickly with a serious misstep.

My Expectations of My Supervisor

What are your expectations of your supervisor and your supervisory committee? Clear communication is essential here. Steer clear of assumptions and apply the CRAVE method. Make sure communication is clear and you and your supervisor are aligned in setting goals. This often requires you to take a deep dive into finding the common interest, the topic of chapter 6, "Negotiation and Conflict Management."

A key to aligning your expectations of your supervisor and their expectations of you is to come up with a list of mutual expectations that have been agreed upon. One method is to prepare a checklist of expectations[1] and discuss them one-on-one with your supervisor, either in person or virtually. Write these on a document with a date, and have your supervisor check them for accuracy so you both have records to ensure clarity as your project progresses through the years. The expectations you discuss may revolve around formal degree requirements such as funding, length of the program, required courses, supervisory committee meetings, and thesis preparation and defence. Other expectations may include hours of work and vacation time. Be sure you are both on the same page for each expectation.

Mutual expectation examples
Mutual expectations more specifically could include commitments, such as:
  We will create a research plan with realistic timelines and deliverables.
  We will work together to develop my research skills.
  We will discuss my research progress on a weekly basis.
  We will hold supervisory committee meetings every six months.
  We will agree on the timing of assignments and feedback.
  We will discuss authorship of papers before the research starts.
  We will develop my writing and oral presentation skills.
  We will discuss my career goals.
  We will acknowledge the value of equity, diversity, and inclusion in a healthy and safe lab environment.
  We will respect confidentiality on personal issues.
  We will manage potential conflicts based on common interests.

---

1 Read this article from Academiac.net: "Checklist to Clarify Supervisor and PhD Student Expectations" (2018), https://academiac.net/2018/11/13/checklist -to-clarify-supervisor-and-phd-student-expectations/.

Examples of your supervisor's expectations of you could be the following:

You will maintain at least a B+ in courses.

You will apply for a graduate student scholarship each year.

You will notify the supervisor or a lab member when you would like assistance with your scientific or professional development, such as learning a new technique or practicing a seminar presentation, or if you experience any wellness matters that might affect your work.

If you do not meet our agreed-upon expectations, please tell the supervisor. If after discussion, you need to speak to a third party, we can contact the graduate coordinator for mediation.

Examples of your expectations of your supervisor could be the following:

I will meet with you once [a day, a week, every 2 weeks – this will depend on what you agreed upon] to discuss my scientific work.

I will meet with you once [a year or every six months] to discuss my individual development plan.

You will give me feedback on my papers within 3–4 weeks [this timeframe also depends on what you agreed upon].

If I do not meet the mutual expectations we agreed upon, call me out on it. If after discussion, you need to speak to a third party, contact the graduate coordinator for mediation.

Managing Expectations

A useful tool used by many universities in managing supervisor-student expectations is the Kiley-Cadman questionnaire. This document originated from work by Ingrid Moses (Centre for Learning and Teaching, University of Technology, Sydney), which was adapted by Margaret Kiley and Kate Cadman (Advisory Centre for University Education at the University of Adelaide), and was further adapted by Steve Lee (Graduate Diversity Officer for the STEM Disciplines at UC Davis) with input by Chris Golde (Stanford University). The questionnaire is particularly useful early in the student-supervisor relationship because it deals with a shared responsibility and finding the right balance.

Questionnaire for Aligning Expectations in Research Mentoring Relationships

Mentor/Supervisor:		Mentee/Student:	
Time Period:		Dept./Program:	

For each pair of statements, determine your preference. For example, with statement pair #1, if you believe the ideal mentoring relationship focuses on common research interests, select 1, 2, or 3. Or if you think the ideal relationship focuses on similar working and communication styles, select 4, 5, or 6. Avoid filling in "3.5" for your responses.

1.	In an ideal mentoring relationship, the mentor and mentee should have similar research interests.	1 2 3 4 5 6	In an ideal mentoring relationship, both should have similar working and communication styles.
2.	In an ideal mentoring relationship, mentors should provide close supervision and guidance.	1 2 3 4 5 6	In an ideal mentoring relationship, mentors should provide much freedom and independence for the mentees to explore and learn themselves.
3.	Mentors should only accept mentees when they have specific and deep knowledge of the mentee's research topic.	1 2 3 4 5 6	Mentors can provide overall guidance, and so should feel free to accept mentees from a broad range of disciplines.
4.	A personal and friendly relationship between mentor and mentee is important for a successful relationship.	1 2 3 4 5 6	A professional relationship is advisable to maintain objectivity for mentee and mentor during their work.
5.	The mentor is responsible for providing emotional support and encouragement to the mentee.	1 2 3 4 5 6	Personal counselling and support are not the responsibility of the mentor.
6.	It's important for the mentoring relationship to focus only on professional and academic issues; thus issues of cultural and personal identity are inappropriate.	1 2 3 4 5 6	It's important for the mentee to thrive fully, and so it's appropriate to directly discuss issues of cultural and personal identity in the mentoring relationship.
7.	It's important for the mentor and mentee to challenge each other, and so disagreements will be common and acceptable.	1 2 3 4 5 6	It's important for the mentor and mentee to have consensus, and so both should seek to maintain harmony in their relationship.
8.	The mentor should play a significant role in deciding on the research focus for the mentee.	1 2 3 4 5 6	The research focus should be selected by the mentee.
9.	When choosing research topics, I prefer to work on projects with potential for high payoffs, even if it involves high risk.	1 2 3 4 5 6	When choosing research topics, I prefer to work on projects that have a strong and safe chance of success, even if the payoff is low.
10.	The mentor should decide how frequently to meet with the mentee.	1 2 3 4 5 6	The mentee should decide when they want to meet with the mentor.

11.	The mentor should provide the rules and guidelines for the program or dept. to the mentee.	1 2 3 4 5 6	It is the mentee's responsibility to gather and learn the rules and guidelines of the program or dept.
12.	The mentor is responsible for finding funding until the mentee graduates or completes the program.	1 2 3 4 5 6	Mentees are responsible for finding their own sources of funding.
13.	The mentor should be the primary guide for the mentee in their academic and professional goals.	1 2 3 4 5 6	The mentee should gather multiple mentors as they work towards their academic and professional goals.
14.	The mentor should be the first place to turn when the mentee has problems with the research project.	1 2 3 4 5 6	Mentees should try to resolve problems on their own, including seeking input from others, before bringing a research problem to the mentor.
15.	The mentor should check regularly that the mentee is working consistently and finishing tasks.	1 2 3 4 5 6	The mentee should work independently and productively, and ask for help when needed.
16.	The mentor should develop an appropriate plan and timetable of research and study for the mentee.	1 2 3 4 5 6	The mentee should develop their own plan and timetable of research and study, and seek input from the mentor only as needed.
17.	The mentor should initiate the preparation of presentations, papers, and reports.	1 2 3 4 5 6	Presentations, papers, and reports should be started with a first draft by the mentee.
18.	The mentor should insist on seeing all drafts of work (presentations, thesis, papers, etc.) to ensure that the mentee is on the right track.	1 2 3 4 5 6	Mentees should submit drafts of work (presentations, thesis, papers, etc.) only when they want constructive criticism from the mentor.
19.	It's the mentor's responsibility to first explain about co-authorship early in the process.	1 2 3 4 5 6	It's the mentee's responsibility to make sure there is mutual understanding about co-authorship.
20.	The mentor is responsible for providing career advice and professional connections to the mentee.	1 2 3 4 5 6	Because professional options these days are numerous, mentees should seek career advice and connections from other sources.

As indicated in the previous chapter, an example of clear lab expectations can be found at this link to a lab supervisor's website.[2] Perhaps you can encourage your supervisor that the next lab meeting be one where all of the lab members together draft a document such as this.

> Time and project management are transferable skills that can and must be learned in order to meet expectations in a realistic manner.

A Workable Work Plan

Graduate students typically have supervisory committee meetings at least once a year to review progress and come up with a work plan. A year, however, is too long an interval for timely feedback on progress. Making matters worse, some students may delay this meeting if they feel their progress is slow. Try to avoid this, since such a time may be the best moment to have a committee meeting – it's an opportunity to ask for advice on next steps from the experts. Problems arise when lines of communication become fractured. An ideal mentorship experience may include a formal meeting with your supervisor about once a month and informal meetings more often. A daily or weekly check-in is helpful to enhance communication and the flow of information, especially at the beginning of your program.

Putting together a work plan with clear timelines and deliverables is a best practice for meeting expectations. A monthly or weekly plan works best, all in the context of longer-term planning of an academic term or year. Of course, it is good practice to set out a plan for each day of work. Remember, tomorrow (the procrastinator's friend) never comes and yesterday is gone. Having a specific target date is also the best practice for meeting your deliverables. A tool commonly used in project management is a Gantt chart.[3] A Gantt chart is a bar graph that displays a series of activities or tasks in rows with time intervals in columns. Each

---

2 Read "Lab Social Contract" from the website of Pat Schloss, University of Michigan (2019), https://www.schlosslab.org/lab_business/social_contract.html.
3 Read "What Is a Gantt Chart?" (n.d.), https://www.gantt.com/.

activity has a defined beginning and a projected end. The activities can have different durations and can overlap. Progress in each activity is tracked against expectations and is displayed on the chart.

A simple example of a Gantt chart that Reinhart constructed for his sabbatical year is shown below. Major activities are indicated on a monthly basis. These include the writing of a book, design of a new online course, writing of an invited review article, and working on research projects, including time in a collaborator's laboratory. Of course, there are regular meetings and other activities over the year that aren't shown on this chart. Grey indicates planned activities, with the shade of grey indicating the intensity of the work, and the three-month time elapsed in the darkest shade. Reinhart also blocks off time for other activities not in the Gantt chart: shaded black for vacation time and time away from tasks, although he never fails to take his laptop to check his emails! A checkmark in the corner of a box indicates a task has been completed. Note that a checkmark is better to recognize that a task is completed rather than using an "X" or crossing out the activity as if it never existed. The Gantt chart is also a living document that can be modified as tasks are completed, delayed, added, or abandoned. Specific research projects, writing reports and papers, preparing for presentations and committee meetings, and reading papers are all items found in Gantt charts for graduate students.

Reinhart's sabbatical projects Gantt chart
September 2021–August 2022

Month	1	2	3	4	5	6	7	8	9	10	11	12
Time Elapsed												
Book												
Course												
Review			√									
Research												
Vacation												

Timely Feedback Is Essential

One major issue that students commonly face is not getting timely feedback on their work, particularly for their writing. All labs should promote a culture of writing, including persuasive writing to convince readers of your view, and should provide opportunities to develop this skill to a very high level. Writing opportunities can include applying for an award and drafting a paper or a chapter in your thesis. If your supervisor is not busy teaching, writing, or reviewing grants, occupied with other professional activities or on vacation, a two-week review period is reasonable, but longer than a month is not. The feedback you receive from your supervisor will improve your writing. Let your supervisor know in advance when they will receive your work, and do this in writing. You need to set realistic deadlines for writing assignments. If you make a commitment to have a report in by Friday, make sure that this is realistic and achievable for you to accomplish. On the other hand, if your supervisor makes this request and you cannot meet the deadline, let your supervisor know and provide a compelling reason for why you need more time. A sample reason and providing an alternative would be: "As you may know I am running a tutorial session this week. I can set aside some time on the weekend and have the report to you by noon on Monday." Be as precise as possible. This is a key element of time management. One way to manage deadlines is to estimate the amount of time you think it will take and notify your supervisor of that amount multiplied by two. For example, if you think you can provide feedback within three days, tell them "I will have something for you in a week." Thus, if you provide anything earlier than a week, you have exceeded their expectations!

Unrealistic Expectations

Do you need to meet all of the expectations you and your supervisor set? Sometimes what you set out as realistic early on in your research is simply not achievable during the course of a graduate education. Perhaps you were too ambitious or too optimistic. Perhaps there was a technical roadblock. So do not judge yourself too harshly if you are unable to meet all your expectations or those of your supervisor. Perhaps, upon reflection, they were not realistic or achievable. If you are having problems, employ the CRAVE method to modify your expectations and try to come up with a modified work plan. Many times, research during the first few years of a PhD program is challenging and may not result in any significant results. These years may take a toll on mental wellness as some students are not used to "failure" or "growth insights." You are not alone. The pathway to discovery is often unnerving, unexpected, and puzzling. Your expectations during these years can be to explore the unknown and embrace the uncertainty, all while remaining excited for future possibilities. Indeed, sometimes when things are going well and expectations are met you may increase your goals. For example, you may end up publishing an additional paper based on an unexpected finding or a new collaboration you set up. Resiliency is certainly a key skill to develop. Dr. Uri Alon's TED talk addresses embracing uncertainty during research.[4]

Sometimes expectations are unreasonable, unacceptable, and counterproductive, such as a supervisor who expects you to work 12 hours a day, 7 days a week. Though this is certainly an unrealistic expectation, keep in mind that research is rarely a 9-to-5 job. Again, be open and honest and explain your needs to your supervisor so you can come to a mutually acceptable agreement. Although some students and supervisors might be on friendly terms, the relationship should be professional and not personal. There is always the power dynamic to keep in mind. Occasionally, there may be a push to get the final results for a paper or your thesis, and extra effort and hours are required, but this should not be the norm. Similarly, all graduate students are entitled to vacation, taken annually at a mutually agreed time. For postdocs, hours of work, vacation time, and sick leave are often part of a contract. It is essential that you discuss your working conditions with your supervisor as part of managing their expectations.

Career Expectations

Looking forward, what are your career expectations? Managing your career expectations can be a shared responsibility between you and your supervisor, graduate unit, and university. Many students enter graduate school with the singular goal of becoming a university professor. The reality is that only a small fraction of PhD graduates are likely to follow this traditional path, and most will find employment outside academia. Becoming aware of diverse careers is helpful in your exploration and career planning.

Some, but not all, supervisors are open to you exploring various career paths. They may be aware of where you can find information on skills development and career exploration, and know that such exploration and skill development take time. If your professor is not able or willing to provide meaningful career advice, you can find others in your professional network, starting with members of your supervisory

---

4 Watch this TED Talk from Uri Alon: "Why Truly Innovative Science Demands a Leap into the Unknown" (2014), https://youtu.be/F1U26PLiXjM.

committee or other faculty members in your department. In addition, there are other sources of career information. Most universities now provide professional advice on career exploration for graduate students. Information on career options are available beyond websites – such as career panels, workshops, and courses. Expert advice and career guidance are available to you through opportunities such as mentoring and internships, and these will also help you to develop your professional network. Document your professional development activities, which become an important part of your résumé. As discussed, one tool to develop your skills and document your career path is an IDP. The key is to begin your career exploration early and document the results.

Conclusion

Setting expectations for yourself that are realistic and achievable is very important, but also keep in mind that your expectations will change. This is particularly true for your longer-term career expectations. Again, many of the tools you can use during your graduate education (e.g., CRAVE, Gantt Charts, IDPs) can also be used throughout your career. It's never too early to start building your skills toolbox. Learning to set realistic and achievable expectations and communicating them is a skill you will use throughout your career.

FURTHER DISCUSSION

1. What are your expectations of graduate school and how do they align with your values and interests?
2. What are your expectations of your supervisor?
3. If you were supervising undergraduate students, what would you expect from those students?

TAKING ACTION

1. Consider your career expectations and if they are realistic and achievable. Revise them if needed.
2. Prepare a checklist of mutual expectations between you and your supervisor and meet to discuss them.
3. Encourage the entire lab to brainstorm expectations of each other and document the results.

6 Negotiation and Conflict Management

Key Messages

- Good negotiation skills are vital to building positive relationships.
- Work towards common interests during a negotiation.
- Emotional intelligence is vital to negotiating with others.
- You must learn to deal effectively with conflicts, as they will inevitably arise.

In chapter 3, "Knowing Yourself," we highlighted the importance of reflecting on your values, interests, skills, and personality. These are key elements in win-win negotiations. Values like empathy, honesty, integrity, and trust can lead to success in negotiation. So, too, can values like competition, power, and wealth, although these particular values often result in win-lose results. Negotiation may also require flexibility, open-mindedness, and patience. Whatever the values, understanding and aligning interests between parties are key to a successful negotiation. In addition, negotiation is a problem-solving skill, one that you will use throughout your career. Negotiating is not only an important part of landing a job, but is also an important skill in managing and resolving conflicts in any relationship. And finally, it's important to note that some personalities can be incompatible and work against one another when it comes to resolving conflicts and building relationships. The key here is to focus on the problem and the positions and interests, rather than the person. Examples of common problems that may occur between graduate students and supervisors include hours of work and vacation time, priority access to equipment, data ownership, authorship on papers, and time to completion. Problems can also arise between graduate students, and it is best to resolve these between the parties involved before turning to the supervisor. Many of these problems can be avoided if expectations are set and communicated early. But some problems will inevitably arise, and good negotiation skills will be essential at those moments.

Getting to Yes

In their best-selling book, *Getting to Yes*, Roger Fisher, William Ury, and Bruce Patton[1] outlined four key principles in successful negotiation:

1. Focus on interests, not positions
2. Separate the people from the problem
3. Create options for mutual gain
4. Use objective criteria

Many educational programs on negotiations are based on these principles.[2]

Positions and Interests

The key to successful conflict management is to know the difference between positions and interests, and then to negotiate the interests that underlie the positions. What are positions? What are interests? A position is the stance a person takes. It is *what* they say they will do. An example of a position is "I am going to work eight hours today." The interest is the underlying reason for the position. The interest in this example would be "I want to work 8 hours today instead of 10 hours because I want to have time to add a swim class and a home-cooked dinner to my day." The interest is *why* they will do something.

As for avoiding conflicts in the relationship between you and your supervisor, let's start with interests. Do you know what your interests are in a negotiation? What about the interests of your supervisor? Are your interests and those of your supervisor aligned? Do your positions differ? Open and honest communication is key to identifying interests in a successful negotiation. Let's look at an example. A common interest in research is to produce high-quality data that can be published in a peer-reviewed journal. But what are the positions of you and your

---

1   R. Fisher, W. Ury, and B. Patton, *Getting to Yes*, 3rd ed. (Penguin Books, 2011).
2   K. Shonk, "Six Guidelines for 'Getting to Yes,'" Program on Negotiation, Harvard Law School (2023), https://www.pon.harvard.edu/daily/negotiation-skills-daily/six-guidelines-for-getting-to-yes/.

supervisor? Say the supervisor's position is the expectation that a student works 12 hours a day, 7 days a week. The student's position is the expectation of working a regular 8-hour day, 5 days a week. Or your supervisor may want you to complete three experiments by the end of the week, but you feel that you only have time to complete two. To address these positions, let's negotiate the mutual interest of research productivity.

The interest underlying the supervisor's position may be that they need to submit the paper before the next grant deadline. The student's interest is about working 40 hours a week and leaving at 5 p.m. because they want to have time for exercise classes and home-cooked meals. Or the student can only complete two experiments because they need to attend a professional development workshop. The shared interest is producing a high-quality publication. In addressing the supervisor's interest of getting the paper published, the student can propose a detailed plan with a timeline to complete the necessary experiments for the paper during a 40-hour work week or to complete the third experiment on the weekend if necessary. The plan may include prioritizing the important experiments within this publication, recruiting help, or perhaps alleviating the graduate student of other lab duties or putting other studies on pause. The plan would also include the expected timeline of when the supervisor would review the draft and return it with feedback. With this plan in hand, both the student and the supervisor can agree on a realistic timeline for submission of the manuscript, a common interest. Students who work a healthy number of hours are more productive in the long run and are less likely to suffer from burnout.

> Research is not a 9:00 a.m. to 5:00 p.m. job, and experiments and deadlines may require working longer days or on the weekend on occasion, but this is not to be the norm.

A second common example of a conflict in graduate school is a student's position of "I want to take on a teaching position" versus a supervisor's position of "I do not want any student working outside my lab": fixed positions. The student's interest would be "I would like experience teaching and to obtain some extra income to help my family." The supervisor's interest may be the worry that "time away from the lab would result in less productivity." In such a case, the student could outline how many hours the teaching position will entail (objective criteria), and how they would make up for that time by working a longer weekday or on a weekend afternoon (options). The student might also point out that teaching undergraduates may result in recruiting a potential future lab member, another interest of the supervisor. Or that working as a teaching assistant would help the student develop better communication and time management skills, which would improve the quality of the lab work and the delivery of presentations that arise from it. When the student and supervisor work towards a common interest, this ensures that both parties are happy with the result.

During a negotiation, it is important to focus on the *interests* of the underlying positions, rather than the positions themselves, to address the common interests between the two parties.

Managing Your Emotions

Good negotiators have a high emotional intelligence. They are aware of their own feelings and how their behaviour may affect others. They are able to move past positions to understand interests. They can focus on the problem and not the person. They are active listeners. They build relationships. They are consistently respectful. They may walk away for a minute or take some deep breaths to manage the emotions, but they do not let anger take over the conversation. They can separate the people from the problem.

One useful strategy in negotiation is to speak for yourself, not for the other person. Use "I" not "You." "I" puts across your point of view, your interest. "You" is often accusatory and makes assumptions about the other's interest. An example: "You continually ask me to do additional work on this project!" versus "I would appreciate a meeting to review the progress I have made on my project and to create a plan to complete it."

During negotiations, emotions can arise and lead to problems rather than solutions. Anger is a natural human emotion that occurs when people do not acquire what they want. The "fast food" rule helps alleviate anger. What happens when you drive up to a window for fast food? You tell them your order and they immediately repeat your order, to confirm they have understood you. Then you move forward to pay, pick up your order, and say thank you. The fast food rule applies to all relationships, whether at home or at work. When someone is upset about something, simply listen with no interruptions, even if you think they have their facts wrong. When they are finished speaking, repeat what they said in a summarized shorter statement, "If I correctly understood, your concern is...." Acknowledging that you have listened and understood by repeating what they have just said helps calm down the speaker.

Here is an example of how you might apply the fast food rule to a situation with a student you are mentoring. Say they are upset about how much work they have, and they want to tell everyone. If you are in the middle of work, you can request a chat during coffee time and when they confide in you, simply listen until they are finished speaking. Then repeat, "I understand you are upset because of 1, 2, and 3, yes?" As soon as you repeat their worries, they will be less angry already. Then you can work towards meeting the underlying interests – the reason why they are upset. With this information in hand, you both can explore options to problem solve together. Providing options helps to empower people to make meaningful choices, especially if the student provides the options rather than the supervisor providing options. Once a choice has been selected, you can come up with a plan that is realistic and achievable.

> Managing and resolving conflicts can help build positive relationships and promote teamwork based on identifying common interests and goals.

Create Options for Conflict Resolution

A conflict occurs when interests collide. Most of the time, if expectations are clearly expressed by both parties involved, a collision can be avoided. However, what if a conflict arises during the course of a research project? Avoidance can be one option in dealing with a conflict, but it may lead to anxiety, distress, and resentment. When do students opt to avoid a conflict? Here is an example: Kay was almost finished her thesis when a new student, Bill, whose personality clashed with Kay's, joined the lab. Instead of dealing with the conflict with Bill, Kay decided that she would manage it by avoiding Bill as much as possible. She did not want to invest time and energy in a conflict when she was almost finished in the lab. Kay also had the option to bring her concerns to the attention of her supervisor. This would put the onus on the supervisor, but Kay would need to provide possible solutions. Often supervisors are not aware that a problem has arisen, but once informed they are keen to resolve it. A private meeting with Kay may be necessary, but ideally the supervisor should meet with Bill and Kay together to directly address both of their concerns. A lab meeting where the supervisor clarifies roles, responsibilities, and codes of conduct for all is another option that Kay can provide. However, be prepared to find that many supervisors lack conflict resolution training or skills and may be reluctant to intervene. In that case, Kay may need to involve a graduate administrator or departmental chair.

As research becomes more interdisciplinary and involves teams, conflicts can arise between team members, especially if expectations of each individual were not discussed prior. It is best to try to resolve differences between the two parties, but often mediation is required. If the conflict escalates to intimidation or bullying, it is your obligation to report this behaviour. Sadly, bullying in graduate school is not uncommon.[3] We all need to create a healthy lab environment.

If the conflict is with a supervisor, avoidance may not be the best option, as supervisors and students most often have mutually shared interests and need to work together to accomplish their goals. Indeed, conflicts can open up an opportunity for honest communication and dialogue. It can reveal the true interests of both sides. Be prepared. Think about your underlying interests. Consider the interests of your supervisor, but do not make assumptions. Ask questions. Get the facts. Defer judgement. Create options to align interests. Creating options involves creative thinking rather than holding a firm position. Work towards a solution not just for you but for everyone – a win-win scenario. Often, reframing the problem will provide new insights. Problem solving is a key skill that you can develop during negotiation.

Research remains a largely hierarchical enterprise. The supervisor may have the last say as some things may not be negotiable. For example, a department may have a set policy of stipend levels, so asking for a raise is out of the question. Do you have any other options? What if your position is "I want a raise," because the underlying interest is "I need more money to pay for living expenses"? An option may be to take on a teaching assistant position. Power dynamics exist in many

---

3 R. Trager, "Worldwide Survey of PhD Students Reveals Bullying, Discrimination and Anxiety," *Chemistry World*, Royal Society of Chemistry (2019), https://www.chemistryworld.com/news/worldwide-survey-of-phd-students-reveals-bullying-discrimination-and-anxiety/4010693.article.

work situations. Learning how to deal with them through effective negotiation will allow you to be a better communicator and team member.

Restorative Conflict Resolution

Restorative conflict resolution not only resolves a conflict but restores a
positive working relationship between the student and the supervisor
by repairing the damage done to both parties by the conflict. Restorative conflict resolution can repair a broken relationship as it focuses on
doing *with*, rather than doing for, doing to, or doing against. Restorative
practices build on a foundation of positive values, empathy, and the application of win-win negotiation techniques. Some of these techniques
include an open one-on-one dialogue, expert mediation with a third
party, or group learning circles for teams. Restorative approaches can
solve problems, resolve conflicts, rebuild relationships, reduce harm,
and create a healthy and productive workplace.[4]

Authorship

Let's take a common source of conflict in science: Who is the first author
on a paper? Imagine that a postdoctoral fellow and a graduate student
have worked together on a project where they have applied their complementary technical skills. The work has gone well and in discussion with
the supervisor, they have decided it is time to write up the manuscript. All
agree that the supervisor is the corresponding author since the supervisor
developed the project, obtained funding, will write the discussion section,
and will edit the final manuscript. Both the graduate student and the
postdoctoral fellow are firm in their position that they deserve to be first
author as they performed an equal amount of work towards the publication. But let's look at interests. A common interest of all three is to publish
the research in a top peer-reviewed journal. But there are other interests.
The supervisor needs a paper to show productivity on the grant, which
is up for renewal. The postdoctoral fellow's interest is to strengthen their
research record and curriculum vitae as they are applying for academic
positions. The graduate student will be applying for a position in industry

---

4 L. Mochon, "Mediators as Facilitators of Restorative Justice and Restorative Practices,"
  Osgoode Law School, York University (2021), https://www.yorku.ca/osgoode
  /jib/2021/06/23/mediatiors-as-facilitators-of-restorative-justice/.

and needs to demonstrate their productivity. Are there other considerations? What are the options?

It turns out that the supervisor has been invited to present the research at an upcoming conference and to write a review article. The supervisor suggests that the graduate student could write the review article as first author, as this document could also form the basis for the introduction to their thesis. The postdoctoral fellow can present the research at the conference in place of the supervisor, which will also serve as a great networking opportunity. The graduate student can also continue to work on the project and be the first author on the follow-up paper. The postdoctoral fellow will shift gears to develop an independent project that can form the basis of their future independent research program. Based on these options, the three people involved agree that the graduate student and postdoc will have joint first-authorship in the manuscript footnotes, with the postdoctoral fellow listed first, which is the same order as the abstract for the meeting.

Now, could this collision have been prevented? If all three lab members had discussed authorship expectations *before* the work began, the "bike crash" and recovery could have been averted. A good starting point is to agree that the person who will contribute the most to the project (e.g., who will generate the most data, make the initial discovery, write the first draft) is to be the first author, regardless of career "needs." Of course, this may change as the project progresses, so regular communication is essential as is the ability to adapt to changing realities. For example, new data provided by a lab member that supports the original findings may add a new author to a paper.

Become a Problem Solver

Problem solving is a valued skill in research as well as in addressing conflicts. Using objective criteria is a scientific approach to negotiation and problem solving. Do you have all of the facts? Do you understand the interests of the other party? Do you understand *your* interests? Have you come up with options? Look at problems as challenges that need to be addressed. It may be difficult to be objective. And getting to the root of the conflict requires discussion and understanding, not blame and guilt. Problems rarely go away on their own. Indeed, unresolved conflicts can lead to a breakdown in communication and more serious problems. We know of cases where students have avoided going into the lab because of a conflict with another lab member. To avoid such situations, suggest having a brainstorming lab meeting with all lab members to come up with mutually agreed-upon expectation guidelines so everyone contributes to a positive working environment in the laboratory, including a process to resolve conflicts. Get advice and offer solutions.

Conclusion

Conflict management is a skill that strengthens over time and work-life experience. You will make mistakes. If you do, own them and apologize and learn from them. Others will make mistakes too. They may not always apologize. You cannot control others, but you can control your response to any situation. Preventing conflict is more ideal that dealing with a battle. Learning the basic terms of positions versus interests, enhancing EQ skills, and embracing differing opinions will help you build this vital skill for work and life.

FURTHER DISCUSSION

1. Negotiate the use of a laboratory instrument with a colleague using the "fast food" rule.
2. Identify a common issue that students may have with their supervisors and come up with three possible solutions.
3. Discuss what the four principles in negotiation (focus on interests, not positions; separate the people from the problem; create options for mutual gain; and use objective criteria) mean to you.

TAKING ACTION

1. Read *Getting to Yes* by Roger Fisher, William Ury, and Bruce Patton (3rd ed., Penguin, 2011) and summarize the key points.
2. Identify one of your key interests that does not align with that of your supervisor and prepare a plan to address it.
3. Negotiate a meal plan with your friends, partner, or family members using strategies outlined in this chapter.

PART III

Wellness: Taking Care of Yourself

7 Integrating Life with Work

Key Messages

- Effectively managing your time is an essential skill needed for getting the most enjoyment out of your career and life.
- Career transitions are challenging but they are important for your growth as a person.
- Integrate partners and family with work.
- Make time for your own interests and friends to maintain a healthy lifestyle and avoid burnout.

Integrating work and life is a challenge. For most, work is an essential part of life, as is family or your community of loved ones. One of the reasons for calling this work-life "integration" as opposed to "balance" is because the term "balance" suggests a difficult act during which the scales could tip at any moment. The term "integration" depicts life as a tapestry of interwoven events, loved ones, work, responsibilities, wants, needs, and deadlines, which it truly is. For some, a clear separation of work and home life is important for their wellness. The key is to be adaptable to changing circumstances. As John Lennon wrote: "Life is what happens to you while you are busy making other plans."

Conducting research is demanding, but you also have life outside the lab. How can you work in the lab at least eight hours a day, and occasionally on weekends running experiments, while taking care of your relationships with friends and family? How can you move your research project forward and keep up with writing scholarship or grant applications and your teaching duties? How can you prepare presentations for important international meetings and find time to travel while there? The pressures of work in research also exist outside of academia. If you are working as a research leader in industry, you still have proposals to write, deadlines to meet, staff to train and manage, presentations to give for investors, legal issues to deal with regarding intellectual property and pending patents, and budgets to balance with sales and marketing. Clients from different countries may prefer to have conference calls late at night or early in the morning. You may even need to travel overseas for meetings. In fact, the same skills you build as a graduate student or postdoctoral fellow to land your first job are put to use with real-life issues that arise throughout your career. Essential skills in the workplace are emotional intelligence (discussed in chapter 3, "Knowing Yourself"), time management, multitasking, managing transitions, and integrating life responsibilities with a successful career, all while incorporating your interests, curiosities, and passions.

Time Management

Time management is about controlling how much time is spent on certain activities and creating a realistic and achievable plan to complete each task in a timely manner. Good time management makes space for new opportunities and important things like family and friends. Good time management also leaves space for the unexpected, prioritizing activities, and setting time limits. Some activities in the life of a graduate student, like attending a class or seminar, are fixed, but the majority of the time will require exercising time management skills to reduce stress and anxiety and increase productivity.

Stephen R. Covey, in his best-selling book, *The 7 Habits of Highly Effective People*, outlines a useful time management matrix.[1] This matrix can be used at a high level to prioritize the importance and urgency of ongoing activities but can also be used for weekly or even daily activities. Important activities need to be scheduled and then acted upon to reduce stress. Activities that you feel are not important need to be delegated to others, automated (e.g., lab instrumentation, out-of-office email replies, calendar entries), or declined (learn to say no).[2]

---

1   S.R. Covey, *The 7 Habits of Highly Effective People: Powerful Lessons in Personal Change*, 30th anniversary ed. (Simon & Schuster, 2020).
2   M.L. Wisdom, "Graduate Study and the Time-Management Matrix," Versatile Humanists, Duke University (2018), https://versatilehumanists.duke.edu/2018/03/19/graduate-study-and-the-time-management-matrix/.

Important Urgent *(Causes stress)* Act upon	Important Not Urgent *(Where you want to be most of the time)* Schedule
Not Important Urgent *(Necessary)* Delegate, automate, or decline	Not Important Not Urgent *(Wasting time)* Delegate, automate, or decline

The best place to spend most of your time is in the upper right quadrant: important and not urgent. This quadrant includes spending time with family and friends, taking care of wellness, taking time for physical activity, and working on professional/career development. Most research time is in this quadrant until a deadline emerges for a paper to be submitted, a grant to be renewed, a poster to be presented, or a thesis to be defended – then it is moved to the left into the important and urgent quadrant. A tight deadline is certainly a great motivator to get things done.

Try a personal audit of your time matrix. Categorize activities into each of these boxes. Think about how you spent a day, a week, and a month at work. If much time went towards watching television, being online, watching the news, or playing video games, these are probably in the bottom right quadrant. Everyone needs a break and time to relax, but if most of your time is spent on "not important and not urgent," you need to ask the question: Why? Why are important tasks and urgent matters being avoided? Is the motivation lost or have values shifted? Am I missing the skills needed to complete the task? At the other extreme, are important matters *always* dealt with urgently? Why? Is it because important tasks are delayed? Perhaps it is being a perfectionist. If you relate to these thoughts, then you may need to ask the deeper question of why you are procrastinating or being a perfectionist. Alternatively, maybe you spend your time attending to "urgent" matters that are not too important. This could be a meeting you were asked to attend, but the meeting holds little interest or importance for you. Or an email message may seem urgent, but is it important? Ask these questions honestly as you add them to your time matrix. See where the time goes.

Another method for structuring time is the Pareto Analysis, which states that 80 per cent of tasks can be completed in 20 per cent of the available time, and the remaining 20 per cent of tasks will take 80 per cent of the available time to complete.[3] It is recommended that tasks falling into

---

3 "Pareto Analysis," Wikipedia, https://en.wikipedia.org/wiki/Pareto_analysis.

the first group be given a higher priority and be tackled first, while not neglecting important tasks that may take more time to complete, like writing your thesis. Breaking big tasks into smaller sections makes them seen less daunting, and this can be accomplished by setting up SMART goals, which we will discuss in chapter 9, "Developing Core Competency Skills."

Time is limited, so how do you make the most of it? Planning is key. A realistic daily plan can help guide you through the details, a weekly action plan can help accomplish the 80 per cent and also work on the 20 per cent, and a bird's-eye view of monthly or semester plans can help with seeing the big picture deadline so the weeks can be planned accordingly. If you are continually putting something off, think about how important the task is to you and if it will become urgent. Alternatively, the task may not be urgent or important so it can be eliminated from your schedule. Ensure you have all the information needed to make a wise decision.

Confirm expectations and focus on deliverables rather than on hours of work. Reassess the workload. Is it realistic and achievable? Schedule work meetings, but also block time for wellness and relationships. If a long commute is involved, work from home one day a week or work en route. Set aside time to deal with responding to emails, perhaps early in the morning or late in the evening, leaving the day free for more productive, deep work. A change in work environment can increase productivity. Read a research paper in a coffee shop rather than at your desk. Spend time in the library, even if you have a private office. Try to avoid distractions. Find a quiet space if you need one.

In addition to using your time efficiently, it's important to take breaks. The view from afar is a good one. It helps put things into perspective. Think of the many scientists who had a revelation outside work. August Kekulé came up with the structure of benzene in a dream about a snake biting its own tail. Kary Mullis, who won the Nobel Prize in Chemistry for inventing the polymerase chain reaction (PCR), came up with the concept in 1983 during a late-night drive in his Honda Civic with his then-girlfriend Jenny Barnett, who was also a chemist at Cetus Corporation, a biotechnology firm. Many of Nana's ideas arise when she is playing piano or taking a walk. Reinhart keeps a notebook handy to jot down ideas for when he is not working at his desk. Spending all your time in the lab may seem productive, but can lead to burnout. Remember to take breaks from your daily routine to refresh yourself. Try to find or create experiences to take a mini "sabbatical" at any stage of your career.[4]

---

4 N. Lee, "Creating a Sabbatical at Any Stage of Your Career," *Inside Higher Ed* (2023), https://www.insidehighered.com/opinion/career-advice/carpe-careers/2023/05/01/creating-sabbatical-any-stage-your-career.

Time is precious. Engage each moment meaningfully and purposefully.

Multitasking

"Multitasking" does not refer to performing more than one action at once, such as responding to emails while chatting and listening to a lecture at the same time. Many studies have shown that the brain does not perform well when challenged to perform multiple tasks at the same time, as productivity decreases and errors increase, which in turn wastes time and, in business, money.[5] "Multitasking" hereinafter refers to managing various projects synchronously, but actually doing each project one at a time, such as responding to emails, chatting, and listening to a lecture in a sequential order, while managing the time dedicated to each activity. In this example it may be the lecture that is urgent, but you need to decide if it is as important as responding to emails.

Successful professors are great at multitasking. In the sciences, professors need to effectively manage their research program to remain competitive. Some activities include obtaining funding, recruiting and training personnel, building a team, supervising trainees, collaborating with other scientists, and writing and publishing papers. Professors also have teaching assignments, which involve creating and delivering courses, creating and marking assignments and exams, and working with students. Furthermore, professors are expected to help with administration of their department by serving on committees or in leadership roles. They also are active in their discipline by helping to organize scientific meetings, reviewing papers, and sitting on grant review panels. Outside of academia, professionals will also have many duties and tasks. Some of these activities may include brainstorming with the team, writing business proposals, pitching ideas to potential investors, following up with clients, marketing, communications, and mentoring interns or junior associates. These activities are not done all at the same time, but rather with prioritizing and effective time management.

Multitasking involves transitioning successfully from one task to another, without necessarily having completed the first task. Of course, some tasks (e.g., 80 per cent) can be completed in a short time

---

5 "Human Multitasking," Wikipedia, https://en.wikipedia.org/wiki/Human_multitasking.

but other tasks can take much longer. Some people are quite linear in their thinking and find it difficult to switch from one task to another and back in a short timeframe. If this describes you, try to schedule enough time to complete each task before moving on to the next. Prioritize tasks and try to apply the Pareto Analysis (80 per cent of your tasks in 20 per cent of your time). On the other hand, if you are someone who can juggle multiple balls in the air at once, you need to be careful not to disperse your efforts into too many tasks because you may then find it difficult to complete any. A key skill that can help you to complete your tasks is managing transitions – small daily transitions and life's big transitions.

Managing Transitions

A career path involves many transitions. You have managed the transition from being an undergraduate student to entering graduate school – a big step in your career path. You decided on a project and a supervisor. Your life plan may be to pursue a PhD for an academic career after one or more postdoctoral fellowships. Or, after completing a PhD, you may decide to move into an internship position to work towards a career in industry. A major transitional period usually arises after the MSc, PhD, or postdoctoral fellowship, either to go on to more education, such as professional school, or take a job.

Managing transitions is an important skill to have because you will face many transitions throughout your life and career.

Here are some of life's transitional moments related to your career:

I	Undergraduate to graduate school or job
II	Graduate school to job or postdoctoral fellowship
III	Internship or postdoctoral fellowship to a job
IV	Early-career to mid-career scientist in academia or industry
V	Mid-career to late-career scientist and senior administrative positions
VI	From one career to another
VII	Official "retirement"

Nana Lee	*One of my supervisors retired recently, and I found out that she was faced with a similar career transition to those transitioning from postdoc to industry, or from a lifebreak back to career. She still wants to give back to the community, but is finding that she can't do this in the way she is used to – as a professor and researcher. It may take a while to find her niche after officially retiring. She is looking into using her skills as a teacher but with younger students from disadvantaged populations.*

The need for career transition skills continues throughout life. Most people have multiple transitions in their careers as they "climb" the academic or corporate ladder leading to leadership positions of increased responsibility. Some people pursue careers in flatter organizations, where a "matrix" rather than a "ladder" exists. In these organizations, people move "laterally" through various positions. Flatter organizations do not have a hierarchy, as seen in academia, but they still have career transitions. They value teamwork; ideas are voted on, and those who are good at managing teams become team facilitators. The need for transition skills only really hits graduate students and postdoctoral scholars when they are no longer told which classes to take, which projects to pursue, and which papers to write. Students and postdoctoral fellows have to use their own career transition skills, combined with their newly acquired scientific expertise, to come up with a career niche that allows them to follow their interests and values. That's challenging for some, especially if they have not fostered these skills before.

Sometimes, what you were counting on in your career might not materialize. Naturally, you will be disappointed and may even feel devastated. However, an alternative path may turn out to be the better fit for you. Always prepare for a Plan B. For example, you may have started your graduate studies with the goal of becoming a professor. Partway through, you realize that it is not for you. If you have developed a transferable skillset and network, you can readily make a career transition to something other than what you initially set out for. And don't try to solve all this on your own – you have the network you developed to help you. Talk to your supervisor, mentors, or others who have made similar transitions, such as from graduate school into medical school, from a postdoctoral fellowship into industry, or from academia into the business world. Many people have gone through what you are going through and can offer advice and encouragement. Life changes bring forth an intermission where you can reflect and self-assess. These changes are the rare moments in life when you can see what your real values are.

Take a Break

The time between life's transitions offers you a moment to reflect and recharge. For some reason, most high-achieving students feel a need to jump quickly into the next step. We have heard stories where students give themselves a week between their thesis defences and their postdoctoral fellowship positions, or even start the postdoc before the defence, going straight from one job to the next. Why do we feel this burning desire to just keep on moving? Scientist-types often feel a need to keep moving to the next step, always in search of that "final" destination. This leaves little time for self-reflection, as you follow a default pathway rather than creating your own way. Instead, take time to reflect. You will come back to work refreshed and ready for new challenges. Pat yourself on the back for what you have accomplished and take a break before you tackle your next challenge! Nobody will grant you this extra time during a job, so take it, if it is financially feasible, during the intermissions in your life. Do not think that an intermission is wasted time. If you are using the time wisely for your own mental wellness, spending quality family time, travelling, writing, or doing any activity that is meaningful to your mind, body, and soul, then it is not wasted time, but time well spent.

Here are some possible examples of intermissions that include taking a "gap" year:[6] (1) Jafar took a year to travel and work abroad between the PhD and postdoctoral fellowship as an English teacher in Asia. The year experiencing another culture now helps them with setting up international collaborations with the scientific work during a postdoctoral fellowship. (2) Claire deferred graduate school and worked in a restaurant as a chef's assistant for one year. Her kitchen skills of teamwork and following recipes and staff protocols helped her with her PhD benchwork protocols and collaborations. In fact, she later combined her PhD in yeast studies with restaurant experience to start her own brewery. (3) Dave took an academic break between his MSc and PhD and worked for a construction company, remodelling homes. Although his intermission did not involve scientific discovery, he strengthened his skills in project management, meeting deadlines, and working with clients, which are all skills he uses today as a research scientist in industry.

---

6 N. Lee, "Embracing the Intermissions in Life," *Inside Higher Ed* (2022), https://www.insidehighered.com/advice/2022/07/11/gap-year-wont-disadvantage-your-professional-development-opinion.

(4) Reinhart did not take any major vacation breaks during his first two-year postdoctoral fellowship, but took a six-week break to visit family in Europe before starting his second fellowship, returning keen to get back in a lab and start a new project.

There is never a final destination, especially in this era. Even if you do achieve a tenure-track academic position, which some may think of as the "final" career destination, it doesn't end there. Many professors are continually supplementing their careers with side businesses, participating in start-ups, task forces, new initiatives, administration and science policy, or volunteering and fulfilling other interests as they move up the academic ranks. Career development never ends. Therefore, it is essential you do not burn out. Pace yourself. And the next time you have a rare intermission in life, take some time and enjoy just being there. Reflect on whether you are on the right path or if you need to shift gears and make a change. Perhaps write your thoughts down in a journal or talk to friends about diverse career paths. You never know what ideas you will come up with.

> Your degree or job title does not define you. You are not a PhD, but a person with a PhD.

Defining Yourself

Many people find career transitions difficult because the way they define themselves is often related to their training or job title. Many have been focused on their Plan A for so long that it's difficult for them to think of being in any other position. Try to think of one, two, or three words that describe you – not an occupation, just words that describe your essence. *That* is real life. That is the legacy you will leave behind. It's not just the science, the publications, or the long hours in the lab. Do descriptions like "leader," "mentor," "collaborator," "ideas person," and "problem solver" come to mind? "Hard worker," "long hours," and "technically competent" will not put you above the crowd. What about other descriptors? What is the extra something you bring to life? Remember, these words explain you wherever you are, during the times you are at a job as well as when you are on an intermission. A clue is what you would like someone to say about you at your funeral! It certainly wouldn't be "I heard they died with a high h-index." Again, reflect on your values, interests, skills, and personality. Nana's three words are empathetic, creative, and mentor. Reinhart's are energetic, collaborator, and mentor.

Some example descriptors:
Adventuresome
Ambitious
Athletic
Balanced
Calm
Community-builder
Creative
Devoted
Driven
Explorer
Friendly
Leader
Organized
Persistent
Relaxed
Science enthusiast
Sporty
Spunky
Successful

Integrating Family Responsibilities

One of the most common values that people hold is the importance of family and relationships. This may include relationships with parents, siblings, partners, spouses, close friends, and children. Most students are single when they enter graduate school, but may find their partner during this time of their life. Some may also have to take care of others, which can be challenging – always important, sometimes urgent (recall the time management matrix). If a close loved one is sick, work receives less time. If you have a huge deadline, you might have to delay the trip to the park with family or friends, or even a holiday. Other life events, such as aging or sick parents, retirement, or company reorganizations all require you to enact your transitional skills. The most important transitional skills are self-assessment and creativity. Expect the unexpected and make back-up plans. It is important to build flexibility into your schedule and to be adaptable.

As scientists in training, we are all curious and want to do experiments to test our ideas. If society did not have monetary awards for work, and all of your wants and needs were provided for, then most of us would still strive to explore the world of science. Most of us entered science to be in discovery and innovation, to gain and generate new knowledge and, in the biomedical sciences, to improve human health through research. We would all still have to think about life integration as we are all people who care for our families and friends, even while being dedicated to a successful career.

Some of the biggest assets graduate students and postdocs have are close friends, relatives, and a partner or spouse. Remember you are never alone. Sharing personal and confidential concerns with those you trust and seeking advice helps you when stressful events occur. Honest and open communication is important to building strong relationships. Communication, empathy, and understanding are transferable skills that can sustain relationships at home and at work.

On another note, if your partner is also a scientist and you would like to eventually work in the same city, the possibilities are endless. We encourage you to reframe the commonly called "two-body problem" into a "dual opportunity." Naming it something positive makes it a more delightful situation as opposed to a challenging problem. You may both apply to jobs together, but that would mean coordinating the end times of your PhDs or postdoctoral fellowships. This can be challenging if you and your partner are not in sync. One strategy is to have one partner first find a job in a city where other opportunities exist. The other could then follow after a few months. Or you may look for jobs at the same time, but narrow down the geography for your search. Often you need to live in large urban centres to find job opportunities for two people. In some cases, one person may be offered a tenure-track faculty position and the partner a limited-term contract position. In some cases, a part-time position for one partner may allow for time to take care of family duties. There are rare occasions where the couple applies for a single faculty position, usually teaching, as a job-sharing arrangement. These "spousal hiring" arrangements can certainly be part of the negotiation process.

Parenthood and Caregiving

Most people go through life with a partner. We are all part of families and may want to raise a family of our own. Becoming a parent is certainly a major life transition. Many professionals, mainly women, delay parenthood to establish their career. For others, parenthood is a priority. Becoming a parent brings a range of new responsibilities. Your time management skills will be put to the test. Learning to integrate caregiving and a career is challenging to even the most organized and energetic among us. Successful work-life integration is a team effort – teams on the home front and teams at work. Partners that share in caregiving form the basis of a successful team. But also reach out to other parents for advice and support. Finding quality and affordable daycare is a challenge for many families. Other support systems for children include friends, neighbours, grandparents, and other relatives. Don't be afraid to ask for help. In fact, if you ask for help that means that you are still trying.

Nana Lee	Nana's transitions into parenthood
	When I was working as a Product Manager, I became pregnant with our first child and realized that I wanted to stay at home with this wonderful little person. I reworked my job description and pitched it so that the company could hire and train a student intern to cover for me while on mat leave for four months. Afterwards, I came into the office once or twice a week and worked from home the rest of the time. The CEO was fine with it as I had already gained experience in many aspects of the company. The job was not advertised as "Part-time Scientist, Full-time Mom Wanted." Instead, I recreated the job into one that I wanted and proposed it, making sure the company's needs were met, and followed this blended work model for a few years. *After working part-time for two and a half years, our second child was born. I went back to work as a consultant after three months, working mostly from home, proposing various projects that I thought the company needed. After a few years, I transitioned back into academia by coordinating and lecturing for the graduate professional development course at my alma mater, bringing back my boardroom and life experiences and network to the graduate students. My third baby was born after I finished classes for the year. While I was on maternity "break," I had a great team of graduate students helping me organize the Biomedical Career Workshop. After any one of these babies, I could have easily quit science to become a full-time mom. Three kids – it takes more than one mom to take care of them! However, I stuck with it, even though there were periods of time when I was changing diapers and nursing more than I was pipetting or calling clients. I used all of my transferable skills (communication, transitional, negotiation) and was constantly reinventing my career to fit my life. Not all women or men are like that. Some go with the job. But I wanted the job to come with me. It is completely possible.*

How do you stay connected to science even if you decide to take a "break" to be a full-time caregiver? Parents with PhDs – these three words prompt an explosion of discussions. The transition back to work after years of childrearing or other life events is a difficult one. It is important to keep up with developments in your field by reading the latest science articles or attending conferences. As a PhD student, you can find resources for support at your campus family care office. Part-time work or maintaining service work at the university is also ideal to remain connected.

Let's look at some examples of parenting challenges:

I	*Luisa is a mom of a two-year-old toddler, and defends her PhD a few weeks before delivering her second baby. It has been a climb, but she is finished! She takes the next few years off to be with her newborn. She remains involved in community projects, but how will she re-enter science after years away from research?*
II	*Luke is a primary caregiver to elderly parents, while his partner is a company director. He has biotech industry experience, but during the last year he has not had time to pursue even his own interests, let alone read an article! Now what?*

There are few programs or support systems in place to help caregivers, but this is changing with the recognition that graduate students and postdocs are often parents.

Re-entry into the competitive research field is difficult. One route is to do an additional one- to two-year postdoc with a supervisor who will allow you to develop an independent research project that you can use to move to the next stage of your career. Fellowship funding often takes into consideration career breaks to care for children or deal with a prolonged illness. However, parents who were already in mid-management science positions do not qualify for fellowships. Recently, the University of Toronto's Rotman School of Management initiated a "Back to Work" program for business women.[7] If such a program does not exist in your organization, think about starting one. The transition back to a career may be the toughest one yet, but don't give up! You have the intelligence and the motivation. Just add some creativity and you'll get there.

---

7 "Back to Work: Initiative for Women in Business," Rotman School of Management, University of Toronto (n.d.), https://www.rotman.utoronto.ca/ProfessionalDevelopment/InitiativeForWomenInBusiness/Programs/Back-to-Work.

Steps to consider for reintegration into the academic or non-academic workforce:

Attend a conference.

Dedicate at least two to five hours a week to stay current with the science and global scientific issues.

Keep in touch with members of your network – ask them what they and their organizations are up to.

Mentor. You still can, even by phone or email.

Be mentored (MentorNet: http://mentornet.org/).

Sit on an advisory board.

Speak at career development talks for students.

Visit labs to discuss their science.

Volunteer for a science-related cause.

Work part-time or volunteer in a lab.

Maintaining Your Interests and Passions

It is important to maintain your interests outside of science, such as hobbies and outside activities. These hobbies will most likely stem from knowing the essence of yourself and will likely remain with you throughout life changes, such as marriage or parenthood. These activities can help you with your wellness, and develop your skillset and your network. Jobs are often obtained through a network of friends or as a result of outside activities. Try to maintain at least one outside interest when you are busy as a researcher. These activities enrich your life and provide some relief, especially when your work is moving slowly or if you have hit a stumbling block. Try something you have never done before. Learn a new language for an upcoming vacation. Take dance lessons to stay fit. Volunteer – grab a hammer and help Habitat for Humanity. These activities can be as rewarding and energizing as a breakthrough experiment. Throughout graduate school and into her career as a teaching-stream professor, Nana maintained her interests in music and song writing and found unique opportunities within the intersection of her music and science worlds. Reinhart learned to deal with people during his summer job at a golf club, a skill he has used throughout his career. Golf also provides a great networking opportunity in a relaxed outdoor environment. Through all of these extracurricular activities, important skills and connections are made. A career pathway may even emerge.[8]

---

8 N. Lee, "Do Extracurricular Activities Help Advance Your Career?" *Inside Higher Ed* (2022), https://www.insidehighered.com/advice/2022/02/21/how-use-extracurricular-activities-advance-your-career-opinion.

Try to maintain your physical health through proper diet and regular exercise. A busy life often means no time for cooking. Remember that most fast food is highly processed and high in sugar, salt, and fat. Try to include some fresh fruits and vegetables in your daily diet. Perhaps take a cooking class or create a cooking cooperative with other students. Also, make time to sit down for meals with friends and family. Make exercise a part of your daily routine. You don't need to join a gym. Walk or bike to school. Walk up a flight of stairs instead of taking an elevator. Reinhart knew a graduate student at Harvard who went swimming every day at 4:00 p.m. and then went home to cook a meal. Participation in team sports is a great way to connect with others. Perhaps start a fun baseball league for graduate students. You may value competition and join a competitive sports league. Universities provide state-of-the-art facilities for students that you may take advantage of.

Conclusion

Time management, skills for transitions, relationships, and your own wellness, both mental and physical, all rely on you knowing yourself. You have some "worldly" identities such as your job, your business card, the lab you work in, the university you graduated from, your publications and awards. But who are you? What are your qualities that transcend these societal constructs? Most of the hobbies or interests that you have reflect these qualities regardless of job or societal status. For example, Nana's passion for the piano and song writing reflect her desire to create art in the form of music. No matter her school, job, or marital status, she has maintained this part of herself, which helps with her wellness and life planning. Her passion for mentorship reflects her desire to help the next generation, which has fueled many of her career and non-career activities. Nana recently told a new mom who was on maternity leave from her postdoctoral fellowship, "Do not forget about you. Do not forget about Celia." Celia (name changed for anonymity) mentioned she had to read those words several times to really comprehend what they meant. And when she did, she became emotional as she realized that nobody had ever said that to her before and she really needed the reminder as a busy new mom and as a scientist.

Scientists usually have type-A personalities – competitive high achievers and well-organized, but stressed if they cannot do everything for themselves in their lives. If you identify as such a perfectionist – let go a little. You cannot do it all. Knowing that part about yourself helps as well. Trying for 100 per cent all the time will lead to stress and anxiety, putting strain on even the strongest relationships. Life is a tapestry. Know your own tapestry and do not be afraid to voice it, even if it may seem difficult at times. Care for yourself. And then care for those around you. Be bold. Make your rewarding career fit your happiness. Make a difference. Give back what you learned. That is success.

FURTHER DISCUSSION

1. Use one word that is not related to any societal construct (such as a school or job title) to describe your unique self and explain.
2. Outline one of your interests outside science and how this activity enhances your skillset.
3. As a team, come up with a plan to create a start-up company while you are graduate students.

TAKING ACTION

1. Create a time management matrix of all your activities (important and not important) for the past week and plan one for the coming week to increase your effectiveness in and outside work.
2. Write out a list of the tasks you enjoy and another list of ones you find challenging and tend to put off, and create a plan to address the challenges you face.
3. Discuss your five-year career plan (breaking it down by year) with your partner or mentor. Do not forget to include life goals, not just career goals.

8 Wellness

Key Messages

- Wellness is a necessary condition for success and happiness.
- Resources are available to deal with mental health challenges.
- A healthy lab culture helps create high-performing research teams.
- Make time for activities to boost your mental health.

Why a chapter on wellness? In brief, supporting graduate student and postdoctoral fellow wellness is closely linked to productivity, happiness, and success.[1] Research requires effective, hard work, and success in the lab demands considerable time and effort. Success comes from more than just hard work. Success in other aspects of your life will give you the confidence you need to succeed in research. And engaging in activities outside the lab not only provides a welcome break, but will also help build your network. In this chapter we will highlight the importance of wellness, both physical and mental, in achieving your career goals.

Wellness is key to performing at the highest level.

---

1 C. Chan and L. Purdy, "Supporting Student Success Requires Looking Out for Their Mental Health," *University Affairs* (2019), https://www.universityaffairs.ca/career-advice/responsibilities-may-include/supporting-student-success-requires-looking-out-for-their-mental-health/.

Time for Wellness

Graduate students are three times more likely than the average adult to experience wellness disorders and depression.[2] Factors that affect graduate student wellness may include 1) the relationship with their supervisor, 2) self-imposed stressful expectations, 3) cultural or language barriers if they are an international student, 4) issues with equity, diversity, and inclusion, 5) financial circumstances, 6) responsibilities outside of graduate school, such as caring for children or elderly relatives, 7) expectations imposed by parents, supervisors, or the university, 8) thinking about their future after graduate training, and 9) health issues.

Graduate students in the sciences are typically high achievers. Some are perfectionists. Indeed, many also suffer from imposter syndrome – "Do I really belong here?"[3] Anxiety and stress have been highlighted as a growing problem among PhD students.[4]

> Working to manage perfectionism or the imposter syndrome will help you stay mentally healthy.

The application of your interests and passions to focused activities with careful planning is up to you. Accomplishing this will make for a well-rounded graduate education or postdoctoral fellowship. Excellent research is a top priority that requires time and commitment. Your wellness is also a priority, and includes outside activities and a self-care regimen. A well-planned, balanced approach is needed. During the time of experiments and workshops, maintain a sense of wellness in physical, emotional, spiritual, social, and intellectual areas of your life. If you feel the stress is overwhelming, talk to others and get professional advice. Student life and health and wellness centres that can

2 P. Puri, "The Emotional Toll of Graduate School," *Scientific American* (2019), https://blogs.scientificamerican.com/observations/the-emotional-toll-of-graduate-school/.
3 Read "How to Cope with the PhD Impostor Syndrome" by James Hayton at the PhD Academy website: https://phd.academy/blog/phd-impostor-syndrome.
4 Read this editorial: "The Mental Health of PhD Researchers Demands Urgent Attention," *Nature* (2019), https://www.nature.com/articles/d41586-019-03489-1.

help with coping techniques exist on all campuses, and there are many stress-busting programs available.[5] Focus on progress rather than perfection.

In previous chapters we covered the importance of time management and work-life integration. A key in wellness is to make time for it. Make sure you divide the hours of the day to leave enough for wellness. Sometimes it helps to draw a pie chart and fill it with your day's activities to see where your time is going. A good night's sleep is the foundation to health and wellness. So, too, is setting aside time for food preparation and eating. How can you carve out more time for wellness, if need be? Perhaps it may be meditation on your commute. Perhaps it is an hour each morning for yoga. Reinhart had a colleague with a daily schedule of starting work in the lab early at 8 a.m. and then going for a swim at 4 p.m. Perhaps go out for lunch with friends once in a while instead of eating at your desk alone. In France, some scientists and other working professionals take a two-hour lunch break! Vacation time is essential – make sure it is in your schedule and that you keep your supervisor informed. All graduate students are entitled to vacation time. Extending a conference in another city by a day or two to explore the local area can provide a welcome refresh after a demanding meeting. Ensure you carve out time so you can be well and motivated for the other important activities like your research.

Wellness of Others

As a peer, mentor, and future leader, try to find wellness training on your campus so that you can learn how to help others. For example, the "Identify, Assist and Refer" training at the University of Toronto can help you identify, assist, and refer individuals who may need assistance with their wellness.[6] Think of these scenarios: (1) student arrives late to several classes in a row when they used to be punctual, (2) student is wearing a parka and has disheveled hair when it is 30°C outside, (3) student mentions that they feel overwhelmed with grad life, (4) student complains that their supervisor is never around and is frustrated by the lack of attention they're receiving, (5) co-worker

---

5 For example, Mental Health Clinical Services, University of Toronto, Student Life, Health & Wellness (n.d.), https://studentlife.utoronto.ca/service/mental-health -care/.
6 "IAR: Identify, Assist, Refer," University of Toronto Student Mental Health Strategy and Framework (2018), https://iar.utoronto.ca/main/.

is exhausted from taking care of an elderly parent, or (6) co-worker continually misses meetings without explanation. In all of these situations, a simple inquiry in a safe space may be warranted. However, an open question such as "How are things?" may not work. Instead, a more specific inquiry revolving around a behaviour would be more helpful. A couple of examples are (1) "Sally, I noticed that you have been late for five of our last classes. Is there anything you are concerned about that you would like me to know?" or (2) "I noticed you are wearing a parka. May I adjust the thermostat for your comfort?" With more information from the student, you can then make a referral to the many resources available at a typical university campus. As a mentor, it's also important to proactively check in with your mentee from time to time, as distress, anxiety, and depression do not always have external signs. You might ask "How are you dealing with ...?" with the "blank" being whatever large project they have going. We have only touched the surface of assisting others; thus, please look for mental health training opportunities on your campus to increase your awareness and to learn about what actions you can take to help others. Always be mindful of maintaining confidentiality and seek expert advice if needed.

Wellness training will teach you what behaviours or comments to look for in someone who might not be doing well.

A Healthy Lab Culture

The research enterprise is highly competitive. There is keen competition for funding of grants and awards. There is pressure to publish ("Publish or Perish"). Graduate students often feel tremendous pressure to produce results to support the favourite hypothesis of their supervisor – fertile ground for scientific fraud. Most graduate students are high performers with a drive to publish and obtain grants – but at what cost? Problems and conflicts may arise in the lab that need to be addressed. Labs remain hierarchical in nature, with the supervisor at the top deciding on projects, personnel, and publishing – even deciding when you can complete your thesis. Many students feel powerless. Most supervisors have little or no lab management training, especially with regard to competencies in managing people and conflicts. There is a call for professors to move away from a strictly supervisory role to that of a mentor.[7] There is also a move to create a healthy lab culture, whereby labs are physically and psychologically safe and productive.[8]

Qualities of a healthy lab

- Uses research, teaching, and other activities to support the development of technical and transferable skills to prepare trainees for diverse career goals
- Provides the resources and training needed to produce novel research findings publishable in peer-reviewed journals
- Creates a safe environment of collaborative research, teamwork, and sharing of good practices
- Engages and consults all current lab members when hiring a new team member
- Clarifies roles, duties, and acceptable standards of performance
- Provides regular constructive feedback and recognizes contributions
- Supports scholarly reading, writing, and oral communication practices
- Provides equitable opportunities to lab members for continuous learning, career development, and personal growth
- Operates with integrity and adheres to codes of conduct
- Is open to change, new ideas, and challenges
- Treats all fairly, with respect and value as unique individuals
- Promotes a culture of openness, honesty, and transparency
- Encourages members to be supportive, be approachable, and demonstrate a "can do" attitude
- Promotes well-being in a healthy and safe work space with reasonable working hours and mandated vacation days
- Supports student mental health needs
- Recognizes diversity, equity, and inclusion as core values where individuals from all backgrounds are safe, welcomed, celebrated, and cherished

F. Frei and A. Morriss, *Unleashed: The Unapologetic Leader's Guide to Empowering Everyone around You* (Harvard Business Review Press, 2020).

A wellness checklist such as the one below may help you realize if you need assistance with your mental health.

---

7 D. Mehta and K. Vavitas, "PhD Supervisors: Be Better Mentors," *Nature* 545 (2017): 158, https://doi.org/10.1038/545158a.
8 Read this news feature: "How to Grow a Healthy Lab," *Nature* (2018), https://www.nature.com/articles/d41586-018-05142-9.

Wellness checklist

On a scale of 1–5 rate yourself on the following with 1 being **never**, 3 **sometimes**, and 5 **all the time**:

I wonder if graduate school is for me ___
I always aspire to be the best ___
I feel anxious about my future ___
I am unable to effectively plan my daily activities ___
I feel that my supervisor puts pressure on me to produce results ___
I worry about money ___
I am concerned about my family ___
I am unable to find time for physical/fun activities ___
I skip meals ___
I spend most of my time alone ___
I have trouble sleeping ___

If you discover with this checklist that you have a high score overall or need assistance in some areas, please find appropriate resources at your university, such as a wellness office, student life programs, or a professor who you can talk to who can help you find other resources. Don't be afraid to ask for help.

Canadian mental health resources include

- https://www.canada.ca/en/public-health/topics/mental-health -wellness.html (Mental Health and Wellness – Canada.ca, n.d.)
- https://www.mentalhealthcommission.ca/English/covid19 (Resource Hub: Mental Health and Wellness during the COVID-19 Pandemic – Mental Health Commission of Canada, n.d.)
- https://www.wellnesstogether.ca/en-CA (Wellness Together Canada – Home, n.d.)

Mental health resources in the US include

- https://www.nih.gov/health-information/science-based-health -wellness-resources-your-community (Science-Based Health & Wellness Resources for Your Community – National Institutes of Health (NIH), n.d.)

- https://www.hhs.gov/programs/prevention-and-wellness /index.html (Prevention & Wellness – HHS.Gov, n.d.)

Conclusion

Know how to maintain your wellness. Find training to help identify signals from others who may need help so you can find resources for them. Be aware of healthy lab practices. If you are a leader of an organization, be mindful of creating a psychologically safe environment.[9] Being mindful of the hours in a day and being realistic about your goals can help relieve stress. Sleep and rest are productive activities. Wellness is not an "extracurricular" activity. Wellness is an essential component of your life that is required to enable you to function with a life force that is energized and flows on a daily basis.

FURTHER DISCUSSION

1. Discuss your personal stress-busting strategies.
2. Discuss the stress points at various stages in your graduate program.
3. Work together to create a healthy lab charter.

TAKING ACTION

1. Complete the Wellness Checklist to identify and deal with sources of stress in your life.
2. Access student wellness resources at your university, even to understand the services available to you.
3. Find time to engage in a new activity that promotes your wellness.

---

9 A. Gallo, "What Is Psychological Safety?" *Harvard Business Review* (2023), https://hbr .org/2023/02/what-is-psychological-safety.

PART IV

Skills: Learning to Do Activities Well

9 Developing Core Competency Skills

Key Messages

- Assess your strengths and weaknesses to determine skills gaps.
- Use your time in graduate school and while doing your postdoc to develop your people skills.
- Try new activities that challenge you to help develop new skills.
- Develop your core competencies across the three layers of dealing with self, others, and organizations.

In chapter 3, "Knowing Yourself," we discussed how it is important to think deeply about your values, interests, skills, and personality, and to be able to clearly articulate them. This chapter focuses on knowing your strengths and weaknesses and growing your skills. In graduate school you will develop a specialized technical skillset that is used to advance science in your discipline. Transferable or core competency skills are important, too. Students often focus on developing hard skills and neglect developing their soft skills that are essential for success in and after graduate school or a postdoctoral fellowship.

Strengths and Weaknesses

You can start building your skillset by identifying your strengths and weaknesses. The first is easy, but identifying weaknesses often takes courage. What are you good at? What do you need to strengthen? What skills do you need to develop? People tend to focus on the skills they are already good at and neglect the ones they need to develop, looking for rewards rather than meeting challenges. To learn something new, try emerging out of your comfort zone and developing a growth mindset, which are essential for personal development and future success.

You are in graduate school or completing a postdoc to learn, but too often trainees focus on demonstrating competencies they already have. For example, most graduate students become experts at doing certain experiments, but are often weak in data analysis and statistics. Other times they are reluctant to try a new technique. Identifying and filling gaps in your technical skills is a key part of a graduate experience but so too should be developing your soft skills, especially communication.

Start by listing your strengths and the skills you need to develop, then ask others who know you to provide a similar list. Choose one strength and consider how it would lead to success in a job. Of course, identifying your strengths and weaknesses has much to do with self-awareness and how others perceive you. Certainly use your natural gifts and strengths that you have developed but also identify your "weaknesses," which are competencies that you have yet to strengthen. Indeed, common questions in interviews are "What are your greatest strengths?" and "Do you have any weaknesses?" Think about how you would answer these questions.

> Become aware of your strengths so you can leverage them in your career exploration, and also know your weaknesses so that you can learn from them.

Technical Skills

Some skills, particularly technical ones, are fairly obvious and straightforward to learn. Perhaps a new technology has emerged that will transform your research. An example is applying the newly discovered genetic technology CRISPR to introduce mutations into a gene of interest or learning programming to handle large datasets. Having said this, you do not have to learn every state-of-the-art technique during your training. Students may ask, "Should I stay in school for longer to learn another skill such as the programming language R or big data statistical analysis?" You can learn the skills you need for your research, graduate, and then learn new techniques as you progress as a scientist. New techniques will continually arise for you to learn. Indeed, postdoctoral training provides a golden opportunity to learn a new skill. It is the ability to *learn* new skills that is prized by employers, rather than the skills you come with. Completing a graduate degree in the sciences demonstrates that you can learn and apply relevant techniques to tackle a research problem. This is one of the values of an MSc or PhD degree.

During your training you may also adapt a method from another field or even invent an entirely new method. This highlights your problem-solving skills. Many Nobel Prizes have been awarded for the development of new methods that have transformed a field. The 2017 Nobel Prize in Chemistry was given to Jacques Dubochet, Joachim Frank, and Richard Henderson "for developing cryo-electron microscopy for the high-resolution structure determination of biomolecules in solution."[1] Serge Haroche and David J. Wineland won the 2012 Nobel Prize in Physics for "ground-breaking experimental methods that enable measuring and manipulating individual quantum systems."[2] If you value innovation and have an interest in developing a new technique and the skills to do so – go for it! If you are entrepreneurial, you may even start your own company focusing on your methodology. Developing skills shows your value to others and allows you to achieve your goals.

Using Activities to Develop Your Skills

Activities are how you develop your skills. It is useful to divide activities into four quadrants as outlined in the bestseller by Stephen R. Covey, *The 7 Habits of Highly Effective People*.[3] Think about the various activities you perform and place them into four groups: activities I like and am good at; activities I like and am not good at yet; activities I don't like but am good at; and activities I don't like and am not good at yet. We added "yet" here, as any skills can be learned and mastered, depending on the dedication to practice by the learner. Some may take fewer hours, some may need more. For example, some children are just "born" with the gift of mastering a musical instrument at a young age. They are "good at it" early. However, most people need to practice hundred and thousands of hours to become "good." They are not good at it … yet. As a guide, the first group are activities you find rewarding; the second challenging; the third unfulfilling; and the last frustrating. Start the exercise with adding your daily activities. This may be cooking,

---

1 Read this press release from the Nobel Prize Committee (2017): https://www.nobelprize.org/prizes/chemistry/2017/press-release/.

2 Read this summary from the Nobel Prize Committee (2019): https://www.nobelprize.org/prizes/physics/2012/summary/.

3 See Franklin-Covey Courses based on S.R. Covey, *The 7 Habits of Highly Effective People*, https://www.franklincovey.com/the-7-habits.html.

tennis, house cleaning, and ironing. From your research activities, you could add doing experiments, giving talks, attending conferences, and writing reports.

Activities I like and am good at (Rewarding)	Activities I like but am not good at yet (Challenging)
Activities I don't like but am good at (Unfulfilling)	Activities I don't like and am not good at yet (Frustrating)

Focusing on the activities you like and are good at is easy and is where most people reside, especially if reward is one of their values (upper left). People who are keen to learn and have a growth mindset focus on activities they like and want to get better at – they value challenges (upper right). Some people work in jobs that they are not motivated by and do not find fulfilling (lower left). They might do this because they are good at their jobs and have the skills, even if they are not interested in the work. This can even happen in graduate school or during your postdoc. Perhaps you are good at research, but don't find it as interesting as you thought it would be. When this happens, ask yourself, "Am I not interested because of the research topic, the techniques, the future of the field, or the people I am working with?" Finally, activities you have tried and are not good at and do not enjoy might be ones to avoid (lower right). Staying in this quadrant for too long can lead to frustration, anxiety, and depression.

> Developing new skills is important if you want to develop in your career path as a professional.

Try to spend your time on activities that are rewarding and challenging. If you're stuck in activities that you find frustrating and unfulfilling, it could be hard to make a change, especially if you don't like to take risks. But you do have options. Try exploring them. Exploring would be finding other research topics, techniques, or communities in which you want to work to change the future of the field. Exploring could also mean sampling other experiences – for example, attending a session at a conference that is not in your area of research, attending a class in a different discipline, or taking a continuing education course in an area of interest online. Indeed, changing course in your career exploration provides a terrific opportunity to develop your skills. In reality, we spend time in all four quadrants. Try to focus on activities you like based on your interests and improve your performance on them by staying within the upper two boxes and oscillating from right to left.

Example of developing skills to advance your career

Dembe was a member of a university sports club. The club was looking for a new Treasurer. Although Dembe had no experience, she volunteered for the position. She signed up for a night class in bookkeeping and connected with the departmental research accounts manager who became her mentor. Dembe discovered that she liked working with numbers and completed a Certificate in Accounting over the last three years of her PhD program in the School of Continuing Studies. Dembe ended up becoming a Project Manager for a large multidisciplinary research project with an annual budget of $5 million!

Competencies

Another way to think about skills is as competencies. Indeed, many professional academic programs focus more on competencies than just the accumulation of knowledge in a discipline. Competencies comprise the *knowledge* that you have accumulated and the *skills* that you have developed that you can apply in your work and daily life. Basically, competencies are the various skills that you can demonstrate in your activities. In graduate school you become an expert in your field. At the PhD level you develop the knowledge to teach in your discipline at the college or university level and to use the research skills you have learned to advance your field. You also have the competencies to develop a career outside academia, including in the public and private sectors. A successful graduate student has demonstrated the ability to learn and to develop a solid knowledge base. Employers are looking for people who are also good at collaborating and working in teams, have great communication skills, are problem solvers, are innovative, and have a desire to learn. These are all skills you can learn in graduate school or during your postdoctoral fellowship and can demonstrate in the workplace.

There are many competencies that one can demonstrate, some very specific, like running an instrument, and some very general, like communication. There are competencies that leaders demonstrate, such as emotional intelligence, communication, and team building. An example of competencies listed by clusters, as applied to business, is described in the article "31 Competencies Explained."[4] We have adapted these competencies to apply them more generally to graduate education. Rather than clusters, we have divided competencies into three layers that build upon one another.

The three layers of competencies are

1. Dealing with self
2. Dealing with others
3. Dealing with organizations

> Before you can deal with others or organizations you need to know yourself.

We dealt with the first layer in chapter 3, "Knowing Yourself." This layer forms a solid foundation for the second layer, dealing with others, which in turn supports the third layer, dealing with organizations. The most important competency in dealing with others is communication, which we will discuss in detail in chapter 10, "Communication and Leadership." In graduate school you deal with your supervisor and other graduate students as well as with other people in your department on a daily basis. We all deal with organizations. In graduate school this includes departments, faculties, universities, funding agencies, professional organizations, publishers, and suppliers of lab equipment and materials. After graduate school, organizations expand to include other universities, companies, government, not-for-profits, and other employers.

My 31 competencies

Rate yourself on each of the 31 competencies and then use this information to make a plan for improving yourself in the areas you are weak in. For each competency listed below ask yourself the following: "How well do I …?" Then rate yourself (honestly) out of 5 points, with 5 being the most optimal for your professional life.

---

4 E.J. Cripe, "31 Core Competencies Explained," Workforce (2002), https://www.workforce.com/news/31-core-competencies-explained/.

Dealing with self

1. Demonstrate self-confidence
2. Manage stress
3. Sustain credibility
4. Show flexibility

Dealing with others

5. Articulate goals
6. Motivate others
7. Work in teams
8. Empower others
9. Manage change
10. Develop others
11. Manage performance of others
12. Inform others
13. Communicate effectively
14. Write for different audiences
15. Persuade others
16. Be aware of others (includes cultural humility and EDI)
17. Get support for my ideas
18. Collaborate
19. Build healthy relationships

Dealing with organizations

20. Gather information
21. Analyze
22. Plan ahead
23. Strategize
24. Find solutions
25. Develop my technical expertise
26. Show initiative
27. Be entrepreneurial
28. Be innovative
29. Get results
30. Be thorough
31. Demonstrate decisiveness

Next, make a personal list of your top competencies from each layer and provide evidence from your activities to demonstrate that you have each skill. This is a useful exercise for when it's time to create statements for your résumé or in interviews. Start with one of your achievements or challenges. What skills did you use in achieving your goal or meeting the challenge? Look at all your activities, including those outside of school. What skills do you use? Or in reverse, what skills do you want to develop to better enjoy activities you like? What was the outcome, result, or impact?

Remember, we all have strengths and "weaknesses." Do not be afraid of any "weaknesses," as they are skills that can be developed for the future. Your "weaknesses" are skills yet to be refined. For example, most scientists are introverts and if you think, as many students might, that you have a "weakness" in networking, remember you will acquire this skill throughout your career lifetime. And as you develop into a career professional, your "weakness" of networking will become stronger, no matter where you started in this skill.

SMART Goals

A useful method to setting your goals is to use the mnemonic SMART as a guide.[5]

SMART
Specific
Measurable
Achievable
Relevant
Time-bound

Your goals need to be specific. What do you want to achieve and why is it important to you? Progress towards your goals needs to be measurable. Goals also need to be realistic and achievable. Are your goals relevant to your career path? Can they be accomplished in a timely manner? Of course, your goals may change or new ones may emerge, so it is important to review your SMART goals from time to time. A common goal for graduate students is to obtain a PhD. Smaller goals include publishing a paper in a peer-reviewed journal or preparing for a research seminar. There can even be daily SMART goals, such as carrying out an experiment or having a meeting with your supervisor.

---

5 SMART goals first appeared in a November 1981 issue of *Management Review* (vol. 70, issue 11) in an article titled "There's a S.M.A.R.T. Way to Write Management's Goals and Objectives," by George Doran, Arthur Miller, and James Cunningham.

Skills development takes careful planning and can be accomplished using SMART goals. Set yourself a specific activity relevant to improving one of your skills. Is it realistic and achievable? How will you measure success? Be sure to engage in the types of activities you like. For example, if you like to work alone, take a course online. If you like working in groups, join one or, better still, create one. Remember that you can develop skills not only in formal academic settings, but also by following your other interests like participating in a sport or club or working on a skill together with friends. So take charge. Start now. Define a goal. Prepare a plan. Evaluate the results. Be SMART.

Conclusion

Developing your core competencies will prepare you for success in academia and beyond. Some of these skills are strengthened during the course of your graduate work, such as technical skills, research abilities, and logical reasoning. Your curriculum and project will provide the skills related to your discipline. Other core competency skills like emotional intelligence, people skills, networking, and conflict management may not be practiced as much as an inherent part of your training. These are skills you can seek to develop or to enhance, either through workshops or participating in interactive group projects such as student groups, teaching, mentoring, and collaborative research. Core competencies continue to grow throughout your career and your professional and personal life.

FURTHER DISCUSSION

1. Describe one of your achievements and discuss the skills you used to get there.
2. Describe one of your interests and discuss what skills you could develop as part of pursuing this interest.
3. Discuss one competency you would like to develop from each of the three layers of the 31 competencies (dealing with self; dealing with others; dealing with organizations).

TAKING ACTION

1. Identify one of your weaknesses (e.g., stage fright) and create a plan that will allow you to develop a skill to address it.
2. Prepare a list of your three top skills and provide examples to demonstrate your competencies in each.
3. Set one SMART (specific, measurable, attainable, relevant, time-bound) goal for your professional development that you can achieve in the next few months.

10 Communication and Leadership

Key Messages

- Learn to communicate your science to diverse audiences.
- Be professional in all your communication.
- Develop good listening skills to understand others.
- Effective communication is an essential leadership skill.

Graduate school is a great place to develop both your communication and leadership skills. Learning how to communicate your research through writing and presenting, not only to experts in your field but to broader scientific audiences and the public, is an essential skill in any scientific career. Learning persuasive communication will help you become more competitive for success in winning scholarships and grants and for recruiting collaborators and building effective teams. Learning how to communicate effectively as a leader will allow you to inspire others and articulate your vision with clarity and enthusiasm and move your team forward to success. How can you start to develop your communication and leadership skills? By introducing yourself.

Introducing Yourself

"Hi, my name is — and I am a — year PhD student in the department of —." We hear this answer about 95 per cent of the time when we ask students "Tell me about yourself." Let's start with your name and how people will remember you. As mentioned in a TED talk about vocal executive presence (go to the 8-minute 20-second mark), the way to introduce yourself is with a pause between your first and last name.[1] If you speak quickly, for example, "Hi, my name is Nana and I work at the University of Toronto," your listener might hear the last part, "University of Toronto," but will they remember your name a few days later? Probably not. However, if you say "I am Nana (pause) Lee. I help students realize their dream careers" or "I am Nana (pause) Lee. I compose musical stories to connect people," these introductions become memorable and inviting. In your introduction, state *how and who you are helping* as opposed to what you study or your title. In another example, instead of saying "Hi, I am Jyoti, and I major in math," Jyoti could try "Hi, my name is Jyoti (pause) Singh. I create mathematical models to help public health officials predict pandemic growth." If you include who you are and how you are helping, your listeners will lean in and want to ask more questions about what you do, rather than who you are.

The first impression you make has a large impact on other students, professors, potential collaborators, recruiters, and CEOs. Your introduction should be brief, yet informative to the listener. Whoever the audience is, include a memorable and meaningful piece of information to pique their interest. Have a one-minute introduction ready to go at any time – your "elevator pitch." Be able to summarize your project in one clear and compelling sentence. As the conversation progresses, be prepared to provide more information about your research and be sure to engage the other party. Develop good listening skills and pay attention to how others respond to what you say, including their body language.

> The first impression is a lasting one – be prepared and step forward with poise and confidence.

Listed below are some examples of scenarios that are likely to happen in your scientific career. Think about what you want to say and plan a short introduction about yourself for each scenario. You also need to be able to introduce yourself in writing (a topic covered in chapter 14, "Marketing Your Brand: Professional Emails, Cover Letter, Résumé, and Curriculum Vitae").

---

1 Watch this TED Talk: Laura Sicola, "Want to Sound Like a Leader? Start by Saying Your Name Right" (n.d.), https://www.youtube.com/watch?v=02EJ1IdC6tE.

	Communication scenarios
I	*You just listened to a talk given by the Innovations Officer at ImagineLife Technologies, a company that commercializes academic inventions. You are working on a project that shows great promise in the market and the patent has just been approved. You meet the Innovations Officer at the coffee break. What do you say?*
II	*You are a PhD student and you happen to be in the elevator with one of the keynote speakers for the conference you are attending. How do you leave a positive impression? How will they remember you?*
III	*You are at a networking session with guest panelists from various industries and 50 other graduate students. You would like to get into science policy or research and development with the government. How do you make sure the science policy guest remembers you in a positive light?*

Introducing yourself to others in person for the first time is not easy. Be prepared with an opening that is clear and memorable. Make eye contact and respect personal space. Other important factors include having a strong and confident handshake or a respectful slight bow or light nod (depending on the culture), a pleasant smile, a pleasant personality, and professional attire. Designer clothes are not necessary, but showing that you care enough to make yourself presentable speaks volumes. Show respect and be humble, but also be confident in being yourself.

Communication in Various Media

Communication takes various forms. In science we think of communicating our research in writing in reports and papers and orally in lab meetings and research seminars. But these days we also use electronic devices to communicate, whether via a phone call, an email, or social media. All of your communication, even in casual conversations, needs to be respectful and professional. For example, if you are writing a professor an email for the first time, always address them as "Dr." until they ask you to call them by their first name, if they do at all. Respect goes a long way. Even if they sign their email with their first name, maintain their title when you address them unless they specifically tell you to call them by their first name. Remember, you are entering a professional world and it is important to be consistently respectful.

Everything you say, write, or post is part of your public communication record.

More recently, encounters have been made easier through virtual meeting platforms. Indeed, your reach can now be global. Having said that, using these online interfaces alone does not make a meaningful connection. You must provide the other party with something they will remember you by, and be sure to follow up with a sincere thank you message. Here is one suggestion for connecting after a virtual conference. Select a part of their speech that left a lasting impression on you and comment on that first by email: "Dr. Keynote, I enjoyed your talk that you gave at —, especially the part about —. My name is — and I am a graduate student/postdoc in Dr. —'s lab at the University of —. I would like to explore science policy work. May I connect with you via a brief Zoom meeting?" If you asked a question after the talk, you can refer to that as well. After your Zoom meeting, you can send a LinkedIn invite to Dr. Keynote with a message in the connection request that would allow them to recall the conversation you had. This is key. If the correspondence goes well, Dr. Keynote may even become a mentor. Remember to remain connected with them, with constructive and helpful correspondence. Details on effective networking and maintaining professional networks are in chapter 15, "Building Your Professional Network."

Nana Lee	LinkedIn dos and don'ts
	I have had many students invite me to connect through LinkedIn with no additional information other than "I would like to become your connection on LinkedIn." I only link in students and professionals I have interacted with in a positive light. If you want to stand out from the other students, provide enough information so that I may remember you. If I talk to 30 students in one day, you have to help me remember who you are.
	Here's an example. I gave a talk one day and a postdoc approached me with some questions about the industry job market with a pleasant, respectful demeanor. He sent me an email and a LinkedIn invite the same day, restating our interaction. I connected with him on LinkedIn right away. He now has connections to all of my network. I talked to about 20 students that day, and only two connected with me via LinkedIn. Others lost a golden opportunity to build their professional network through meaningful engagement.

Effective Communication

As a graduate student you will have the opportunity to present the results of your research at different times, to different people, in different ways, and in different venues. Some are casual, some are formal. All leave an impression. So, be *professional* at all times. Communication is a two-way street. Work to engage your audience, whether it is one person at a coffee shop or 1,000 people at a symposium. In academia, professors tend to lecture, even at a party. This is one-way and certainly not suggested by Dale Carnegie in *How to Win Friends and Influence People*. Again, the first impression is important. So how should you start a conversation?

Judith Humphrey wrote a popular self-help book called *Speaking as a Leader*.[2] In it she highlights the importance of communication and introduces the concept of a "grabber" statement. A grabber statement immediately engages the listener in two ways. They think (1) that's interesting and (2) tell me more. For example, if I told you "I met someone yesterday who absolutely changed my life," how would you respond? You would want to know who I met and how they changed my life.

The grabber statement is like the title of a newspaper article, as it grabs the reader's attention and prompts them to read the article. The first sentence of the article leads into an interesting story. The article starts off with a compelling, often personal, introduction and gets more detailed as people read along. This method of going from simple to complex works for conversations as well as for writing and presenting. If you start with the complex, people become confused and lose interest. That's why the title of your research presentation is crucial. Think very carefully about how you begin your engagement to make it meaningful and memorable. Use a grabber statement in your conversations, in your presentations, and in your writing as part of your effective communication strategy.

Scientists use baker's yeast to discover new cancer drugs

This article starts with a grabber title, and then sets off into the introductory paragraph, moving from simple to complex: "Discovering effective new drugs takes a long time. Frustrated by this reality, Sally Scientist knew that many cancer targets in humans were also found in yeast, the same kind we use to make bread. Sally's lab had developed a rapid method to test the effect of drugs on the growth of human cells grown in culture. But these cells took a long time to divide and the effects of the drugs were hard to measure. Yeast is a very rapidly growing organism and a library of different yeast strains missing individual genes was available. Sally set up a drug screen using robots to test the individual yeast strains."

---

2 J. Humphrey, *Speaking as a Leader* (Jossey-Bass, 2012).

The article then dives into the details of the paper's findings. Finally, it ends with a conclusion paragraph containing a main takeaway: "The novel use of the yeast system to find compounds that interfered with protein-protein interactions in yeast molecular pathways showed real promise of discovering an effective anti-cancer drug. The results of the study were published this year in the March issue of the journal *Yeast*."

Oral Presentations

When presenting, remember that you are always talking to a non-specialist, even when the presentation is for your own research group. Research is becoming increasingly specialized, where depth rather than breadth is required. Start in the shallow end of the pool and move your audience into the deep end in a slow and deliberate manner. Start with a grabber statement. Why would someone want to listen? The introduction needs to be short. Take the audience by the hand and lead them, helping them build confidence in their understanding with every step. Think of your talk as a play. Who are the main characters? What roles do they play? Who is the star? When do you need to introduce them? Not all right away! Know your audience. Don't force them to jump off the highest diving board into the depths of your project right away.

Oral presentations are all about telling a story that engages the audience.

Too often researchers use abbreviations or jargon that are known only to specialists. You are working at the leading edge of your field. You may be using specialized techniques that are not broadly used. You do not need to explain the details of your experiments, but do have a slide in reserve in case you need to explain how you did the work. The title of your talk should be understandable to all in the audience, not the one you used for your last publication. Tell the audience what you discovered and why it is pertinent to society. Remember, you are always talking to non-experts, and you need to engage your audience and make them as excited about your topic as you are.

Why frogs don't get infections: Designing a new class of peptide antimicrobials

In your presentation, start with an interesting grabber statement: "About one million people die every year from infections by antibiotic-resistant bacteria." Then get right to the purpose: "The purpose of my research is to develop a new line of peptide antibiotics that target drug pumps in bacteria." This intrigues the audience and makes them want to learn more about your approach – so you tell them: "Our strategy is to design synthetic peptides that are based on natural peptide antibiotics like those found in frog skin." Next you provide a summary of what to expect in the rest of the talk: "Today, I will tell you about some promising results using synthetic peptides and provide insights into their mechanism of action." Now you're ready to provide an introduction to your research project: "The biochemistry of Temporin, the parental frog-skin anti-microbial peptide, is shown on the next slide." The majority of the talk is then spent on sharing your results, which are followed by a take-home message: "In conclusion, synthetic peptides that disrupt protein interactions in drug pumps hold considerable promise as a new class of antimicrobial drugs." And before you wrap up the talk, leave the audience with a clear and concise answer as to what the next steps in your research are: "My future goal is to design the next generation of peptides and test their ability to inhibit the growth of *Pseudomonas*, a common clinical pathogen."

Scientists commonly use slides for their seminars, but it takes skill to create a great slide presentation. Here are some tips for great slides:

- Your slides tell a story.
- Your title slide is a grabber statement and avoids jargon.
- The title of each slide provides the main finding or conclusion.
- Each slide is like a paragraph that makes one point, idea, or concept. What is the message you want to deliver?
- Slides are simple and not cluttered. Think of an advertisement that grabs your attention and is memorable. Use lots of empty space. Less is more.
- Use short (six-word) bullet points (6 points maximum), not sentences.
- Do not read your slides out to the audience.
- Your figures should be clear enough that a caption is not needed.

- A combination of clear data and colourful schematics enhances understanding.
- People recognize the shape of words so do not use ALL CAPS!
- Check for typographical errors.
- Prepare your slides with care and the audience will thank you.

One of the challenges you will face when presenting a talk is taking questions at the end. If you receive no questions, it does not mean that your presentation was necessarily clear and understandable. In fact, it may be quite the opposite! Try to engage your audience with the excitement of your work. You can even pose key questions during your talk. Then, when it's time to take audience questions, listen closely. Repeat the question in your own words: "So what you are asking is —?" If you need time to compose an answer say "That's a good question." Provide a one-sentence answer and then elaborate if necessary. If you don't know, say so! And perhaps follow up with "But if I were to take an educated guess …" And, of course, always leave time for questions, since this is the time for meaningful engagement with your audience.

Nervous on stage? That's usually the case. Even the best actors are nervous before a live performance. A little adrenaline is fine and avoids a flat talk. Breathe in deeply and breathe out slowly if you are stressed. Practice your talk. During your practice talks, encourage questions so you are prepared to answer them during the real talk. Use keyword reminders on your slides and not a full script. Maintain eye contact with all audience members – be sure to look to the back, side, and front of the room. Focus on a friendly face in the audience. Smile occasionally. Make sure the audience members at the very back can hear you. Show that you are excited to be sharing your latest findings. Practice builds confidence and will help you overcome nerves.

Tips for when you're on stage

- Start with a "grabber" statement.
- Modulate your voice.
- Use pauses, not filler words such as "uhm," "like," "right," and "ok."
- Use emphasis on important words.
- Watch your posture.
- Use your hands deliberately.
- Use a pointer steadily and only when necessary.
- Maintain a steady pace of speech.
- Use language your audience understands.

Communication in Effective Leadership

Great leaders are able to clearly articulate a vision and to motivate and inspire team members to reach a common goal, always demonstrating integrity, respect, empathy, and personal humility. Leadership is focused on *what* goals you want to accomplish, while management is focused on *how* to accomplish those goals. Leaders have a high emotional intelligence.[3] They are able to recognize their own emotions and those of others. They have empathy skills that they use to manage and resolve conflicts. They are good at managing change. Great leaders are also good at recognizing when to bring in a team to have a brainstorming session. Great leaders guide the team forward during a crisis. Great leaders provide a psychologically safe environment so all people feel included and celebrated.

Effective leaders are great communicators. Communication is a two-way street – great leaders are great speakers *and* great listeners. Good listening is a skill. Be an *active* listener (see the box, "Strategies for Active Listening," below). After you listen to a talk, could you provide a summary of it to someone else? Take notes if you need to. Be able to summarize it in one line. As a leader, go in with what you want to convey, and listen to what your team members have to say. Be the last to speak. Your initial message might change during the course of the discussion. Encourage discussion and debate, but don't let loud or angry voices dominate. Ensure that *all* voices are heard. Maintain an inclusive environment. Work towards building a consensus, but be aware that all may not agree.

How can you as a team leader accomplish an inclusive environment in a virtual meeting? One tool that seems to work for ensuring all voices are heard on any team is a Google Sheet that Nana uses in virtual meetings. This tool is an adaptation of her design thinking methods described in chapter 17, "Getting Ready: Strategic Career Planning." A link to a Google Sheet is shared with all meeting participants at the time of the meeting. Everyone brings their cursor to a cell in column A and writes a nickname. Column B contains a question regarding the goal of the meeting, such as "How can we address imposter syndrome?" Another example would be "How can we redesign course evaluations?" Next to each participant's nickname,

---

3 Read this article: "The Meaning of Emotional Intelligence," Institute for Human Health and Intelligence (n.d.), (https://www.ihhp.com/meaning-of-emotional-intelligence/.

they write one or more ideas in the cells in column B to answer this question. After some brainstorming time, each participant votes on the ideas they find most delightful by adding a "1" to the right of their favourite idea in column B. The 1s are then added up to see which ideas received the most votes. Using the ideas with the most votes, the participants enter breakout rooms to plan possible next action items for implementing these ideas or a "tamed" version of these ideas. These teams later reconvene in the main room, share their potential plans, and receive feedback from the rest of the group. The team now has a prototype to test, a key to design thinking. In this type of team leadership, everyone's ideas are heard, the delightful ones are selected by voting, and action items are created with team input and feedback. If this is an in-person meeting, each idea in the "cell of the Google Sheet" is written on sticky notes and a team member tabulates votes by adding checkmarks directly on the sticky notes.

The boxes below highlight key features of communicating as a leader, active listening, and running effective meetings.

Communicating as a leader

- Be consistently respectful.
- Consult people first.
- Focus on solutions, not problems.
- Focus on issues, the system, or the environment, not people (meaning focus on the action items and not on changing personalities).
- Listen to the speaker's message, not just on "hearing the words."
- Check in with your team members, even if they are not requesting a meeting.
- Show understanding and demonstrate empathy.
- Have a positive "can-do" attitude.
- Do not assume.
- Watch your tone, facial expressions, and body language.
- The environment (office, conference room, on a walk, coffee shop) matters in setting the tone of the conversation.
- Use the general rule of three as people remember in threes: "There are three points that I would like to make." Four points are too many; one can be enough especially if it is your top priority.
- Use email to summarize discussions, not to carry the discussions.
- Everything you say and write matters.
- Maintain confidentiality unless there is a risk to someone's safety.
- Do not use sexist, racist, and offensive language; particular caution is warranted when using humour.
- Be aware of issues in equity, diversity, and inclusion so you may apply them to your conversations and mentorship.

Strategies for active listening

- Use empathy.
- Pay close attention.
- Maintain eye contact.
- Watch for visual and emotional cues.
- Confirm understanding.
- Repeat back: "So what you are saying is —?"
- Acknowledge feelings.
- Reserve judgement.
- Give the speaker space for their own pauses and refrain from jumping in too quickly.
- Follow up with "tell me more about that" or questions about what they just said.
- Provide a summary or constructive feedback, if they request it.
- Be aware that neurodiverse individuals (15–20 per cent of the world population) may not communicate with eye contact or engaged body cues, or they may use blunt language or unfiltered topics. Asking questions and summarizing more often will make them feel heard. See https://dceg.cancer.gov/about/diversity-inclusion /inclusivity-minute/2022/neurodiversity.

Running effective meetings

- Gather background information.
- Set an agenda.
- If you are the mentor, train the mentee to set the agenda.
- Ask more than tell.
- Listen.
- Provide feedback.
- Receive feedback.
- The meeting environment affects the tone.
- Reserve sufficient time.
- Define topic and purpose.
- Keep on point with the agenda until the end, leaving time for "arising matters."
- Set context.
- Propose solutions.
- Develop action plans.
- Set timelines and deliverables.
- Take action.
- Follow-up – have your mentee send an email with action items arising from the meeting and an agenda for the next meeting.
- Adjust, if need be.

Other Thoughts on Leadership

Along with the communication skills discussed above, a leader of a group also develops the other qualities discussed in this book, such as skills in emotional intelligence, equity, diversity and inclusion, empathy, conflict management, wellness, and effective teamwork. As you pursue your graduate degree or postdoctoral fellowship, you have the potential to develop your scientific thought leadership, which can take you into more general leadership roles beyond your training.[4]

If you do land a leadership role, here are some tips to practice empathetic leadership, a key feature of people with high levels of emotional intelligence. The first tip is to reach out to your mentees or team members, even if they are not expecting it, to see how they are. This strengthens personal connections beyond the classroom. Nana makes time to visit her students with casual pop-ins to the lunchroom, a leadership style called "walk-arounds." She may reach out to ask "Is there anything you are concerned about that I should be concerned about?," especially if there is a change in behaviour or mood. The second tip for leaders is about inspiring their team members to create a vision that they can share with others and build a community around. Nana and Reinhart's graduate professional development community was built from their shared vision of the course to ensure that graduate students are fully prepared to take advantage of the career opportunities open to them after graduation. Ensuring that people are engaged and empowered helps ensure the vision and, therefore, the success of the program is realized. The third tip is to include all the voices of your community members to ensure that diverse views and experiences are captured. Besides leading others, these and other tips in this book should help you with the other type of leadership, *leading yourself – leading your own life*.

A leader is one who inspires and motivates others into action towards a shared vision.

Conclusion

Effective communication as a leader of your own career development or as a leader of a group or an organization involves (1) empathetic listening, (2) reflection, and (3) inclusive community-building. In leading your own career development, you listen to your own needs and to other people's career paths, reflect upon these thoughts, and build a

---

4   N. Lee, "Developing Your Thought Leadership for Any Career," *Inside Higher Ed* (2021), https://www.insidehighered.com/advice/2021/05/17/advice-grad-students-determining -whether-they-should-pursue-career-academe-or.

community around you to guide you through the process. In leading a team, listen to all team members, reflect upon their needs, and provide a forum where all members have their voices heard to build a safe community where everyone is celebrated and all ideas are considered.

FURTHER DISCUSSION

1. Introduce yourself using a memorable "grabber" statement that addresses what motivates you.
2. For your research project, write down a general title and three points that highlight the importance of it (the why).
3. To practice active listening and public speaking, interview a classmate for three minutes and then introduce them to the class in one minute.

TAKING ACTION

1. Create a single slide to describe your research project.
2. Take a workshop or course to improve your writing or speaking skills.
3. Read a book on leadership or communication and provide a one-page review.

11 Mentoring, Supervising, and Teaching

Key Messages

- Mentors play an essential role in your pathway to success.
- Develop and maintain strong mentoring relationships.
- Supervising and mentoring others is a noble way to give back and to improve your leadership skills.
- Develop your teaching skills, as these will be important in your career in academia or beyond.

In the previous chapter we covered the importance of developing your communication skills, especially for serving in leadership roles. Mentoring, supervising, and teaching all rely on effective communication and are in and of themselves activities of leadership. These activities involve the second level of competencies, "dealing with others." You will have many mentors in your life. In graduate school, your supervisor or other professors may be mentors. As a graduate student or postdoctoral fellow, try to look for opportunities to mentor, supervise, and teach. Spending all your time "at the bench" may seem productive but will seriously limit the development of your transferable skills – skills you will need to move forward in your career. By pursuing mentoring, supervising, and teaching activities, you will improve your communication skills, build your professional network, and work on your leadership abilities. So find time in your busy schedule to expand these skills, through which you will also empower others to meet their goals.

A Great Mentor for You

Mentoring is the personal one-on-one guidance and encouragement given freely by a more experienced person to another, usually more junior, professional. Mentors provide invaluable, and perhaps essential, guidance at all levels of a career and help their mentees overcome challenges, big and small, even challenges that may not have been anticipated. They are leaders and can serve as inspiring role models. Our first mentor is often a parent, older sibling, or school teacher. Certainly, a PhD or postdoc supervisor should serve as a mentor, though this is not always the case. However, there is a call for professors to move from merely supervising graduate students on their research project to being mentors that provide guidance on a grander scale.[1] Mentors who are also supervisors, however, hold a level of authority that precludes impartial, arm's-length guidance. Since supervisors who serve as mentors are also responsible for evaluating performance, be sure to also have other mentors *outside* the line of authority. In academia, it could be someone from another department or even another institution. In terms of graduate professional development, a mentor could also be someone who is outside academia, but who understands your career path and your particular goals and challenges. Do not be afraid of reaching out.

An ideal mentor for graduate students is someone who understands the challenges you are facing because they have faced them themselves – "been there, done that." This can be a more senior member of the lab during your training. Many senior students and postdoctoral fellows are willing to be mentors, some having clear expectations with their mentees from the beginning. You need to be very selective in choosing your mentors. While it is best to have a range of mentors, you need to ensure that your mentors care about you and your career and have the time and experience to dedicate to the task.

For postdoctoral scholars, your supervisor and more senior postdoctoral fellows can serve as mentors. At this transitional phase of your career, try to find a variety of mentors who are positioned at various stages along your possible career paths. In academia, this may be a junior faculty member. If you are interested in transitioning out of academia, your mentors could include scientists working in industry or government.

Create a mentorship team, with members selected for their various areas of expertise.

---

1 D. Mehta and K. Vavitas, "PhD Supervisors: Be Better Mentors," *Nature* 545 (2017): 158, https://doi.org/10.1038/545158a.

Reinhart Reithmeier	*My first mentor was my high school biology teacher, Mr. Gibson. He was a great teacher. He challenged us. We had to come up with a research project of our own design, plan and carry it out, and write up a report. Mine was on squirrel populations and habitats. I discovered that black squirrels live together in communities in deciduous forests, while red squirrels are solitary, live in coniferous forests, and even defend their territory against other red squirrels. Mr. Gibson said I had discovered a fundamental principle of nature. I was amazed at what you could find out by just looking around. Mr. Gibson encouraged me to take advantage of my natural curiosity and to go into science at university (https://www.nrcresearchpress.com/doi/full/10.1139/bcb-2014-0058#.XspWnCd7mRs).*

A good mentor is readily available and committed to their mentee's personal growth and development. They are not afraid to give their honest opinion. Good mentors don't just give answers, they ask questions; they don't say "What's the problem? Just try harder," but rather "Perhaps this is not for you. What are your real interests?" (And you should be ready to answer this question based on what you learned in chapter 3, "Knowing Yourself.") Mentors care about you and your career. They should be critical, but also provide encouragement and support. You need to build a strong and trusting relationship with your mentor. If you can't talk openly with your mentor, find another. Openness and honesty are essential. Over time you build rapport, which leads to trust. A mentor will also help you build your professional network. They can even help you find a job through networking, although that is certainly not their primary task. Good mentors are empathetic, respectful, open-minded, accessible, experienced, enthusiastic, consistent, reliable, optimistic yet realistic, trustworthy, sensitive, patient, honest, seasoned, and savvy. Look for these personality traits. Great mentors like to give back and will celebrate your successes as much as their own.

What a mentor does

- Provides advice
- Helps you set specific and achievable goals
- Encourages you to think strategically and critically
- Upholds professional standards and ethics
- Imparts specific skills to you
- Gives you moral support
- Helps you resolve conflicts

What a mentor does not do

- Apply for scholarships or jobs on your behalf
- Raise funds for your start-up
- Get you a job

Finding a Mentor and Starting the Mentor–Mentee Relationship

Professors are usually great mentors for students pursuing academic careers because that is their specialty and they are very familiar with this career path. Many who are now professors had supervisors who were helpful in finding them postdoctoral opportunities that would chart the way for a successful academic appointment. However, some supervisors may not be able to answer questions about other options available to graduating PhDs, such as medical school, law school, management consulting, industry science positions, medical writing, technical specialty positions in law firms, research administration, science policy, college instruction, and forensic science (see more in chapter 21, "Creating Your Science Career"). Nonetheless, your supervisor could recommend people in their network to help you. Searching among alumni from your department is another great way to find a willing mentor. They are familiar with your program and your career path options. During your PhD and postdoctoral fellowship, it is beneficial to have at least *two* mentors, one that is associated with your work – perhaps your supervisor – and another who knows you but does not need to know the exact details of your research. A key is to have enough mentors to cover your various and evolving career interests. You will also have different mentors at various stages in your career that will comprise a mentorship team you can turn to for advice along your path to success.

> Mentors can help set your career goals and inspire you to meet them.

If your supervisor cannot be a helpful mentor with respect to career exploration and/or development, find someone in a career that you might like to pursue and ask them questions about how they got there, what their typical day is like, and what the pros and cons of various career choices may be. Ask them questions about appropriate topics, such as career objectives, other non-academic career paths, and balancing the demands of personal life with a science career. Informational interviews are a key tool to find and engage a mentor and are covered in chapter 15, "Building Your Professional Network."

Finding an appropriate mentor depends on what your career goals are. The first step in any career move is self-assessment. Ask yourself, "Where do I want to end up? Am I on the right pathway to success?" Then find someone, either within academia or beyond, that you know and respect who is already "there" and can meet with you once in a while to talk about your career path. Graduate students are on a track that leads to continuing in research as a university professor. Over time, you may wish to change your career path. Mentors can help you navigate along this path to success.

During your graduate studies or postdoctoral fellowship, it is highly recommended that you find mentors to cover all aspects of your life. Try to find mentors for research, service, teaching, and life changes. Seek out those who have a similar background as you. If you are a caregiver for children or other loved ones, try to find someone who also has caregiving responsibilities and a career so you can bounce ideas around with them and ask for advice. If you were the first in your family to attend university, try to find someone who did the same. If you are from an underrepresented group, try to find a role model from a similar group, within your home university or another.

If you need to broaden your search for a mentor outside of people you know, potential sources of mentors can be found in campus career centres, internship programs, student and postdoc associations, science career forums, and professional societies or mentorship programs such as Ten Thousand Coffees[2] or Graduway.[3] To gain access to mentors from those sources, get directly and actively involved in those groups – help organize a conference or volunteer to be on a panel. Attend workshops and take courses that will help strengthen your areas of expertise, broad-base knowledge, communication skills, networking, and project management. Any of these interactions can build your professional network and can lead you to finding a good mentor.

You can also send a cold-call email to someone with an interesting career asking for an informational interview. Informational interviews can be done in person or remotely. Potential questions to ask during such

---

2 See Ten Thousand Coffees website: https://www.tenthousandcoffees.com/.
3 See Graduway website: https://graduway.com/.

interviews can be found in the Science Careers Individual Development Plan.[4] By using online tools you can expand your professional network to a global scale and even find mentors in distant places – places you may wish to go. If the interview goes well, follow up with a thank you email and a link to your LinkedIn profile. Showing gratitude is very important.

Questions to ask yourself about your career path

- Where do I want to be in 5 or 10 years?
- How can I get there?
- Am I on the right path?
- Do I have a Plan B?
- Who do I admire as a role model, and why?

Questions to ask during an informational interview

- What is your typical day like?
- What do you like about your job?
- What key decisions did you make that led you to where you are?
- What steps did you take in your past to gain an edge in your current career?
- What advice would you give someone who wants to be in your position in 10 years?

Once you have found a mentor, set clear goals and expectations. You may use your individual development plan to help identify and discuss your goals with timelines. An example of a long-term goal is obtaining an academic position or a leadership role in industry. If you just started graduate school, your short-term goal may be writing the CIHR scholarship application. Having just started a postdoctoral position, an immediate short-term goal would be to design research projects that would result in high-impact publications required for an academic position. If the long-term goal is industry, the projects could also include collaborations with industry partners.

You may want to write out the boundaries of the mentor-mentee relationship so that it remains constructive, predominantly work-focused, and professional. NIH provides suggested mentoring guidelines.[5]

Work-life issues will always come up. A mentor may be able to provide advice on how to handle them based on their experience. Confidentiality will allow honesty and an open and frank discussion. Don't

---

4 See MyIDP Science Careers website: https://myidp.sciencecareers.org/.
5 See National Institutes of Health Office of Intramural Training and Education website: https://www.training.nih.gov/.

expect your mentor to solve your personal problems. Having said this, a mentor has the moral and legal obligation to report a student who feels threatened, is threatening, or poses a danger to themselves or others.

Your mentors will change across time, as will your needs.

Sheryl Sandberg's book *Lean In: Women, Work, and the Will to Lead*[6] comments that if you have to ask a potential mentor to be your mentor, then they are probably not suitable to be your mentor. If you approach someone outside of a formal mentor-mentee program with the question "Will you be my mentor?" then it somehow brings an aura of awkwardness comparable to the question "Will you be my friend?" A mentor-mentee relationship that is outside of a formal program should be one in which both the mentee and mentor "click." Sometimes mentorship can be arranged through an intermediary, but many times it happens after a few organic interactions. Again, a good place to start is with an informational interview. When a mentee finds a mentor with whom they "click," it will be clear – the mentor will truly enjoy witnessing the mentee grow and the mentee will appreciate the feedback.

Nana Lee	*I found my most recent mentor at a networking luncheon of a conference. She was one of the speakers and I liked what she had to say, so I approached her with a question about my career path and followed up with an email so she would not forget about me. We then scheduled regular virtual meetings. She was very accommodating and supportive. Following the initial interaction at the conference, I developed a relationship with this new mentor who introduced me to several new contacts, provided me with further opportunities, and offered some great, specific advice about my own career transition.*

You as a Mentor

Graduate students and postdocs can be mentors too. While the benefits of being on the receiving end of mentorship are quite clear, it is also useful to understand the impetus behind why one would want to act as a mentor. Being able to share insights and help others avoid the pitfalls

---

6   S. Sandberg and N. Scovell, *Lean In: Women, Work, and the Will to Lead* (Alfred A. Knopf, 2013).

that you experienced may give a sense of satisfaction and personal involvement in the futures of others. Another great motivator to being a mentor is remaining up-to-date on the issues of early-career professionals that you may no longer be exposed to, and having a chance to improve the system from within.

Over the years, offering mentorship will help you to create a solid professional network that you yourself may benefit from – early-career mentees may become close colleagues in 5–10 years. Additionally, you may gain access to the network of other mentors your mentee has. Thus, the act of mentoring one student may create new interactions for you as well.

Peer mentorship occurs when another graduate student serves as your mentor. A friend can act as a peer mentor and be a valued source of advice, but they may not always be perfectly honest with you in their attempt to be supportive: "You are doing great, good things will happen soon." A peer mentor should be able to freely give advice without risk to the relationship. Peer mentorship can be casual, but it is more effective if structured around a program with administrative support.

Tina Sing, PhD candidate, GPD graduate	On being a mentor
	The thing that always boosts my confidence is when I'm told "One day, you will pass your wisdom on to the next generation." I know it's silly, but it gives me a different perspective and makes me unafraid to approach potential mentors. When I'm in their shoes in the future, I'll be happy to give my time to mentor younger scientists.

Mentorship Programs

Many departments have set up formal mentorship programs, some organized by faculty members, others by student groups. If your department does not have a mentorship program you can start one. Always look for support from a faculty member champion and department leadership, especially to cover incidental costs. Drawing from Nana's experience leading graduate student mentorship programs over the last few years, here are 10 concepts that have been demonstrated as wise practices in creating peer mentorship programs:

1. Match mentors and mentees randomly – not necessarily based on personality, interests, or career preferences.

2. Match senior students with junior ones and recent alumni with seniors.
3. Start before the students arrive on campus, with senior students reaching out over email to first-year students before they depart their homes, perhaps in July.
4. Train mentors and mentees about the mission and goals of the program.
5. Train mentors and mentees about mentorship considerations, including equity, diversity, and inclusion, mentee-driven mentorship using the individual development plan, setting up agendas, and action items.
6. Train mentors and mentees about mental wellness and how to identify, assist, and refer resources to those who may need it.
7. Provide opportunities for both mentee and mentor to continually provide constructive feedback for each other and make changes as necessary. Train how to give constructive feedback with clear action items and not comments like "My mentor was no good."
8. Assess the program on a yearly basis and brainstorm with mentees and mentors on what worked and did not and next steps for improvement.
9. Social events with open-ended "parties" and no agenda do not accomplish very much; networking sessions with breakout groups are better.
10. Train the next cohort of mentorship program coordinators while the current ones are active so the departmental or institutional memory is not lost. Keep protocols and documents for the next year for continuity.

As a graduate student, you can get involved in mentoring high school students and undergraduates, as well as graduate students just starting in your department or lab. The benefits here are twofold. First, you will gain valuable experience in guiding others. Second, being a mentor will help you to be a better mentee – you will use your mentor's time and resources more conscientiously, and will better understand what types of questions and discussions lead to productive interactions. Always document your meetings to provide a record of your mentoring activities so you can meet your mentoring goals. Stay connected and follow up with your mentee to determine the impact you had on them.

Being a mentor is a core part of your professional development. For example, you may end up mentoring undergraduate students that you have taught or supervised. Here is an example of an expectation list you might have as a mentor: "I can help you with career interests, skills development, and setting goals, but not personal problems, fundraising, getting a job, or university applications." At your first meeting with your mentees, discuss and agree on (1) expectations, (2) meeting times per year, and (3) a list of three short-term and three long-term goals and how they will accomplish them based on their individual development plan, and then follow up with an agenda, issue, or question before each following meeting or phone call. For example, if the mentee wants some guidance on a poster they are developing for a future conference, then that item can be on the next meeting's agenda. You can help students you know find scholarship opportunities and provide letters of support. Other places in which mentors can help mentees are (1) seminar presentations, (2) oral presentations, (3) grant writing, (4) networking at the first conference, and (5) setting up collaborations. These are some practical outcomes of a good mentoring relationship.

> Always keep the mentoring relationship respectful and professional.

Supervising Others

A supervisor holds a management position and is responsible for the activities, workflow, productivity, wellness, and performance evaluation of a small group of trainees and employees. This is quite different from the role of a mentor. The research lab presents a great opportunity to gain supervisory experience. Indeed, the lab culture is hierarchical, typically with the supervisor at the top, although some labs do operate in a flatter, more collaborative team approach. Senior graduate students often train their replacements to allow research projects to continue. Postdoctoral fellows may operate independently or could be responsible for the supervision of graduate students or technical staff. As a graduate student you may have the opportunity to supervise undergraduate project students. Perhaps when you were a teaching assistant you encountered some exceptional students. Be proactive and recruit two or three of them to be your summer students, building a team with you as the leader. Of course, be sure to get approval from your own supervisor – remember the hierarchical nature of research.

As you supervise undergraduates, try to build your mentorship skills, such as the skill of "empowering others." An example would be instead of giving your student the recipe to make a buffer at a certain pH, tell them what you are looking for, such as "I need a 0.5 M acetic acid buffer at pH 4.75," and ask them to solve the calculations. Afterward, check their work, make any corrections if need be, and then watch them measure out the chemicals and make the buffer. This exercise will help empower the student to develop their problem-solving skills. Another example would be to have your student set an agenda for a meeting with you, which could look something like this:

1. Go over calculations for next experiment.
2. Discuss results from this week's experiment.
3. Go over written abstract for poster competition.
4. Talk about selecting a potential research project.

Gaining supervisory experience during your graduate training will be valuable throughout your career, especially as you move to more senior managerial roles.

Teaching 101

One of the outcomes of a graduate education, especially at the PhD level, is to accumulate enough knowledge in a discipline to be able to teach at the university level. During your program there may be opportunities to teach. This could be working as a teaching assistant (TA) in a course, monitoring activities in a teaching lab, or giving a guest lecture. Some universities even offer instructor positions to graduate students where they teach an entire course. Or perhaps you identified a need and created your own TAship, a new course, or a workshop. This demonstrates initiative.

Teaching involves careful planning and preparation. As a teacher, you will develop course curricula, learning outcomes, materials, assessments, and assignments. You will give written and oral feedback and meet individually with your students. You will have a teaching schedule and office hours. Teaching provides a golden opportunity to develop your skillset, including time management and multitasking. As an engaged educator, you will help build community amongst the students. Yes, your job is to deliver curriculum, but engaged teaching is relationship-building with and between your students so they develop a sense of a place where they not only learn the content but share their challenges and joys in being a student.

Formal lectures held in auditoriums are still the dominant teaching style at universities, but this is changing. Flipped classrooms[7] are now common, and online teaching is emerging as a complementary approach to the traditional classroom experience.[8] The emphasis is shifting from teaching to learning. Assessments have moved from high-stakes final examinations to continuous evaluations with feedback. There is still a focus on individual performance, with an emphasis on grades, although many graduate courses are now pass-fail. Rich peer-to-peer learning can also take place when properly organized and facilitated. Group activities within classrooms and beyond develop team-building skills, and leaders often emerge. Working effectively with others is a skill that all organizations value. There are different styles of teaching, including remote learning. Decide on a style that suits you and the students to ensure a good learning experience.

How do you learn to teach? There are a number of valuable guidebooks on this topic: for example, *What the Best College Teachers Do* by Ken Bain[9] and *Teach Students How to Learn* by Saundra Yancy McGuire.[10] Try to draw on your experiences of having listened to and presented research seminars. Further sharpening your presentation skills will make you a better communicator and a better teacher. Observe lectures given by faculty members and then discuss their approach to teaching with them. And if you are teaching a class for the first time, present it to your peers or supervisor for a trial run. Receive feedback and implement any changes that resonate with you. Early on in his academic career, Reinhart had senior professors sit in on his lectures and provide feedback to help him make some major changes to his teaching style (e.g., slow down, face the audience, repeat and review, and less is more). Practice and prepare. Use pauses. Pause to see if anyone has questions every 10 minutes or so. Reinhart dedicates an hour before each lecture to reviewing the material so it is fresh in his head and can be delivered without notes. Most universities provide formal training for TAs and have resources to assist professors in their teaching duties. Seek out and take advantage of these expert resources. There are also some online courses on teaching you can take

---

7   C.J. Brame, "Flipping the Classroom," Vanderbilt University Centre for Teaching, 2013, https://cft.vanderbilt.edu/guides-sub-pages/flipping-the-classroom/.

8   For example, see J.V. Boettcher and R.-M. Conrad, *The Online Teaching Survival Guide: Simple and Practical Pedagogical Tips*, 3rd ed. (Wiley, 2021).

9   K. Bain, *What the Best College Teachers Do* (Harvard University Press, 2004).

10   S.Y. McGuire, *Teach Students How to Learn* (Stylus Publishing, 2015).

(e.g., https://uwaterloo.ca/extended-learning/teach-online/teaching
-resources). You were an undergraduate, too, so look back to your experiences as a student and think about what you would like to see in
a teacher. Don't be afraid to try out new ideas and tools, such as gam-
ification, time trials, rapid answers, real-time quizzes, and online platforms such as Miro[11] and Kahoot.[12] Nana approaches teaching mostly
with the use of a flipped classroom, so students watch short videos
or have prework to read before the class; she then uses class time for
discussions and group activities to reinforce the learning. The goal is
to increase student engagement in the learning process with instant
feedback, yielding better results and learning outcomes.

For your own teaching development, design anonymous feedback
surveys and distribute them, perhaps after the first class, midway
through the term, and during the last class so that students can share
their thoughts on your teaching approach and in-class activities. Some
instructors request short feedback after every class to modify the
activities for the next session. A feedback survey during the early days
of the course can provide the instructor with information in real-time
going forward with the current cohort. Some examples of the benefits
of early feedback are (1) the anonymous reveal of neurodivergent
students (who may wish to remain so) in the cohort who may benefit
from a different teaching approach, (2) identification of preferences
with meeting new students in group work, and (3) feedback on the time
allotment of group exercises. Allot 5–10 minutes at the end of the class
so students have time to fill out the survey before they leave the room,
and make this a part of their participation assessment, as most online
surveys have only 20 per cent–50 per cent participation. Key questions
to include in a final survey are (1) Would you recommend this course to
others? and (2) Any suggestions for course format, content, or delivery?
Many universities require course evaluations as part of the assessment
process. Remember, teaching evaluations are a tool to help you enhance
your teaching methods.

As you accrue experience as an educator, try to constantly develop
and change using current pedagogical tools and online platforms. Ask
yourself "What is the purpose of higher education?" or "How can my
teaching bring something extra to the students, something they cannot obtain from a generic, online course?" As more and better online
options become available, educators should tackle the challenges of

---

11   See Miro website: https://miro.com/.
12   See Kahoot website: https://kahoot.com/.

remote learning, along with other challenges of the value of higher education, as presented in the news.[13]

Teaching Philosophy

A teaching philosophy[14] is a personal statement of your approach to teaching. It is a reflective piece of writing that is grounded in your values and draws on your teaching experience. It's never too early to think about your approach to teaching, but remember it will continue to evolve as you gain experience. The statement should describe what you want to achieve as a teacher and what you want your students to achieve as learners. It is not a list of your teaching experiences, which are already contained in your curriculum vitae. The document should be written in a narrative style and tell your story as a teacher. It is also a living document that you can revisit as you gain different teaching experiences and can form an important element of your teaching dossier. Furthermore, applications to teaching positions will commonly ask you to provide a teaching philosophy. It is a good practice to develop a teaching philosophy while you are in graduate school, based on observing others and your own teaching experience. This philosophy will likely evolve as you gain more and different teaching experiences.

Conclusion

Mentoring, supervising, and teaching are all core competency skills involved in dealing with people, such as relating to others, empowering others, conflict management, emotional intelligence, and cultural humility. You will be taught, mentored, and supervised by others. You will teach, mentor, and supervise others. All of these mentors and mentees are part of your network. They will one day help you. You will one day help them. Building a community by setting action items and follow-up throughout months, years, and even decades will help build a meaningful life for you and your colleagues as well.

---

13 S. Coughlan, "More Students Say University Not Value for Money," *BBC News,* June 11, 2020, https://www.bbc.com/news/education-52999315/.

14 "Developing a Statement of Teaching Philosophy," University of Toronto Centre for Teaching Support and Innovation (n.d.), https://teaching.utoronto.ca/resources /developing-a-statement-of-teaching-philosophy/.

FURTHER DISCUSSION

1. Role-play a mentor-mentee relationship with a classmate and then flip it. For example, role-play a situation where an undergraduate has come to you for advice on applying to summer research programs or a situation where you are teaching an undergraduate a technique in the lab.
2. Create a list of your top three expectations from a mentor.
3. Discuss one strength and one weakness of your relationship with your supervisor.

TAKING ACTION

1. Mentor another graduate student or supervise an undergraduate project student and create a record of your goals, activities, and outcomes.
2. Modify your work schedule to take on a teaching assignment or commit to delivering one or two guest lectures.
3. Write a one-page draft of your current teaching philosophy and get feedback from an experienced teacher.

12 Working with Integrity

Key Messages

- Integrity in research is a shared responsibility.
- Proper validation and documentation of experiments is a valued skill.
- Information reported in presentations and publications must reflect original data.
- Integrity and courage in science and/or the arts and life build character.

This chapter summarizes the shared roles of graduate students, postdocs, supervisors, universities, and other organizations in the responsible conduct of research.[1] It defines the responsible conduct of research as "the practice of scientific investigation with integrity. It involves the awareness and application of established professional norms and ethical principles in the performance of all activities related to scientific research." These activities include data acquisition and presentation, financial integrity, authorship, conflict of interest, and animal and human ethics in research.

> The public's trust in science depends on integrity in research.

---

1 National Academy of Sciences, National Academy of Engineering, and Institute of Medicine, *On Being a Scientist: A Guide to the Responsible Conduct of Research*, 3rd ed. (National Academies Press, 2009), https://nap.nationalacademies.org/catalog/12192/on-being-a-scientist-a-guide-to-responsible-conduct-in.

Research Is a Shared Responsibility

Biomedical research is a shared responsibility, and the best outcomes flourish in an environment that promotes integrity in research.[2] Professors act as supervisors, role models, and mentors, and as such, they are responsible for the activities of their students. It is often the case that you are working on a project designed by your supervisor as part of a research team. The research is typically supported by a grant held by your supervisor. Your stipend may even be provided by your supervisor's grant. Although you may do the majority of the bench work, your supervisor may write some or all of the papers, or at a minimum edit drafts prepared by you. They may also prepare figures in whole or in part, presenting the findings from your experiments. Supervisors often present the results of research in their labs at scientific meetings and conferences. As such, they count on their team to provide accurate data, based on carefully conducted experiments.

Research is about more than carrying out experiments and publishing results. Science is a practical and systematic activity, but it is also an intellectual one. Remember, you should frame your work as a hypothesis – a proposed explanation of a phenomenon – that you will test rigorously through properly designed experiments. A good experiment can certainly disprove a hypothesis, while many experiments are typically needed to support a hypothesis. According to the philosopher Karl Popper,[3] a falsifiable theory is scientific, while an unfalsifiable theory is unscientific, but may not be in and of itself false. A hypothesis that cannot be disproven is called a theory. A theory is supported by at least one observation. So you should frame a hypothesis such that it can be disproven, but also can be supported by observations that evolve your hypothesis into a theory. Your research may quickly indicate that your original hypothesis is false (e.g., "gene X is essential for yeast viability" may be proven to not be the case). That is not necessarily a bad thing and could lead to a modified hypothesis (e.g., "gene X is essential for yeast viability under certain conditions," or "gene Y can substitute for gene X"). Selectively accumulating data to support your supervisor's pet hypothesis is not ethical or honest.

---

2 Committee on Assessing Integrity in Research Environments, *Integrity in Scientific Research: Creating an Environment That Promotes Responsible Conduct* (National Academies Press, 2002), https://www.nap.edu/read/10430/chapter/1.
3 M. Shuttleworth and L.T. Wilson, "Falsification: Karl Popper's Basic Scientific Principle," Explorable: Think Outside the Box (2008), https://explorable.com/falsifiability.

How many times have you heard "I don't understand it – my experiments aren't working anymore"? Sometimes this is simply due to experimental errors or the use of a new reagent. But it may also mean "I'm not getting the results that I (or my supervisor) expect." Don't fall into this trap – it can lead to unethical behaviour. It is often the unexpected result that is the most exciting and significant finding. So expect the unexpected, and then try to explain it. The results of many experiments cannot be predicted, and that is the fun of science.

There are people who like to work alone, while others enjoy teamwork. A student working in isolation can be problematic if they are secretive and unwilling to share or even discuss work with others. Teamwork also has challenges. Not everyone gets along, and authorship or ownership can be brought into question (see more under "Authorship and Publishing Policies" in this chapter). Who has done the actual work, you or the summer student under your supervision? A conventional guideline is that the intellectual property rights of the person who generated the raw data must be considered if the data are used in publications, theses, or grant applications. It is essential to share your raw data in an open manner with others in the lab and, most importantly, with your supervisor. You should be prepared to have your supervisor appear unannounced at your bench asking to see the latest result. You should also feel free to present your latest finding to your supervisor. It is this open exchange of new knowledge that drives science forward.

A Competitive Research Environment

The research environment today is very competitive. Scholarship and grant competitions are competitive, as is the drive to be first to publish a novel finding. Unfortunately, this can lead to unethical behaviour. Students are often motivated to please the boss. Smart students know the result expected and work to get it. Supervisors are often amazed when a new student arrives and everything works. "They've got golden hands." Then, often years later, the supervisor may discover that the results are not reproducible when someone new enters the lab to continue the project. Good lab notes with raw data and well-described protocols are a valuable resource in these cases, more so than the published paper. Was the old work valid and the new work flawed, or the other way around?

Researchers are under incredible pressure to publish their work in top journals in order to obtain grants to continue funding their research. This pressure is often applied to students. Does your supervisor take enough time to review your raw data? Or do they only view your formal presentations with PowerPoint slides of nicely constructed figures and tables? In your figures, do you include all of your data from multiple experiments, even the outliers? Your supervisor should be helping you with your data so that you do not make mistakes in statistical methods, data interpretation, or future experimental design. But sometimes even supervisors make honest mistakes, putting the wrong piece of data into a figure. If your supervisor is preparing figures for a paper based on data you provided, be sure the final product represents the original data. Don't be selective: "Show the whole gel, not just a slice." Speak up right away if you think something is amiss. Remember, it is your scientific reputation on the line. No one wants a retraction as part of their academic record.

Breaches of academic integrity can delay or even prevent future career transitions.

Keeping Accurate Lab Notes and Storing Data

Most experiments should be repeated multiple times, and the data should be subjected to proper statistical analysis. We are not talking about technical replicates done in one experiment, but rather independent biological measurements made with different samples at different times.[4] In addition, well-designed experiments with proper positive and negative controls carried out in a competent fashion should lead to clear conclusions. Be your own critic. Repeat experiments if you are not satisfied, especially if the results are ambiguous. But make sure the data you present are representative, not just the "best" result or the one that "worked." Better still, try to design a better, more incisive experiment that tells you something, no matter the result.

Keeping all raw data and accurate records, including dates, of your research activities is vital. Indeed, it is a best practice to share raw data

---

4 P. Blainey, M. Krzywinski, and N. Altman, "Points of Significance: Replication," *Nature Methods* 11 (2014): 879–80, https://www.nature.com/articles/nmeth.3091; G. Bell, "Replicates and Repeats," *BMC Biology* 14 (2016), https://bmcbiol.biomedcentral.com/articles/10.1186/s12915-016-0254-5.

with your supervisor. Keep dated records of your daily research activities. Do not remove or delete "failed" experiments – referring back to these may provide valuable clues into your research and future experiments. Your notes should be kept for a minimum of five years after your thesis and papers are published.

One responsibility that you have as the individual collecting the data is to ensure that they are represented in the papers in a way that corresponds with the raw data that you provided. If not, immediately report this to your supervisor. An example of research misconduct would be presenting data that are selective and create a bias – for example, leaving out a set of experiments that are at odds with the results of other experiments. Double-blind experiments can prevent bias; they are produced when one person examines the results without knowing the identity of the samples and then gives their interpretation to the person who does know the identity of the samples.

Scientific Reproducibility

Scientific reproducibility is another topic that has had much discussion at the national level.[5] Yes, plagiarism and fabrication are clearly unethical. However, what happens if you are trying to reproduce published results from previous scientists, only to find different outcomes in your hands? What do you do? This requires a careful analysis of your experiments and how they differ from previous work. For example, were the same techniques used? Were the cell lines the same? What about the reagents used: were they validated? Often differences are due to simple differences in experimental protocols.

Another part of good research practice is being trained in the proper use of instrumentation, the use and development of protocols, the application of proper statistical methods, and the preparation of figures and tables. Proper calibration of instruments is essential. In biochemistry, we are familiar with pipettes and the need for them to consistently dispense the correct volume. But this is also true for all instruments, such as centrifuges, chromatography equipment, spectroscopic equipment, and incubators. Was the pH of the buffer accurately measured? Was the pH metre properly calibrated? Validation of results is particularly

---

5 National Academies of Sciences, Engineering, and Medicine, "Reproducibility and Replicability in Science" (n.d.), https://www.nationalacademies.org/our-work /reproducibility-and-replicability-in-science.

important in industry research to ensure compliance and the reliability of products and services.

> Documenting *all* of your research activities is a best practice, equally important in academia and industry.

Accuracy in Presenting Data

Consider the following statements regarding data presentation. "If I leave out that point, the graph looks a lot better." Bad. "If I put in a couple of data points, the results look better." Worse. "I can show the control from another experiment." Bad. "I'll just add a blank lane as the control." Worse. Image manipulation is a major issue to be aware of, especially as figures are now routinely created and modified using programs like Adobe Illustrator and Photoshop, where it's easy to alter images. Journals routinely check figures for alterations, particularly if the manipulation may have been intended to mislead.[6] Data manipulation with the intent to deceive, no matter how seemingly minor, is research misconduct and is to be avoided. In self-reporting studies, close to 5 per cent of respondents have admitted to modifying data to improve presentation. And greater than 5 per cent know of a colleague who they believe has falsified or altered research data.[7] When you publish your work, it is open to the highest level of scrutiny, first by reviewers and editors, and then by interested readers. Others should be able to repeat your work, and the data presented should be an accurate representation of the results you obtained. Reproducibility of experiments remains a major concern in science, especially if the work forms the basis for a new product or service to be brought to market. Remember, a paper is a public record of your work – your reputation is on the line. You can only lose your reputation once.

---

6 U.S. Neil, "All Data Are Not Created Equal," *Journal of Clinical Investigation* 119, no. 3 (2009): 424, https://www.jci.org/articles/view/38802/.
7 D. Fanelli, "How Many Scientists Fabricate and Falsify Research? A Systematic Review and Meta-Analysis of Survey Data," *PLoS ONE* 4, no. 5 (2009): e5738, https://doi.org/10.1371/journal.pone.0005738.

The urge to manipulate data may be due to the pressure to publish in high-impact journals that want the very best high-quality data. Retraction of papers is on the rise, and the retraction index is higher in journals with high impact factors.[8] One of the reasons why high-impact papers have higher retraction rates is perhaps because more readers are reviewing the data, and inconsistencies or methodological mistakes are more likely to be discovered.[9] Retractions may be due to misconduct (e.g., fabricated data, plagiarism) or honest errors (e.g., wrong graph inserted into figure, mistake in protocol). Admit honest mistakes by issuing a correction to the journal. Papers are retracted when it is discovered that they contain fabricated data, false data, or just honest mistakes.[10] Making up data, or deliberately misrepresenting data, is research misconduct. Plagiarism – claiming the work of others as your own or copying it without proper acknowledgment or citations – is another example of research misconduct. Papers have also been retracted due to plain mistakes, which still require correction.

Accurate Reports and Honest Committee Meetings

Students want to do a good job during committee meetings by demonstrating progress and an improvement in their knowledge, expertise, and communication skills. Figures are prepared to show committee members compelling data that are clear and easy to interpret. It is essential to also have the raw data available, not just the final figure or slide. Meetings are often delayed if the student feels that progress has been slow or if there are problems. However, this is precisely when a committee meeting might be helpful. Your committee members are there to provide input and advice in addition to that of your supervisor. Often, a fresh perspective provides new insights that can eliminate barriers to progress. In fact, sometimes a decision is made during these committee meetings to stop working on a project and to change to a new line of investigation. It is essential to be open and honest, especially if your research is not going well or as expected.

---

8 F.C. Fang and A. Casadevall, "Retracted Science and the Retraction Index," *Infection and Immunity* 79, no. 10 (2011), https://journals.asm.org/doi/10.1128/iai.05661-11.

9 "Why High-Profile Journals Have More Retractions," *Nature* (2014), https://www.nature.com/news/why-high-profile-journals-have-more-retractions-1.15951/.

10 See the website Retraction Watch: https://retractionwatch.com/.

> In industry, directions in research can change often and quickly, so being able to pivot is a valuable transferable skill.

Authorship and Publishing Policies

You are ready to write up your first paper. Who gets their name on the paper and why? Your supervisor is most likely to be named on the paper as the corresponding (last) author. The first author is typically the person who contributed most to the paper in terms of generating the raw data, preparing figures and tables and writing the first draft. Joint first authors can be indicated on a paper if contributions are equivalent. The rest of the authors should be listed in order of contribution.

But who else should be listed as an author on the paper? A guideline is anyone who contributes a piece of raw data that ends up in a figure or table in the paper is to be included as an author. A best practice is to include technical staff as co-authors to recognize their contribution, although this is often not the case. Technical staff should at a minimum be listed in the acknowledgments. Reading over a paper and providing comments or providing a reagent alone does not justify co-authorship, but you should acknowledge these people at the end of your paper. Authorship is shared with a co-supervisor, but not with a committee member who makes helpful suggestions.

Today's research is often collaborative, and the role of collaborators needs to be defined early on, as they often appear as co-authors. It is best to make these arrangements well in advance. If there are co-supervisors, who will present the work at meetings? Who has grant funding to support the project? They should be the last author. As explained in chapter 6, "Negotiation and Conflict Management," authorship on scientific papers is a common cause of conflict.

Journals have strict editorial policies about authorship, plagiarism, data storage, confidentiality, conflicts of interest, and copyright.[11] Information on integrity in scholarly publishing is available from COPE, the Committee on Publication Ethics,[12] even on how to handle authorship

---

11 See "Editorial Policies: Authorship," *Journal of Cell Biology* (n.d.), https://rupress.org/jcb/pages/editorial-policies#data-sharing.
12 See COPE: Committee on Publication Ethics, "Promoting Integrity in Research and Its Publication," http://publicationethics.org/.

disputes.[13] Journal editors have also provided guidelines to improve the quality of medical[14] and scientific reporting.[15] A condition of publication by many journals is that authors must be willing to make protocols and unique materials freely available to other researchers. This allows experiments to be repeated and confirmed. There is also a move to open-access publishing, often a strict requirement of funding agencies, with the costs to be covered by the authors rather than the journals.[16] University libraries continue to pay hefty fees for journal subscriptions to make them accessible to their community members.[17] Most research is publicly funded either through taxes or donations, so the results of this research should be made available not only to other scientists but to the broader public sector.

Plagiarism

A serious breach of research ethics is to copy another person's work and claim it as your own. Always cite the original source. Also, be careful of stealing from yourself – self-plagiarism is research misconduct, too. An extreme example of plagiarism is duplicate publications – publishing the same article, often with a title change, in two journals. Once the first article is published, the journal generally owns the copyright, although this is changing with open-access publishing.[18] Universities also have official policies on publication, copyright, and invention that apply to

13 T. Albert and E. Wager, "How to Handle Authorship Disputes: A Guide for New Researchers," *The Cope Report* (2003), http://publicationethics.org/files/u2/2003pdf12.pdf.

14 See International Committee of Medical Journal Editors, "Roles and Responsibilities of Authors, Contributors, Reviewers, Editors, Publishers, and Owners," ICMJE (n.d.), http://www.icmje.org/recommendations/browse/roles-and-responsibilities/.

15 See J. Deyton et al., "Recent Updates to the CSE White Paper on Publication Ethics," *Science Editor* (2020), Council of Science Editors, https://www.csescienceeditor.org/article/ethical-editor-recent-updates-to-the-cse-white-paper/.

16 R. Van Noorden, "Open Access: The True Cost of Science Publishing," *Nature* 495 (2013): 426–9, https://www.nature.com/news/open-access-the-true-cost-of-science-publishing-1.12676.

17 A. Shen, "Universities Must Present a United Front against Rising Journal Costs, Research Librarians Say," *University Affairs* (2018), https://www.universityaffairs.ca/news/news-article/universities-must-present-united-front-rising-journal-costs-research-librarians-say/.

18 R. Van Noorden, "Open Access: The True Cost of Science Publishing," *Nature* 495 (2013): 426–9, https://www.nature.com/news/open-access-the-true-cost-of-science-publishing-1.12676.

plagiarism – these are found on their governing council websites. For example, even though a thesis represents your original work, permission to use data from it must be obtained.

If you like the way something was stated, use quotation marks and provide the citation or source of the quote. Try to put things into your own words and develop your own unique writing style.[19] As mentioned earlier, graduate school is a great place to develop your communication skills.

What to Do If Problems Arise

What if you suspect that your supervisor has conducted research misconduct? First, talk to your supervisor and express your concern. If you are not satisfied, talk in confidence to the graduate coordinator who may, if it is thought to be a serious matter, bring it to the attention of the departmental chair. It is the responsibility of the chair to deal directly with the faculty member. Serious allegations of research misconduct are brought to the attention of the Dean of the Graduate School or the Vice President, Research, who can initiate an inquiry and sometimes a full investigation. Research misconduct is taken seriously by universities and funding agencies, and there are formal processes to deal with these matters. For that reason, it is not a good idea to talk informally to other students or professors, even committee members, about your concerns because a formal process may be required.

There are many reasons given for not reporting suspected research misconduct. For a student, concern of retaliation is a big one. If you feel at risk after expressing your concerns to your supervisor, immediately report this to the graduate coordinator and departmental chair in a joint meeting. You certainly don't want to make false accusations – that is why you need clear evidence. Was it an honest error? If so, it should have been corrected immediately. Or was it deliberate, and no actions were taken to correct it? Always seek confidential advice before proceeding with any allegations. Reputations are on the line and you need to proceed with certainty and caution.

---

19 M. Procter, "How Not to Plagiarize," University of Toronto Writing Advice (n.d.), https://advice.writing.utoronto.ca/using-sources/how-not-to-plagiarize/.

Intellectual Property

Who owns your research? Who owns your data? As an example, the University of Toronto's School of Graduate Studies has prepared guidelines on intellectual property. The guidelines[20] state:

> In brief, your supervisor and other parties may have a large or small claim on the intellectual property rights relating to work you do as a student. This is something you should be aware of and discuss with your supervisor prior to beginning work that could lead to creations or inventions that would be accorded intellectual property rights. Ordinarily, a student will have no claim to his or her supervisor's or instructor's work unless the student is a joint author or joint inventor. Likewise, a supervisor would not have a claim if he/she is not a co-author/co-inventor. If your work was done as part of an ongoing research project, it should be expected that your results can be used, with appropriate attribution, in furthering the research activities of the supervisor and others working in the same laboratory or research group (e.g., in publications, presentations, grant applications and final reports). It is important to clarify rights to intellectual property prior to the submission of papers for publication or disclosure of research findings at scientific meetings or in any way which places any creation or invention in the public domain.

In other words, it's complicated. What is clear is that students have some interest in, but not exclusive interest in, the data they generate in research projects carried out under the supervision of a faculty member. Indeed, research data are considered an invention, and as such, are jointly owned by the supervisor and the university. Government agencies, hospital-based research institutes, and other employers have different guidelines. Often, scientists are considered employees and their institution owns the invention. Most organizations have tech-transfer offices with expertise in contracts and patents and are a valuable source of information on intellectual property.

Confidentiality and Conflict of Interest

All universities and funding agencies provide guidelines for confidentiality and conflict of interest. There are rules governing who can review

---

20 See "Intellectual Property Guidelines for Graduate Students and Supervisors," University of Toronto, School of Graduate Studies (2007), https://www.sgs.utoronto.ca /policies-guidelines/ip-for-graduate-students-supervisors/.

papers and grants. Basically, papers and grants are confidential documents – you cannot use the information contained within them for any purpose, and you certainly cannot tell others about their content. Consider the following statements. "I just reviewed a paper and rejected it because we are doing similar work that I need to get out." Unethical. "I was on the Organic Chemistry Panel, and had a peek at the rating of your grant. I don't think you have anything to worry about." Breaks confidentiality.

Scientists are required to declare any potential conflicts of interest. A conflict of interest arises when your personal interests conflict with your responsibilities as a student, or in the case of your supervisor as a professor at a university. This includes providing any benefits, financial or otherwise, to yourself, close colleagues, or family members. "Can you hire my brother to work in your lab this summer as he needs a job?" Perhaps. He needs to be qualified and shown to be the best candidate through an open and fair recruitment process. It is best to avoid these potential conflicts of interest. Universities, funding agencies like CIHR,[21] and scientific journals all have strict conflict of interest guidelines.

Financial Integrity

The appropriate use of grant funding is the responsibility of the supervisor and the university, but students and postdocs also have a financial responsibility. You must declare all sources of income to ensure there is no overlap. You can't accept two full scholarships, for instance. Be sure to check if the income you receive is part of your stipend or a supplement. For example, you may be provided with a stipend, but you can also have a supplemental income source such as a teaching assistantship. You must also ensure that you submit proper claims for travel and reimbursement to your financial administrator. Students often win travel awards, which are to be used to reimburse funds that covered the travel expenses. An area where transparency is essential is declaring all your sources of funding, especially if they come from an industry partner. Make sure that you are clear where your funding is coming from. Finally, you must also declare if you have a financial interest in the outcome of the research, or if it was supported by a commercial interest, before your presentation or in a manuscript.

---

21 See "CIHR Conflict of Interest Policy," Canadian Institutes of Health Research (2013), https://cihr-irsc.gc.ca/e/46601.html.

Animal Care and Human Research Participants

There are detailed guidelines on the use of animals in research and the recruitment and participation of human participants. It is the responsibility of the student to be aware of the policies and procedures, and to be trained in animal care and the ethics of research involving humans. All universities have training and certification procedures in place. For example, the University of Toronto's Office of Research and Innovation provides information on research ethics and protections[22] that deal with research involving the use of animals and humans.[23] The site also provides information on the ethical conduct of research and how to deal with research misconduct. Similar information is available at all university research offices.

Funding Agencies

Funding agencies also have strict rules and guidelines on research integrity. Canada's research granting agencies – Canadian Institutes of Health Research (CIHR), Natural Sciences and Engineering Research Council of Canada (NSERC), and Social Sciences and Humanities Research Council of Canada (SSHRC) – have created a Framework for the Responsible Conduct of Research.[24] The framework covers rules on applying for and using funds and for performing research and disseminating results. CIHR has guidelines for the ethical conduct of research.[25] NSERC launched Dimensions to promote equity, diversity, and inclusion (EDI) in the research environment.[26] More information on EDI is found in chapter 13, "Equity, Diversity, and Inclusion." In the US, the Office of Research Integrity[27] oversees research activities in government agencies such as the National Institutes of Health and provides up-to-date lists of cases of research misconduct findings.

---

22 See University of Toronto, Division of the Vice-President, Research and Innovation website: https://research.utoronto.ca/.
23 See "Before Engaging in Research," University of Toronto, Division of the Vice-President, Research and Innovation (n.d.), http://www.research.utoronto.ca/policies-and-procedures/.
24 See "Responsible Conduct of Research," NSERC (n.d.), https://www.nserc-crsng.gc.ca/NSERC-CRSNG/Governance-Gouvernance/rcr-crr_eng.asp.
25 See "CIHR Ethics" (n.d.), http://www.cihr-irsc.gc.ca/e/2891.html.
26 See "Equity, Diversity and Inclusion: Dimensions," NSERC (n.d.), https://www.nserc-crsng.gc.ca/NSERC-CRSNG/EDI-EDI/Dimensions_Dimensions_eng.asp/.
27 See Office of Research Integrity: https://ori.hhs.gov/.

> Integrity is an essential value in research and is recognized as important in great leaders as it creates trust. Make it one of your values.

Integrity as a Professional

Maintaining integrity goes beyond your academic training. Some actions that show integrity in the workplace include (1) showing up, (2) setting a positive example, and (3) being respectful even during conflict. More examples are given in these articles.[28] In addition to the widespread use of social media, it is inevitable that if you are a career professional or in a leadership position after your graduate degree, you will have an online presence. Although not necessary, a polished LinkedIn profile at the very least will bring you more opportunities and open up your global network. Since we are all connected this way, applicants cannot really provide "false" statements on their résumé, as it would not match up with the LinkedIn profile. Honesty and genuine professionalism are hallmark qualities on your résumé and cover letter and when networking, interviewing, working with your team, providing feedback, and growing as a scientific thought leader throughout life. Integrity in life/work is the ability to stand by an idea that stems from a belief of goodness and truth. As with our research examples, some life/work situations will be grey zones and it will be up to you to decide what is valuable to you, what is your worldview, and how you want to live by your authentic voice. Sometimes the answers are not perfectly clear and, just as with the research examples, some peer, therapy, or professional coaching will be helpful. The sources of your beliefs or your beliefs themselves may change over time, but your best answer or decision regarding the grey zones will be made with the information and good intentions you had at that particular time. Life can create some difficult situations, and hopefully with your skills of empathy, integrity, EQ, and knowledge of institutional policies, you will make right decisions for everyone.

---

28 Read "What Is Integrity? Definition, Attributes, and Examples," Indeed (2023), https:// sg.indeed.com/career-advice/career-development/what-is-integrity, or "Integrity in the Workplace," Hays (n.d.), https://www.hays.com.au/career-advice/upskilling /integrity-in-the-workplace.

Case studies for further discussion

---

1. *You have done an experiment three separate times and the results are in very good agreement, so you prepare a nice graph for a final figure in a paper that you are getting ready to submit to a journal. To strengthen your statistical analysis, you repeat the experiment one more time, but now get quite different results that may disprove your main hypothesis and the major finding of the paper. What do you do?*
2. *A summer student working under your supervision provides the results of an enzyme assay routinely done in the lab that will form part of a figure in a paper. The student is applying to medical school and needs their name on a paper to be competitive. What do you do?*
3. *You provide the results of an experiment to your supervisor to be included in a paper and notice that a couple of outlier points are missing from the final figure. What do you do?*

Cases That Need Discussion

Hopefully most of us know the difference between morally right and wrong in science and life. However, the challenges we confront and struggle with are the ones that are not in the clear zones, instances that need discussion and open dialogue. Some examples are (1) one collaborator on the manuscript asks if they can add an undergraduate student on the author list, as the student contributed to setting up one assay and "needs" a publication for their application to professional school; (2) one replicate experiment does not have as clear a result as the first two; (3) a control image is from a different experiment; (4) two of the students you are mentoring both want you to nominate them for the same award; (5) you are grading a lab report and it reads much like a report from the previous year; (6) someone submits a paper with your name on it although you did not give them permission. Sometimes a decision needs to made. Be sure to make it an informed one and seek guidance if needed.

Conclusion

The consequences of research misconduct are profound, including sanctions, withdrawal of papers, revoking of degrees and even termination of positions, not to mention public embarrassment and loss of reputation.[29] Accountability is being responsible for one's actions –

---

29 W. Broad and N. Wade, *Betrayers of the Truth* (Simon & Schuster, 1982).

ignorance is no excuse. The more difficult issues in ethics are those cases that sit in the "grey" zone, which need input from all parties involved. These are difficult conversations that must be undertaken so that rules are followed, everyone's opinions are considered, and all interests are respected. Whenever you do not know what to do, seek out mentorship, as chances are one of your mentors has been through similar times and could offer critical advice.

FURTHER DISCUSSION

1. Review the case studies and discuss your approach.
2. Outline a best practice that you follow to maintain a high ethical standard in research.
3. Share a story about a recent "negative" result you obtained and how you dealt with it.

TAKING ACTION

1. Read one of the resource documents dealing with research integrity and prepare a summary for the class.
2. Be prepared to show raw data to your supervisor, not just polished figures.
3. Discuss authoring your first paper with your supervisor.

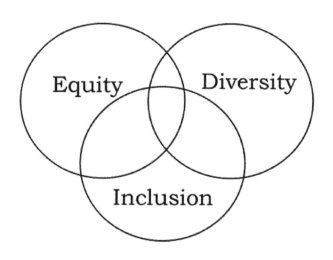

13 Equity, Diversity, and Inclusion

Key Messages

- Equity, diversity, and inclusion is becoming a strong part of university research culture.
- Systemic barriers still exist that must be addressed to diversify science.
- Diverse perspectives advance knowledge and our ability to meet local and global challenges.
- Trainees can assume leadership roles in equity, diversity, and inclusion.

Universities need to be places where everyone has an opportunity to achieve their full potential. Yet universities remain places of privilege. The faculty and students often do not represent the general population. Tuition and other costs are a financial barrier to some. Admission criteria, although changing slowly, are often outmoded, relying heavily on grades, and do not take into full account life experience and other factors. Universities are also places where diversity of ideas is welcomed and the status quo can be challenged. To make the world better for the entire human population, research needs a group of scholars from diverse backgrounds, cultures, and genders. A diverse student population can bring in different experiences and perspectives. Students feel a sense of inclusion if they see themselves reflected in those who teach them. Hiring practices are being critically reviewed and redesigned to diversify faculty. There is a growing awareness of the importance of equity, diversity, and inclusion (EDI) as a means to address systemic barriers and historical inequities. Universities are changing and graduate students can be the change-makers. After all, it is your university experience.

Inclusive Universities

Universities in Canada and the US are attracting increasingly diverse groups of students at the undergraduate and graduate levels.[1] Similarly, the faculty complement is slowly changing as professors hired a generation or two ago are now retiring.[2] Increasing numbers of universities have offices that offer EDI workshops, information sessions, and training opportunities to faculty, students, and staff on topics such as inclusive teaching, implicit bias, microaggression, allyship, and anti-racism. A 2015 review article[3] summarizes EDI action items for organizations, including (1) remove gender-identifying data in applicant pools, (2) require adequate representation on short lists, (3) enforce training on implicit bias, and (4) provide transparency and accountability to applicants.

Some might ask – why embed EDI in higher education? For example, aren't all students accepted based on their academic credentials and letters of reference? Although it may seem objective, the reality is that the application process itself includes biases and inequities, and is an example of the "Myth of Meritocracy." Applications may be rejected because of arbitrary grade requirements, without consideration of other factors, such as life experience. Many applications for admission to graduate school include quantitative ranking of applicants relative to their peers. But this ranking may not tell the whole story. Informative letters of reference from sponsors who know the applicant well are vital to the review process and provide insights into research ability and potential, relevant experience, and achievements both within and beyond academia. Letters of reference, however, vary in their style and content and depend on the ability of the writer to make a persuasive argument and for the writer to be unbiased. In fact, it has also been demonstrated that letters of reference have a gender bias, where women are described as empathetic, while men are described as leaders.[4] We will cover more on gender bias in a later section of this

1 See "Recent Data on Equity, Diversity and Inclusion at Canadian Universities," Universities Canada (n.d.), https://www.univcan.ca/wp-content/uploads/2020/02/UC_2019_EDI-Stats_EN.pdf.

2 See "Stats on Equity, Diversity and Inclusion at Canadian Universities," Universities Canada (n.d.), https://www.univcan.ca/priorities/equity-diversity-inclusion/stats-on-equity-diversity-and-inclusion-at-canadian-universities/.

3 S. Kaplan, "Meritocracy: From Myth to Reality," *Rotman Management* (Spring 2015), https://www.rotman.utoronto.ca/Connect/Rotman-MAG/Issues/2015/Back-Issues---2015/Spring-2015---Smarten-Up/Spring-2015-Free-Feature-Article---Meritocracy-From-Myth-to-Reality-by-Sarah-Kaplan.

4 See "Avoiding Gender Bias in Reference Writing," Commission on the Status of Women, University of Arizona (n.d.), https://csw.arizona.edu/sites/default/files/avoiding_gender_bias_in_letter_of_reference_writing.pdf.

chapter. Unconscious bias, ethnic and cultural differences, socioeconomic background, and lack of opportunities can influence the quality of the student's application package and how it's evaluated.

> Embedding EDI in higher education admissions can help overcome the limitations inherent in the standardized application process that many programs still use today.

We are all aware of the moves to make campuses more accessible by removing physical barriers. But there are other barriers that are not as visible. Structural barriers to accessing education that are not taken into account in many university application processes include (1) food and shelter insecurity; (2) access to resources such as high-speed internet or cell phones; (3) taking on the role of caretaker for family members; (4) domestic violence in the home; (5) enormous expectations from parents; (6) living in a noisy, urban neighbourhood with no quiet time or space for studying; and (7) no one at home to help with homework questions. In an ideal world, children should not experience racism, unconscious bias, financial difficulties, family troubles or hardship, or illness and should always have access to tutoring at home. However, such is not the case. EDI initiatives at universities acknowledge that these barriers exist for some and that support for students that face these challenges needs to be made available.

Further reading

The positive impact of ethnic diversity and scientific collaboration is reviewed in these articles:

- B. AlShebli et al. (2018), "The Preeminence of Ethnic Diversity in Scientific Collaboration," https://www.ncbi.nlm.nih.gov/pmc/articles/PMC6279741/.
- "How Diversity Empowers Science and Innovation," *Scientific American* (n.d.), https://www.scientificamerican.com/report/how-diversity-empowers-science-and-innovation/.
- "Benefits and Challenges of Diversity in Academic Settings" (n.d.), https://wiseli.wisc.edu/wp-content/uploads/sites/662/2018/11/Benefits_Challenges.pdf.

Unconscious (and Conscious) Bias

Unconscious and conscious forms of individual bias continue to exist in universities and in our society, even with the ongoing work of peaceful resistance groups and anti-oppression organizations.[5] As scholars, we should acknowledge these biases and become educated not just about how they impact scientific content, but also about how the biases have societal influences that affect our learning, institutions, and research processes. For example, research studies about sex differences in disease and health were not well studied historically (though this is improving more recently) for diseases such as lupus, Alzheimer's, certain cancers, and depression, among others.[6] Individuals who are responsible for reviewing résumés or serving on selection committees need to be aware of unconscious bias. Universities and funding agencies like CIHR provide training modules dealing with unconscious bias.[7] You do not need to wait until you are in a position of authority to avail yourself of these resources, and you can become aware of unconscious bias in yourself and others early in your training. Leading in this way can facilitate change. Positive change will help you grow yourself, others, and whole organizations.

In 2016, the University of Toronto's medical class had only one Black student. After the implementation of a Black Student Application Program (BSAP),[8] our 2020 entering class had 24 Black students.[9] A University of Toronto Black Medical Students Association is now in full vigour. This program is not affirmative action. All of the same competitive criteria exist for entry into medical school through the BSAP. Rather, it is a program that works to address barriers that result from anti-Black racism within the admissions process by including members from the Black community within the process. Acceptance is not enough. Higher education leaders must

---

5 See Alliance for Healthier Communities, "Anti-Oppression" (2018), https://www .allianceon.org/anti-oppression.

6 V. Regitz-Zagrosek, "Sex and Gender Differences in Health," *EMBO Reports* 13 (2012): 596–603, https://www.ncbi.nlm.nih.gov/pmc/articles/PMC3388783/.

7 See "Health Research Training at CIHR: Training Tools" (n.d.), https://cihr-irsc .gc.ca/e/50517.html.

8 See "Black Student Application Program," MD Program, University of Toronto (n.d.), https://applymd.utoronto.ca/black-student-application-program.

9 See "24 Black Medical Students Accepted to U of T Medicine – The Most in Canadian History," *Global News*, January 29, 2021, https://globalnews.ca/news /7010646/24-black-medical-students-accepted-u-of-t-medicine/.

ensure these students have a supportive environment and allyship during their education and beyond. Their peers, supervisors, and other leaders are trained in unconscious bias and allyship. Thinking about who is missing in the class or organization and removing systemic barriers promotes diversity. While this book was being written, the Black Lives Matter movement has brought into focus countless stories of racism that Black communities continue to face. By having uncomfortable discussions about race and listening to racialized people, we can all learn from one another and make systemic changes.

> Allyship is supportive association and being in solidarity with another person or a group to which one is not a member.

Gender Differences

The 10,000 PhDs Project at the University of Toronto showed that an equal number of women and men graduate with a PhD, although there is some variation in certain disciplines.[10] For example, women are underrepresented in math and physics, while men are underrepresented in speech language pathology and nursing. The number of PhD graduates who assume tenure-track positions is about equal between men and women overall but, again, different in some disciplines. Women tend to be the majority in teaching-stream faculty positions and also in contract sessional work, especially in the humanities.

In the US, more women (53.5 per cent) were enrolled in PhD programs than men (46.5 per cent) in 2017, with a bigger difference (59.2 per cent vs 40.8 per cent) at the Master's level.[11] Yet, in most academic

---

10 R. Reithmeier et al., "The 10,000 PhDs Project at the University of Toronto: Using Employment Outcome Data to Inform Graduate Education," *PLoS ONE* 14 (2019): e0209898, https://doi.org/10.1371/journal.pone.0209898.

11 "First-Time Enrollment Holds Steady, Application Counts Slightly Decline at U.S. Graduate Schools," Council of Graduate Schools (2018), https://cgsnet.org /first-time-enrollment-holds-steady-application-counts-slightly-decline-us -graduate-schools.

institutions, particularly at the senior level, men dominate, likely for historical or societal reasons, but this is slowly changing as more women are hired and move up the academic ranks. Nevertheless, gender differences in STEM[12] and academic careers[13] still persist.

Why does gender bias occur? Multiple reasons may exist. For example, (1) women may have the view that the expectations of the academic tenure track may be difficult to meet while having a family life, so they elect to find another career path; (2) female students may not feel comfortable being part of the "boys club" when they are the only female in the group meeting or if some of the collaboration discussions occur over alcohol at a pub or in the locker room of a sports club; (3) women may not feel as psychologically or emotionally safe with the work environment (a place where they feel heard) that some leaders may unconsciously foster; and (4) unfortunately, some experience harassment or discrimination that deters them from staying in academia.[14] It would be interesting for a future study to gather the factors that female and male alumni considered in their career decision-making. Collecting data in this way may shed light onto what educators can provide to their graduate students and postdocs to help them overcome potential obstacles and provide insights into what systemic changes need to be made. Women tend to be underrepresented in leadership positions in industry, although this is changing. For female professionals who want to enter the private sector, initiatives that are focused on personal growth, skills, and leadership development and transitional support are increasingly available in business schools.

EDI at Canadian Universities

Universities across Canada are working together to remove barriers to EDI.[15] Many universities have created EDI Working Groups and have EDI offices to advise on removing systemic barriers, providing

---

12 "Women in Science, Technology, Engineering, and Mathematics (STEM) (Quick Take)," Catalyst (2022), https://www.catalyst.org/research/women-in-science -technology-engineering-and-mathematics-stem/.

13 "Women in Academia," Higher Education Quality Council of Ontario (2023), https://heqco.ca/women-in-academia-main/.

14 See "Sexual Harassment in Academic Science, Engineering, and Medicine," National Academies (n.d.), https://www.nationalacademies.org/our-work/sexual-harassment -in-academia.

15 See "Equity, Diversity and Inclusion," Universities Canada (n.d.), https://www .univcan.ca/priorities/equity-diversity-inclusion/.

supports, and advancing EDI across all administrative, teaching, and research functions.[16] Universities Canada has developed seven working principles regarding EDI:[17]

1. *We believe our universities are enriched by diversity and inclusion. As leaders of universities that aspire to be diverse, fair and open, we will make our personal commitment to diversity and inclusion evident.*

2. *We commit our institutions to developing and/or maintaining an equity, diversity and inclusion action plan in consultation with students, faculty, staff and administrators, and particularly with individuals from under-represented groups. We commit to demonstrating progress over time.*

3. *We commit to taking action to provide equity of access and opportunity. To do so, we will identify and address barriers to, and provide supports for, the recruitment and retention of senior university leaders, university Board and Senate members, faculty, staff and students, particularly from under-represented groups.*

4. *We will work with our faculty and staff, search firms, and our governing boards to ensure that candidates from all backgrounds are provided support in their career progress and success in senior leadership positions at our institutions.*

5. *We will seek ways to integrate inclusive excellence throughout our university's teaching, research, community engagement and governance. In doing so, we will engage with students, faculty, staff, our boards of governors, senates and alumni to raise awareness and encourage all efforts.*

6. *We will be guided in our efforts by evidence, including evidence of what works in addressing any barriers and obstacles that may discourage members of under-represented groups to advance. We commit to sharing evidence of practices that are working, in Canada and abroad, with higher education institutions.*

7. *Through our national membership organization, Universities Canada, we will work to generate greater awareness of the importance of diversity and inclusive excellence throughout Canadian higher education.*

These working principles can be applied at your institution and provide great topics for discussion at EDI workshops and training seminars.

---

16 See Division of People Strategy, Equity and Culture, "Equity, Diversity and Inclusion Annual Report," University of Toronto (2022), https://people.utoronto.ca/news /equity-diversity-inclusion-annual-report/.

17 See Universities Canada, "Inclusive Excellence Principles" (2017), https://www .univcan.ca/wp-content/uploads/2017/10/equity-diversity-inclusion-principles -universities-canada-oct-2017.pdf.

EDI in Research

There has been a number of EDI-focused actions undertaken by Canada's federal research funding agencies, including addressing inequities such as gender differences in competition success rates, supporting early-career researchers, accounting for leaves-of-absence and addressing barriers faced by underrepresented groups often due to lack of adequate data. These actions have changed the administration of funding opportunities, the makeup of review panels, and the obligations of universities receiving federal funding. For example, training sessions now exist dealing with unconscious bias for members of review panels.[18]

The three research granting agencies in Canada have come together to provide the following statement on EDI:[19]

The Canadian Institutes of Health Research, the Natural Sciences and Engineering Research Council, and the Social Sciences and Humanities Research Council are committed to excellence in research and research training. Achieving a more equitable, diverse and inclusive Canadian research enterprise is essential to creating the excellent, innovative and impactful research necessary to advance knowledge and understanding, and to respond to local, national and global challenges. With these goals in mind, the agencies are committed to:

- *Supporting equitable access to funding opportunities for all researchers and trainees*
- *Promoting the integration of equity, diversity and inclusion-related considerations in research design and practices*
- *Increasing equitable and inclusive participation in the research system, including on research teams*
- *Collecting the data and conducting the analyses needed to include equity, diversity and inclusion considerations in decision-making*

Through these means the agencies will work with those involved in the research system to develop the inclusive culture needed for research excellence and to achieve outcomes that are rigorous, relevant and accessible to diverse populations.

The Dimensions Program

One of the major EDI initiatives undertaken by the federal research funding Tri-Agency (NSERC, CIHR, SSHRC) is Dimensions. This program

---

18 See CIHR Training Module on Unconscious Bias Training (n.d.), https://cihr-irsc.gc.ca/lms/e/bias/.

19 See "Triagency Statement on Equity, Diversity and Inclusion" (n.d.), https://www.nserc-crsng.gc.ca/NSERC-CRSNG/EDI-EDI/index_eng.asp.

will affect the way universities operate and is designed to achieve diverse, fair, and inclusive learning conditions. Postsecondary institutions are invited to endorse the Dimensions Charter to be publicly recognized for their progress in making systemic changes to address EDI. As of 2022, over 100 Canadian institutions have signed on and 17 institutions were selected for pilot projects to better define the vision and develop tools to support institutions. Standards will be established, and four levels of recognition are envisioned for progress with five minority groups (women, visible minorities, Indigenous people, those with disabilities, and LGBTQ2+ people). Successful implementation of Dimensions will require buy-in from institutions and their members and the human and financial resources to make meaningful change.

From the Dimensions website:[20]

Dimensions: equity, diversity and inclusion Canada invites you to take part in a post-secondary transformation to increase equity, diversity and inclusion (EDI) and help drive deeper cultural change within the research ecosystem. Sound EDI-informed policies and practices improve access to the largest pool of qualified potential participants, enhance the integrity of a program's application and selection processes, strengthen research outputs and increase the overall excellence of research. The Dimensions program addresses obstacles faced by, but not limited to, women, Indigenous Peoples, persons with disabilities, members of visible minorities/racialized groups, and members of LGBTQ2+ communities. It provides public recognition for institutions committed to achieving increased EDI.

Dimensions is based on Athena SWAN, a UK initiative established in 2005 to advance gender equality in STEM. In 2015 the charter was expanded to include other disciplines and underrepresented groups. The program provides three key elements:

1. Tools to achieve the goals of EDI
2. Accreditation by an external body
3. Awards and public recognition for following EDI principles

From the Athena Swan Charter:[21]

---

20 See "Equity, Diversity and Inclusion/Dimensions" (n.d.), https://www.nserc-crsng .gc.ca/NSERC-CRSNG/EDI-EDI/Dimensions_Dimensions_eng.asp.
21 See "Athena Swan Charter," Advance HE (n.d.), www.advance-he.ac.uk/equality -charters/athena-swan-charter.

Recognising advancement of gender equality: representation, progression and success for all. Advance HE's Athena SWAN Charter was established in 2005 to encourage and recognise commitment to advancing the careers of women in science, technology, engineering, maths and medicine (STEMM) employment in higher education and research. In May 2015 the charter was expanded to recognise work undertaken in arts, humanities, social sciences, business and law (AHSSBL), and in professional and support roles, and for trans staff and students. The charter now recognises work undertaken to address gender equality more broadly, and not just barriers to progression that affect women.

[The Athena Swan Charter:]

- *helps institutions achieve their gender equality objectives*
- *assists institutions to meet equality legislation requirements, as well as the requirements and expectations of some funders and research councils*
- *uses a targeted self-assessment framework to support applicants [to] identify areas for positive action as well as recognise and share good practice*
- *supports the promotion of inclusive working practices that can increase the retention of valued academics and professional and support staff, demonstrating an institution's commitment to an equitable working environment*

Practical Tips

The organizational statements above (from Universities Canada, the Tri-Agency, Dimensions, and the Athena SWAN Charter) provide an overall framework for how you can align your activities with your EDI vision. What are some practical tips? What are some things that you can do on a day-to-day basis? What are some activities or initiatives that you can provide as a student? As an educator? As a mentor? Here are four steps one can take to become a better ally. Remember: to be an ally is to be in constant action and to grow over time. An ally will make mistakes, but they will know to apologize and learn from them. Being an ally is a process, and you will continue to learn how to be an ally throughout your life.

Acknowledge and be aware that mentorship and allyship are lifelong commitments.

Step One: Awareness

Becoming aware of issues of EDI is a lifelong journey that takes reflection, effort, and dedication. Read articles, watch testimonials, listen to others around you. Read up on examples of microaggressions. Wikipedia's definition is "Microaggression is a term used for brief and commonplace daily verbal, behavioural, or environmental indignities, whether intentional or unintentional, that communicate hostile, derogatory, or negative prejudicial slights and insults towards any group, particularly culturally marginalized groups" (https://en.wikipedia.org/wiki/Microaggression). Think of a microaggression as a mosquito bite. One may be irritating, but not so bad. Now imagine being bitten by several over a lifetime. It can become more than irritating. Here is an example from Nana. As a Korean growing up among communities of people of predominantly European descent, she experienced blatant racism, but also microaggressions. For instance, people assumed she was and spoke Chinese and celebrated "Chinese" New Year. It was really not that bad at first, but hearing this repeatedly over the course of her childhood and adulthood made it more than irritating. Now she discloses that she is Korean-Canadian, does not speak any Chinese language, and that the holiday should be referred to as "Lunar" New Year, as people from a number of countries celebrate the new year designated by the moon.

Listen to others' stories. Listen to their challenges and why they had those challenges. Reflect on why you had either the same or different challenges. Acknowledge the fact that you may not have had similar challenges, based simply on your background and nothing that you did. Acknowledge the fact that due to systemic unconscious bias and racism, some of your classmates or people that you work with will have very different outlooks on their life, their achievements, and their goals.

If you would like to read more about systemic racism, here are some suggested books:

- *So You Want to Talk about Race* by Ijeoma Oluo, https://www.goodreads.com/book/show/35099718-so-you-want-to-talk-about-race
- *Stamped: Racism, Antiracism, and You* by Jason Reynolds and Ibram X. Kendi, https://www.goodreads.com/en/book/show/52220686-stamped
- *White Rage: The Unspoken Truth of Our Racial Divide* by Carol Anderson, https://www.goodreads.com/book/show/26073085-white-rage

- *Speaking of Race: How to Have Antiracist Conversations That Bring Us Together* by Patricia Roberts-Miller, https://www.goodreads.com/book/show/56363655-speaking-of-race

Here is an example of becoming aware of unconscious bias. Sam A is the only daughter in her family. She is also the first family member to attend university. Despite not having an academic mentor during her childhood and teenage years, she succeeded in applying and being accepted to university. She's not quite sure what she should major in, but throughout her childhood she was told by other relatives and older members of her family that the physical sciences such as physics, math, and computer engineering are for boys. Although she has an interest in these subjects, she decides to major in life sciences. During her undergraduate years she discovers the world of research through conversations with the teaching assistants of the courses she's taking. She did not know that one could carry out research as a student and get paid! She decides to apply for graduate programs, but this is met with opposition from her family. Her family members think an undergraduate education is sufficient "for a woman." Her family is also having financial difficulties. Due to these reasons Sam decides to not pursue graduate school, despite having the scholarly drive and being strongly encouraged by her professors, and instead finds a job straight after undergrad.

Let's contrast this with the story of another Sam, Sam B, who is the only son in his family. He is encouraged by his family to study whatever he would like. While he is in high school, both of his highly educated parents are present to help and guide him with any difficult homework and provide insight into his university program selection. Sam B has a knack for computer science and business. Once in undergrad, he also discovers the world of graduate studies and the potential of providing new knowledge for a future economy. As such, he applies to graduate school in a research program in computer science, and upon graduation, he co-founds a tech company where he eventually becomes the CEO.

In both of these examples of "Sam," the name was the same. (Note, however, that even the name of somebody can elicit an unconscious bias towards them; https://www.raconteur.net/hr/diversity-inclusion/ethnic-name-bias/). Both of our Sams had an "equal opportunity" to pursue whatever they wanted, but because of cultural, financial, and family influences, their career outcomes were different. *Equality* means giving everyone the same thing, whereas *equity* means giving someone what they need.

Now, let's imagine that Sam C is part of an underrepresented group in race and perhaps gender. Even if Sam C had supportive parents and financial stability, Sam C may still face societal effects from unconscious or, unfortunately, conscious bias when they are applying for a job, when they are in a social setting, during their graduate program, and during their work life and in business meetings with other staff or clients. If Sam C is in an underrepresented group that has faced systemic discrimination, they may have other stresses in life such as always being nervous about meeting people for the first time who lack awareness of their circumstances. Sam C may have to deal with these biases rather than focusing solely on their work. For example, a supervisor may feel that Sam C is not as capable of learning as others. This takes extra energy throughout the day for Sam C to have to prove something their colleagues from a non-underrepresented group do not have to grapple with. Being aware of your own conscious and unconscious biases will allow you to deal fairly with others.

Step Two: Gather Information

Step Two is about gathering information. One of our students told the following story: "I recall going to a doctor's office and this woman in a wheelchair approached me in the waiting room. I assumed she was a patient, but she turned out to be the doctor! It was a huge learning moment for me." This is a good example of conscious bias. Talk to your colleagues or friends from underrepresented groups about their experiences to help you better understand them and their perspective, and ask how you can help. Be an ally. If you become aware of an incident that concerns you, reach out. You can even start with "I'm not quite sure what to say or what to do, but I'm reaching out to you to see how you are. I would like to hear your story." Once you start becoming aware of different perspectives and experiences in life, and the unconscious biases that exist – even in yourself – you can start to seek information or training modules for yourself and your colleagues on how to be a better ally. Read more and attend online modules or in-person workshops. Find resources on campus about cross-cultural mentorship.[22] With this information, you can start to better understand others' experiences and learn to be a more empathetic teaching assistant, mentor, teacher, or colleague.

---

22 B.N. Crutcher, "Mentoring across Cultures," *Academe* 93 (2007), https://diversity
    .ucdavis.edu/sites/g/files/dgvnsk731/files/inline-files/Crutcher%2C%20Mentoring
    %20Across%20Cultures.pdf.

Step Three: Implementation

Step Three is implementation. Now that you are becoming more aware of your biases and you have skills that you have learned from conversations, workshops, or online modules, you can implement what you learned into actions that drive change. Here are some examples of what you can do. (1) As a teaching assistant for a class, you write an email to your students before class starts to ask if anyone requires accessibility accommodations. Students who need accommodations will appreciate that you started the conversation and they did not have to approach you. For instance, a student may need to be at the front of the class because they have vision or hearing needs or may require extra directions to your classroom as they need to find a route without stairs. (2) As a graduate student or postdoctoral mentor, you keep in mind that cultural differences or neurodiversity may prevent your mentees from speaking up. For example, students from some cultures may think it is not polite to speak up or ask questions of those in authority. Due to this, you reiterate that you welcome questions and even write this policy out in an email. (3) As an educator writing recommendation letters, you remove adjectives that may be gender-biased (e.g., helpful, hardworking, dependable vs. competitive, intelligent, ambitious) and remember to write strictly about accomplishments and not about the student's personal life. Leadership qualities and potential should be emphasized. Guidance of how to avoid gender bias in reference writing is provided in this article from the University of Arizona[23] and many other articles. (4) As a professor on the selection committees for admission to graduate school and also on faculty hiring committees, you make sure that everyone on the committee receives unconscious bias training before they review the applications, conduct the interviews, and cast their vote in the group decision. (5) As a team member of a university faculty or an organization, you realize there is a lack of diversity on your team. Acknowledging this with the entire group can be the first step in opening the conversation about how to include more diverse voices in your space and move to recruit suitable candidates. (6) Be mindful of microaggressions, those subtle comments or actions that express unconscious or unintentional prejudiced attitudes towards others in your daily interactions, and be prepared to call them out.

---

23 See "Avoiding Gender Bias in Reference Writing," Commission on the Status of Women, University of Arizona (n.d.), https://csw.arizona.edu/sites/default/files/avoiding_gender_bias_in_letter_of_reference_writing.pdf.

Step Four: Moving Forward

Allyship is not linear. You will have growth insights along the way. Become acquainted with humility, apology, and acceptance when you recognize that your words or actions might have harmed someone. You may be slightly surprised at yourself as you thought you had good intentions. One way to genuinely apologize could be "I am sorry. I did not have any ill intentions. Thank you for providing a perspective that I was unaware of. I will keep that in mind for next time."

Conclusion

EDI is essential to creating a healthy lab culture and promoting the well-being of workers. Indeed, many studies have shown that creating a healthy and inclusive workplace that empowers employees to work cooperatively with adequate support and resources is linked to increased productivity and the success of enterprises.[24] In contrast, a toxic workplace results in stress, burnout, a high level of worker turnover, and decreased productivity.

FURTHER DISCUSSION

> Note: It is critical that you have these discussions with a trained EDI professional who can guide the group so as not to trigger distress.

1. What is your story? How has your background shaped your current world? This is to be written on paper anonymously in 5–6 sentences and posted around the classroom for everyone to read in silence.
2. Share a story when you acted as an ally even when it was not an easy thing to do – also post it on the wall for people to read.
3. What are some action-based activities you or your institution could implement to promote allyship? Discuss.

TAKING ACTION

1. Read the information on EDI on the Dimensions website and attend an unconscious bias training workshop at your campus equity office.

---

24 See Healthy Workplace website: https://excellence.ca/healthy-workplace-standard/.

2. Think about how you can incorporate more diverse voices in your working group, school, class, or other gatherings and share with your departmental EDI committee. If your department does not have an EDI committee, start one.

3. Read Nana's article on daily action items on being an equity-minded scholar, https://www.insidehighered.com/advice/2020/10/19/how -being-equity-minded-scholar-can-support-your-own-professional -career-growth, and watch "Picture a Scientist" (www.pictureascientist. com). Discuss with your peers and mentors on how to move forward on being an equity-minded scholar.

PART V

Networking: Meaningful Engagement with Others

14 Marketing Your Brand: Professional Emails, Cover Letter, Résumé, and Curriculum Vitae

Key Messages

- A brand is how you are perceived by others.
- Create compelling profiles on websites, LinkedIn, and other platforms.
- Be professional on social media and in all your correspondence, including over email and in person.
- Compose strong cover letters and résumés.

In the previous chapters of this book, we discussed ways to reflect on your professional development by looking at your values, interests, and skills, and on the importance of wellness and taking care of yourself. In the next part of this book we will discuss networking and meaningful engagement. Communicating effectively is an essential skill. You can demonstrate competency in dealing with others through your oral presentations and in your writing. In this chapter we will focus on "marketing your brand."

> Marketing your brand is a way to present yourself to the world so that you can become a known and sought-after candidate for future activities and positions.

Marketing Your Brand

An important aspect of strategic communications while you are in graduate school or during your postdoc is marketing your brand. You may ask yourself, "Brand? What brand? I'm a graduate student. I am not a business student. I'm in research, not marketing. What does marketing have to do with scientific research?" As with most business terminology, let us reframe this concept into language that is more relatable to the scientist. A brand is the way you are perceived by others – it is your scientific and professional reputation. A PhD is part of your brand. So are the universities where you studied. Your supervisor may even be a part of your brand. Publications, conferences, poster presentations, abstracts, meetings with potential collaborators, tweets about your last publication, your LinkedIn profile, your curriculum vitae (CV), your résumé, your cover letter, your three-minute thesis presentation, your student seminar presentations, your chalk talk at a job interview, and your informational interviews – these are all communication tools you use as a scientist to market your brand. Once you have built your network and sent in job applications, you will start marketing your brand at interviews. Interview topics and tips are discussed in chapters 19 ("Succeeding in Academia") and 20 ("Succeeding beyond Academia").

The Three–Minute Thesis

The three-minute thesis (3MT) originated at the University of Queensland, Australia, in 2008 by the Dean of the Graduate School, Dr. Alan Lawson, as an exercise in which the speaker summarizes the typical 80,000–90,000 word PhD thesis in a three-minute presentation for a general audience.[1] This vital exercise provides the following: (1) the "why" behind the detailed research is clarified and reiterated for the student, serving as a vision statement for their own research view; (2) it provides a strong foundation for the student to explain their research to anyone, often requested in job interviews and networking moments throughout their career; and (3) preparing and presenting this oral exercise strengthens presentation skills for future career-related engagements. The assessment criteria for the 3MT in our classes include engagement and clarity, each holding equal weight. Engagement questions include (1) Did the listener want to lean in and listen more? (2) Did the speaker remain in eye contact and show enthusiasm for their work? (3) Did the speaker start with a captivating hook as the first statement? The clarity assessment includes (1) Would a grade 10 high school student understand the research? (2) Did the presentation explain concepts clearly without using jargon and, if used, was that term explained clearly? (3) Was the slide helpful to the presentation? Alumni

---

1   https://threeminutethesis.uq.edu.au/higher-degrees-researchstart-your-3mt-journey-here.

have returned to tell us that the 3MT exercise was essential for job interviews, networking, and presentations, which are all tools for building your brand. Indeed, most "pitches" in industry start with a short three-minute summary.

What contributes to your brand?

- Your science
- How you work with professionals
- Your interactions with collaborators, colleagues, professors, and committee members
- What other scientists think about your work and your camaraderie
- How you deliver your message on what you hope to achieve as a scientist
- How you carry yourself as a professional
- How you communicate (e.g., introductions, email messages)
- The content you create (e.g., reports, student council initiatives)
- How you are as a mentor
- How you are as a mentee
- How you teach the next generation
- Your public profile on LinkedIn and social media

> Marketing your brand is broader than cover letters and résumés – it is about how you present yourself, how you behave, and what impression you make on others, in social media and in real life.

LinkedIn

Your brand is reflected in your LinkedIn profile, as this is your public and professional face. You may not know exactly what path you wish to take for your career and that's okay. Once you have an idea of the direction of your path, reflect this in your planned actions and in your LinkedIn profile. Many university campuses hold workshops on the optimal way of structuring your LinkedIn profile. We highly recommend that you attend one of these and also look at those profiles of alumni whose footsteps you may want to follow. Remember that everyone is unique, so your profile will and must be unique from others. Do include your experiences (paid and unpaid) using CAR statements (Context-Action-Results, see below) as well as your publications and awards. Include the following in your summary profile: (1) your current work, (2) your past experiences, and (3) what you hope to contribute to in the future. Having this information will allow recruiters from various agencies to know where you are planning to transition next. For example, you may say "open to opportunities in scientific communication" or "interested in opportunities in the biotech research and development areas of drug discovery" or "interested in artificial intelligence" or "interested in climate change initiatives." Having clear statements of where you hope to go in the future is helpful for you and for other people discovering your profile.

Strategic Communications

Strategic communications, as we refer to here, means any verbal, visual, or written forms of communication that provide the listener with pertinent information about you, to potentially benefit both parties. These include emails, cover letters, and résumés. How do you reach out to someone properly using email? Can you write an engaging one-page cover letter? How does a résumé differ from a CV? How do you ensure that your application ends up on the top of the pile of applications for your dream job? Writing emails, cover letters, and résumés that capture the attention of the reader is an essential component of strategic communications and key to a successful job search. These communications also provide strong evidence of your writing and organization skills. To be strategic, you need to be able to customize these documents to the particular job opening. Free standard templates[2] and advice specific to PhDs[3] exist at your university's career centre or professional development program.

Strategic communication tips

Check out Nana's videos on strategic communication:
- Job applications: https://www.youtube.com/watch?v=F2Dnc_UixM4.
- The résumé: https://www.youtube.com/watch?v=vcsrlAxtPJI.
- The cover letter: https://www.youtube.com/watch?v=b_pc5I4IBSc.

The Email Message

We all use email to connect with others, including with family and friends and for work-related communication. It's a great way to document information. And it is also a permanent written record.

---

2 See "Professional Résumé Templates," Indeed (n.d.), https://www.indeed.com /profile/resume-templates/.
3 "Resumes and Cover Letters for PhD Students," Harvard University, Office of Career Services (n.d.), https://hwpi.harvard.edu/files/ocs/files/phd_resume _cover_letters.pdf.

As such, email is a great tool to follow up on a meeting – a sort of mini-minutes to ensure clarity. However, email is not always the best communication tool. For example, sometimes a simple phone call or face-to-face meeting can better clarify a situation. This is because statements in email messages often are misinterpreted. Email is also no place for debate or discussion. Think twice about using "Reply All." Avoid humour. Many email messages are far too long – that's why we use attachments. Emails are an effective way to connect and communicate with others, especially to provide important information. Be professional, as an email is a written record of your correspondence.

Email guidelines

- Use a specific subject title, not just "hello."
- Do not write more than half a page (~300 words), and use attachments.
- Use bullet points, if appropriate.
- Start with *why* you are contacting the person – the purpose of the message.
- Next, add some relevant details about *who* you are.
- Then, explain *what* you want.
- Close with a follow-up statement and say thank you.
- Include your full contact information in your email signature.

Professional email etiquette should begin as soon as you become a professional member in a society, meaning that email etiquette should apply for emails sent for purposes of work, school, volunteering, informational interviews, or growing your network – in essence, any emails that don't go to family and friends are written professionally. These types of emails can start as early as in the preteen years, when a student applies for a babysitting or lawn-mowing job or for volunteering. For some students, email etiquette does not become an issue until graduate school. For the following real examples, discuss with your class how you would make them more professional.

Email case examples

 I *Yo, Charlie, Can you be on my committee? Student A*
 II *(assignment sent as an attachment with no text in the body of the email)*
 III *Hey Ms. Singh, Could you be a guest speaker for our event on August 23? Student B*
 IV *Here you go. (with an assignment attachment)*
 V *Dear Dr. Brokovich, I am going to be away on vacation next week so I cannot submit in my report until later, Student C.*

Suppose you are interested in being the graduate student of a particular supervisor and plan to make initial contact via email. Let's compare the following three emails for the application to a PhD position.
Example A:

Subject: Hello
Hi Joe,
I am looking for a place to do my PhD. Do you have any openings? I am a hard worker and love life sciences. I am also interested in law, but I want to keep my options open.

(Name)

Many issues exist in email A. Can you identify them?

1. The subject heading needs more detail, such as "Potential PhD."
2. Who is Joe? This should be addressed to Dr. or Professor.
3. The note has to be inspiring – tell the professor why you want to work with them through how you want to contribute to their research.
4. There is no need to write about an interest in law.
5. An email signature is missing. Who are you?

Let's look at another one.
Example B:

Subject: Interested in PhD Studies in Your Lab
Dear Dr. Nobel,
I read your recent paper in Molecular Cell *and found the discovery of a novel role for the HSP90 protein in colon cancer fascinating.*
I am a 4th year honours student in Biochemistry at the University of Toronto and have extensive research experience working on heat shock proteins with Dr. Reinhart Reithmeier, who suggested that I contact you.
I am very interested in joining your research group as a PhD student, perhaps continuing to work out the molecular mechanism of HSP90 in primary colon cancer cells using high-throughput CRISPR methods that I am currently using with HEK-293 cells.
I have attached my curriculum vitae that lists my first publication based on my summer research project.
I look forward to your response and hope we can speak in person over the next two weeks at your convenience.

Thank you for your attention and I wish you continued success in your very exciting research.

Yours sincerely,
(Name)
(Contact information, including LinkedIn and website)

This letter mentions your work in a related lab, with someone who knows Dr. Nobel and his work. It shows that you are familiar with the work of Dr. Nobel and have thought about how you can bring a new technology to their lab. It also provides a two-week timeline for a response. Now, how could we make such a good email even more succinct and to the point?

Example C:

Subject: PhD Applicant_(your last name)
Dear Dr. Nobel,

After reading your fascinating Molecular Cell *HSP90 publication, I am writing to offer my extensive research experience working on heat shock proteins with Dr. Reinhart Reithmeier as a PhD student for your research group. I would perhaps propose continuing to work out the molecular mechanism of HSP90 in primary colon cancer cells using high-throughput CRISPR methods that I am currently using with HEK-294 cells.*

I have attached my curriculum vitae that lists my first publication based on my summer research project. I look forward to your response and hope we can speak in person over the next two weeks at your convenience. Thank you for your time and consideration, and I wish you continued success in your very exciting research.

Yours sincerely,
(Name)
Fourth Year Honours Undergraduate Researcher
PI: Reinhart Reithmeier (hyperlink to the lab)
Department of Biochemistry, Global University
Room 1000, 15th Floor, Green Building
(City, Province, Postal Code)
(Phone, Email, LinkedIn URL)

If you include detailed information in your email signature, you do not have to open with an academic introduction of yourself. You can open with "why they would care" to read ahead. Open with what you can offer them and why.

The same brief type of email is also useful when applying for jobs, or when you are submitting your application to an online human resources service. For example, you could try writing to the decision makers. If you have a connection within their team, then writing a short note to include mention of this contact would also be helpful. Attach a copy of your cover letter and résumé. Here is an example:

> *Subject: Applicant* (your last name) *for Job #123ABC*
> *Dear Dr. Ross:*
>
> *I am writing to offer my experiences and apply for the Senior Scientist position, Job #123ABC, in the Oncology Division of LifeSciences Inc.*
>
> *I collaborated with Dr. Hunter in your Pharmacology Division as a postdoctoral fellow a few years ago.*
>
> *Attached are my cover letter and résumé, which I have also sent to HR.*
>
> *I look forward to working with you and Dr. Hunter again.*
>
> *Sincerely,*
> (Signature)
> (Name)

This email is straight to the point and offers key information that is not available in the cover letter – the fact that you know someone in the organization. It is likely that as soon as Dr. Ross reads this, she will be calling Dr. Hunter for his impression of you. Although Dr. Hunter is not one of your references, he does matter to Dr. Ross, as teamwork is vital in a company. However, what if you do not know anyone in the company? Not even remotely?

Here is another example:

> *Dear Dr. Ross:*
>
> *I am writing to offer my experiences and apply for the Senior Scientist position, Job #123ABC, in the Oncology Division of LifeSciences Inc.*
>
> *Your recent press release about OncoFab inspired me to apply for this position to help strengthen your team using my experience in monoclonal antibody development.*
>
> *I am attaching my cover letter and résumé, which have also been sent to HR. Thank you for your kind attention.*
>
> *Sincerely,*
> (Signature)
> (Name)

This letter tells Dr. Ross that you know the company's product and its latest news. You have done research and it shows in one line of your email. Also, always include the job number you are applying for, as companies may advertise for more than one position at any given time.

Cover Letters

Cover letters follow a similar format to email messages – they highlight why you are interested in the position, what you can offer, and how you can be contacted. Cover letters should not repeat what is in your résumé. They should only be one page long and have a professional letterhead with your full contact information. Be sure to provide a date and the name and address of the hiring manager or CEO of the company. If a recruiting firm is handling the interviews, then you probably won't be contacting the CEO or principal investigator directly, so you should write accordingly. Like email messages, cover letters are addressed to a real person, not to "Whom it may concern" or "HR Officer" or "Sir/Madam." With the magic of Google and LinkedIn, you can find the hiring manager or CEO/CSO of any company. Take the time to find the real name. If you cannot find a name for whatever reason, your last resort would be "Dear Hiring Team" or "Dear Hiring Manager."

A great cover letter is like a mini business proposal, succinct yet well researched. As Simon Sinek outlines in his book *Start with Why*,[4] a successful cover letter addresses all of the items on his Golden Circle, which are "Why," "How," and "What." Address on the cover letter why are you applying to work for them, how you are going to help them, and what you are going to help them with. "To pay the mortgage" is not a good reason. The "why" of the matter is about how you agree with and support the company's motto, credo, or mission statement. Beyond the Why, How, and What is the "Who." Who is the company serving? Their clients or customers? Who, then, are you helping? A sentence like this would answer the Why, How, What, and Who: "I have read the mission statement of your company and believe that my skills and experience will help you accomplish your goal to develop a new line of anti-cancer drugs." This "grabber" statement could go in the early part of your cover letter.

The letter should have an introduction on why you are writing and interested in working for the company. A good introduction would be "I bring my seven years of collaborative research and creativity to apply

---

4 S. Sinek, *Start with Why* (Optimism Press, 2009), https://simonsinek.com/books/start-with-why/.

for your advertised position of Application Scientist, Job Ad #AB45678, as seen on your company website." If you have a connection with the company use it: "I was also referred to your company by a colleague, Dr. Jane Doctor from Biotech Inc., who worked with your Senior Scientist, Dr. Brilliant, two years ago on a collaborative project." A superb introduction, if you do not know anyone at the company, would be "I offer my seven years of vaccine research experience and ten years of leadership skills to your Research Scientist position #JC124 to help strengthen your research and development of your antibody manufacturing technology, ABCare." This sentence tells the hiring manager what qualities you can offer them and how you will do so. An example of a poor introduction would be "I am applying for your Scientist position." Be specific, don't be generic. Be professional, not casual.

The middle paragraph should cover what you have to offer the company. This is key, especially when you are writing a "cold" application, with no contacts in the company. This second paragraph should be concise and powerful, and not a reiteration of your résumé, which provides your details. This paragraph should relay your talents and overall qualities that may not be readily apparent on your résumé. What can you do for the company? What will you bring to the organization? Why should they choose you? This is the paragraph where you expand in more detail on the What, How, Why, and perhaps even Who. It will be the longest section of your letter and can sometimes be divided into two subsections, the first on Why you are suited for the position and the second on How you can help them. This is where you include what you read about the company's research on MEDLINE or in other public statements. A shortened example of a good second paragraph would be "My extensive work with microarrays and assay development will provide your company the expertise needed for your Diagnostics Department in its R&D of Product X, as described in your last month's press release. My five years of leadership skills and collaborative science projects have strengthened my ability to handle multiple projects at once, my communication skills, and my willingness to take initiative, as evidenced by my leadership awards. I offer my science background, combined with strong interpersonal skills, to help advance Company Y in your mission of providing the highest quality diagnostics for all of your international clients." This second paragraph tells the hiring manager that you know what the company is all about and how you can help them.

The concluding statement tells the reader how to follow up with you. State again which job you are interested in and how the reader can reach you. One example would be "I believe I am an ideal candidate for your Application Scientist position. Please contact me with any questions at

555-555-0000 or student@university.edu." Conclude with: "Thank you for your time and consideration. I look forward to meeting with you. Sincerely, (Signature), (Name)."

Here is a sample cover letter:

(Name)
(Phone, Email, LinkedIn URL)
Dr. Aaliyah Hadi
Director of Science Communications
ABC Corporations
555 Main Street
City, Province, Postal Code
July 20, 2023

Dear Dr. Hadi:

I offer my seven years of research excellence and eight years of science outreach and mentorship experience to the position of Assistant Director of Communications Job #123RTG of ABC Corporations to enhance your vision in scientific outreach for health-care providers, patients, and learners of all ages.

I bring my science background and interpersonal skills, as demonstrated by my several years of experience as Outreach Officer for SciReach, to your firm in helping with your WE high school design program. I would be driven to design communi-cation platforms outlining recent science events, such as the basics of the science of COVID virology as well as the big picture epidemiology with short video clips, live online chats, blog, and podcasts. [Expand this section with more of these types of statements on *Why* you want to work for this particular company and *How* you will help them.]

Thank you for your time and consideration. Should you have any questions, please contact me at 555-555-0000 or student@university.edu. I look forward to discussing many exciting projects with you.

Sincerely,
(Signature)
(Name)

Curriculum Vitae (CV)

A CV is a complete record of your academic accomplishments and is used for all academic positions whether that is an application for graduate school, an award, or a university professor position. The CV includes everything – education, awards, research and teaching expe-rience, community service, and a complete list of your presentations and publications. Every graduate student has a CV that is regularly updated to reflect their complete record of academic accomplishments. For a person in a senior position, a CV may run over 50 pages! You may ask your supervisor for a copy of their CV as an example. Again, CV templates are readily available online.[5] Some institutions provide sample templates as well, such as seen here for the University of Toronto.[6] Your complete CV can also serve as a master document for shorter documents, including the NIH Biosketch[7] and the Canadian Common CV.[8]

Curriculum Vitae Outline

Name
Address and Contact Information (Phone, Email, LinkedIn URL, Website)
Current and Previous Academic Positions
Education and Professional Development
Research Experience
Awards and Recognitions
Professional Affiliations and Memberships
Teaching Experience
Committees and Administrative Duties
Community and Volunteer Activities
Invited Seminars and Presentations
Public Events
Publications
Abstracts and Posters
Review Articles and Chapters
Peer-reviewed Papers
Other Publications
References

---

5 "How to Write a Professional Academic CV," Academic Positions/Career Advice (n.d.), https://academicpositions.com/career-advice/how-to-write-a-professional-academic-cv.
6 See "Faculty Appointments," Temerty Faculty of Medicine, University of Toronto (n.d.), https://medicine.utoronto.ca/faculty-staff/faculty-appointments-and-promotions.
7 See "Biosketch Format Pages, Instructions and Samples," NIH Grants and Funding (n.d.), https://grants.nih.gov/grants/forms/biosketch.htm.
8 See "Canadian Common CV" (n.d.), https://ccv-cvc.ca/indexresearcher-eng.frm.

Résumés

A résumé is very different from an academic CV. A résumé is a unique document targeted for a specific job outside academia, for example, in industry or government. Résumés are short, focused documents, typically one to two pages in length. Effective résumés should tell stories – your stories. They highlight what you have accomplished. It is not simply a list of techniques, but what you accomplished using them. It describes the impact of your actions from every position you have held that is relevant to the job you're applying to, including during your undergraduate years and your PhD studies.

A résumé is not a mini CV. While you have one CV, you will write many résumés, each designed for a specific job application. Many people send out the same résumé for many different jobs, but this is not a great approach. A résumé provides a summary of your experiences *relevant* to the particular position. If the job requires many technical skills, you may want to highlight them more than for a job requiring someone to coordinate people or a program. If you have volunteered for an organization for a while, this is also experience. Just because you did not get paid for it does not mean it should be left out. On the contrary, every work or volunteer experience that helped make you a "people person" or strengthened any core competency skill should be included. These positions can also indicate leadership potential.

Your résumé is organized into different sections with headings, with the section most relevant to the job posting at the top. An exemplary résumé stands out with its CAR statements and by being easy to read with bullets and bolded fonts. Recruiters spend less than 10 seconds reviewing résumés! For example, your publications are a key feature of your CV but are not typically listed in full in a résumé. Use hyperlinks if you need to. Publications certainly can be included as key accomplishments, and indicate an ability to complete a project and report on it. Compare the academic CV described above with the box below to see what typically goes into a résumé.

Résumé Outline

Name, Phone, Email, LinkedIn, Website URL
Career Objective (detailed from the job description)
Relevant Experience with CAR Statements
Professional Qualifications and Recognitions (publications, professional
    development activities, and awards)
Education (one line per degree)
Pertinent Skills

Challenge/Context, Action, and Result (CAR) Method

The CAR Method is a powerful tool to use when creating statements for your résumé. CAR stands for Challenge or Context, Action you took, and Results you obtained.[9] It is essential that you develop a personalized set of CAR statements as bullet points that you can use in different résumés. Which CAR statements you use depends on the job. Some CAR statements add an S; the S is So-what? What was the impact of your result? Why is it important? These considerations often come up during the interview process.

The best place to start writing CAR statements for your résumé is with the job description. Go through the ad very carefully and highlight the specific qualifications and skills required. If you struggle to match your skillset to those of the position, perhaps the job is not for you. That said, just because you don't fulfill 100 per cent of the qualification, doesn't mean you shouldn't apply.[10] This especially applies to women.[11] There is typically a job description, the level of education required, and the skills and experience the employer is looking for.

> A graduate education provides work experience, so don't think that the only relevant work experience comes after you graduate!

CAR statements may start either with an action verb or with the challenge/context, in which case they usually start with "To...." Pick one format and stick to it throughout your résumé. Your CAR statements will also change with the type of action verb you want to highlight for that job. For example, if you want to highlight your collaborative skills,

---

9   T. Omoth, "How to Get More Results with a C.A.R. Resume," TopResume (n.d.), https://ca.topresume.com/career-advice/how-to-get-more-results-with-a-car-resume.

10   B. Mossman, "Apply for Your Dream Job Even If You Don't Match the Criteria," *Guardian*, July 11, 2016, https://www.theguardian.com/careers/2016/jul/11/apply -for-your-dream-job-even-if-you-dont-match-the-criteria.

11   T.S. Mohr, "Why Women Don't Apply for Jobs Unless They're 100 Per Cent Qualified," *Harvard Business Review* (2014), https://hbr.org/2014/08/why-women-dont-apply -for-jobs-unless-theyre-100-qualified.

the CAR statement will be different than if you want to highlight your research outcomes. What you want to highlight will depend on what job you are applying for. Let's look at the same experience written with different perspectives, depending on the job and action verb (in **bold**) you want to highlight.

For a research role in an industry where you want to highlight research productivity and teamwork skills:

- "To **elucidate** potential therapies for disease A (context), investigated the effects of 10 inhibitors of an essential cell transporter system with three researchers over 112 months (action), resulting in a publication in a top journal and the foundation for targeted drug discovery research in disease A (results)."

For a communications role where you want to highlight teamwork and communication skills:

- "To **acquire and translate** knowledge from research in disease A (context), investigated cellular processes through collaborating with three researchers over 12 months (action) resulting in a first-author publication in a top-tier journal, a global conference, invited poster presentation, and a science outreach magazine article with 350 views over 2 weeks (results)."

Here are some more examples starting with "To...." See if you can guess what jobs they were written for, and discuss with your class how you might change them for other job listings:

- "To provide an unprecedented career fair for graduate students (context), **spearheaded** an 8-hour career development symposium **coordinating** with three other departments (action) resulting in over 300 attendees with a greater than 90 per cent satisfaction rate (result)."
- "To promote science outreach (context), **edited** science-related articles and **led** new marketing initiatives for the quarterly campus journal, *Hypothesis* (action), increasing scientific awareness for the general public, as indicated by a 50 per cent rise in Facebook and Twitter hits (result)."
- "To provide fundraising expertise for cancer awareness (context), **initiated** and **trained** 10 staff on cold-call and outreach techniques over a six-month period (action), leading to a 35 per cent increase in donations (results)."

Here are some examples starting with the action verb:

- **"Instructed and customized** individual lesson plans for under-graduate students (action) to **assist** students with a comprehensive understanding of the introduction to biochemistry (context), which improved exam performance by 10–20 per cent (result)."
- **"Investigated** 10,000 effective hours of mammalian cell-signalling research (action) to **discover** the role of a key gene involved in cancer cell growth (context), resulting in two publications, three poster presentations, and two invited speaking engagements (result)."
- **"Led** a group of 15 graduate students (action) to **promote** a new cancer awareness project (context), resulting in the formation of a new nonprofit organization with three staff, a website, and 25,000 members who receive cancer awareness monthly articles written for the general public (result)."
- **"Managed** a five-year research project with seven team members (action) to **expand** scientific thought leadership (context), resulting in three peer-reviewed publications in top journals, a successful grant application, and optimized protocols that are being used by 15 other research labs globally (result)."

Action verbs for scientists

collaborated	organized
coordinated	planned
created	prepared
communicated	presented
developed	programmed
designed	published
disseminated	researched
facilitated	resolved
identified	supervised
initiated	taught
innovated	trained
led	validated
managed	volunteered
mentored	wrote
negotiated	

More examples are here: https://capd.mit.edu/sites/default/files/jobs/files/resume-action-verbs.pdf.

A sample résumé is outlined below.

Jo Surname

555-555-0000 | jo.surname@globaluniv.edu | josurnameLinkedIn

Objective: Offering six years of biomolecular research and teamwork/ mentorship skills to the position of Research Scientist at Company A to further enhance your mission of researching genetic causes of illnesses in the global population.

RESEARCH & TEACHING EXPERIENCE

PhD Researcher – *Professor A Lab, Dept of Zoology, World University*   **2017–present**
- Investigated the molecular basis of disease A to elucidate the unknown pathogenesis of a newly discovered condition with a collaborative team of five members resulting in the discovery of the effect of metals on various polymorphisms
- Purified, refolded Protein B from inclusion bodies and developed an *in vitro* biochemical assay to characterize its unfolding and aggregation, which led to the identification of a misfolded intermediate

Teaching Assistant – *Dept. of Cell Systems Biology, World University* **2018–2022**
- Implemented individualized lesson plans for 12 undergraduate students for a research lab course resulting in their improved understanding of basic techniques, an overall positive feedback on teaching format and delivery, and a Teaching Award

Mentorship Team Co-Lead – *Life Sciences Career Development Society, Toronto, ON*   **2019–2022**
- Led a team of 3 graduate students in the recruitment and pairing of 14 life sciences professionals with current graduate students to help students expand their professional network and receive industry-specific guidance resulting in mentee-mentor relationships that lasted 1–2 years

Undergraduate Honours Research Project – *Professor B. Kind, EU University* **2016–2017**
- Applied an ancestral reconstruction approach to studying the structure and function of Receptor C, resulting in a first author publication in *Cell*

TECHNICAL SKILLS

Protein expression and purification, UV and fluorescence spectroscopy, immunoblotting, ELISA, BCA assay, mammalian cell culture

PUBLICATIONS

Jo Surname et al., *Cell*. Vol. Pages, Dates
Surname et al (4th)., *Biochim Biophys Acta Prot Proteom*. Date

EDUCATION & AWARDS

Biochemistry, PhD *Global University, Dean's Honour List, Scholarship* **2017–2022**
Biochemistry, Honours Bachelor of Science (Cum Laude), *World University* **2013–2017**

Where to find support for CVs, cover letters, and résumés
University career services provide advice on writing CVs, cover letters, and résumés with good examples (e.g., https://www.grad.ubc.ca/cover-letter-cv-resume-templates-ubc-career-services). The experts in these offices will help you get started and are essential to helping you review drafts before you send them out in an application package. Graduate studies offices typically publish guidelines and often run workshops and courses as well (e.g., https://uwaterloo.ca/graduate-studies-postdoctoral-affairs/events/writing-session-resumes-and-cover-letters-phds-and-postdocs-1).

Conclusion

Even after you land the position, you will continue to market your brand throughout your professional and personal life. Instead of your graduate school activities, your brand will be informed by your professional network, your projects, your clients' projects, new initiatives you bring to the research team, and your interactions with the general public as an ambassador of science. Keep being professional, courteous, enthusiastic, effective, and genuine. All of these qualities lead to you adding only the meaningful engagements on your CV or résumé. Some students fall into the "trap" of "doing something" so it "looks good" on or "pads up" their résumé. These activities will not last long and employers will notice. Only engage in activities that are truly you and inspire you. These are the activities which will produce meaningful results, both for you and on paper. Keep being the real *you*.

FURTHER DISCUSSION

1. Work in teams to create an email to ask your supervisor for a meeting concerning a topic of vital importance.
2. Randomly assign action verbs for the class to use to create individual CAR statements, and post them on a board for class feedback.
3. Present a three-minute pitch for a possible job opening in industry and solicit feedback.

TAKING ACTION

1. Update your academic CV.
2. Reflect on your values, interests, skills, and personality to define your brand, and write a 100-word bio that could be used by hosts to introduce you at meetings or conferences where you give a talk.
3. Find a job ad of interest, create an appropriate cover letter and résumé and share with a peer for feedback.

15 Building Your Professional Network

Key Messages

- Build a diverse professional network beyond academia to diversify your employment opportunities.
- Take advantage of the various activities and events that you attend as networking opportunities.
- Build lasting connections with role models and mentors as they are your sponsors.
- Contribute to others in your network as you progress through your career.

Networking is about building strong connections with other people.[1] Networking is not about the number of connections, but rather their endurance and strength. Meaningful engagement refers to actions that fulfill a part of your exploration, experiential learning, or core competency skill development. Examples of meaningful engagements may include establishing a research collaboration, setting up a series of informational interviews to build an effective network, connecting with a community group, creating an internship opportunity, mentoring other students, or even starting a new student organization. Meaningful engagement is not just "doing more" for the sake of a listing on your curriculum vitae, but taking a deliberate set of actions to carve out your own life and career journey. Central to these actions is connecting with the individuals who may be able to assist you along your path.

---

1 I. Hankel, "8 Networking Tips for PhDs to Advance Their Careers," Cheeky Scientist, n.d., https://cheekyscientist.com/8-networking-tips-for-phds-to-advance-their-careers/.

Why Networking Is Essential

Building a strong network will give you choices and help you to develop your career path. The academic pathway is linear, but you still need to develop branches. People in the academic world build networks that often lead to productive interactions and collaborations. Successful scientists get invited to speak at meetings not only because of their great science, but also because they are known outside of their university and have an extensive and worldwide network they built up over the course of their career. If you are a Canadian on your postdoctoral fellowship abroad and wish to return to Canada as a faculty member, visit Canadian national conferences at least once a year to present and make Canadian connections. If you are thinking of career options outside of academia, it is better to develop a network in the area you would like work sooner than later. National organizations such as Science to Business Network,[2] Ten Thousand Coffees,[3] or other student groups can assist you in building your community while you are still in training.

Regarding postdoctoral fellowship positions, think about whether you really want or need to do one. In some fields like the humanities, postdoctoral fellows are rare and graduates typically move straight into jobs. What are the alternatives to a postdoctoral fellowship that will lead to a successful career path? Find people who did not complete a postdoctoral fellowship who are now in careers you are interested in. Perhaps they went on to professional school. Perhaps they went into the job market and succeeded in landing a job as the result of a network they developed outside the lab while they were a graduate student. Find these people and invite them into your network. Again, think about starting early. Explore the possibilities.

Effective Networking

Effective networking requires (1) self-assessment, as outlined in the previous chapters; (2) research on potential mentors, including speakers at conferences; (3) formulating specific questions for informational interviews; and (4) following up. Each of these steps is equally important so that potential mentors will remember you and want to help you. For example, if you are at a networking session as part of a scientific meeting, approach the presenters with a smile, a brief introduction, and a

---

2 See Science to Business Network website: https://www.s2bn.org/.
3 See Ten Thousand Coffees website: https://www.tenthousandcoffees.com/.

business card. Ask them questions that you have already prepared, or questions based on what they just spoke about: "I just read your article on global health in *The Globe and Mail*. Do you mind if I ask you a couple of questions?" If their career path intrigues you, ask them about how they made decisions during their transitional moments. How did they obtain their first writing job? How did they transition into editing? Ask specific questions regarding their publications that you were particularly interested in. After the conversation, thank them and send them a LinkedIn invitation the same day, with content in the message that they will remember you by. Send them an email with any further questions. They will not only give you some good advice, but perhaps connect you with others in their network. If you really connected with them and you think it is mutual, send them appropriate updates on your progress or something that might interest them once in a while (every four to six months, or when appropriate) to maintain the connection. This is meaningful engagement.

Meaningful engagement is all about people. It is not the company, university, or hospital institute that is hiring you. It's the people that you will work with. The company provides the infrastructure and funding to make the work possible. But it's the people that interview you. If you "click" with the team, people invite you in. However, many graduate students are shy and may think, "What do I say in a room full of CEOs, CSOs, COOs, professors, VPs of sales, patent agents and lawyers, science writers, and people with professional-sounding titles? These people are already established and are busy. They wouldn't want to talk to me, a mere graduate student." Just remember: they were graduate students once, too, and are likely going to be happy to talk to you, especially if you ask them about elements of their life story during or following up on networking events. Practicing networking during your training will help you be more comfortable when you are put in situations with higher stakes, such as during interviews.

> While you are a graduate student, learn the art of networking so that as you approach graduation, you already have an array of people you can speak to about your potential career direction.

Role Models as Part of Your Network

Role models are a key part of your professional network. Everyone has role models: people they admire and want to emulate. Your supervisor may be a role model if you are interested in the academic path. But what if you are interested in other career paths? Who else do you admire and why? Perhaps someone in your community. Perhaps someone you read or heard about. Think broadly. You need to think about the career choices that you have and find people in those careers who can share their experiences with you. What do PhD scientists actually do in biotech companies? Find out using informational interviews. They rarely work at the bench, but they are expected to be leaders and make decisions. Is this for you? Do you like day-to-day routine? Do you like the unexpected? Do you enjoy working long hours or are you a nine-to-five kind of person? All jobs have expectations. Can you meet them? Do you want to? What are your ambitions, your expectations? You may be surprised to learn that many jobs are not what you thought they were. You need to find out before you invest time and money in a path that is not for you. Role models are key to helping you figure it out. But if you only have one, such as your supervisor, this clearly limits your potential.

A broad network will help you identify people who can develop into your role models or even your mentors.

An example of networking for a science writer

When you are attending a networking event, scan through the guest list and find all professionals who are related to the science writing world, such as pharma document writers, patent agents, science communication professionals, science bloggers, policy writers, science reporters, and the like. Research their profiles on Google and LinkedIn. Read their publications. Get to know them and their work. Introduce yourself to them and make their acquaintance. Maintain communication with them over time.

Market yourself. You can create your own website. You can start a blog on WordPress or Blogspot. Having said that, make sure you blog intelligently and effectively to showcase your writing and opinions. Highlight your writing projects on your LinkedIn profile. Utilize YouTube. A strong presence on the internet can help your writing career, as seen for "1000 Awesome Things" (*1000 Awesome Things – A Time-Ticking Countdown of 1000 Awesome Things* by Neil Pasricha, http://1000awesomethings.com/). Check out *Science Borealis*, a conglomeration of Canadian science blogs (*ScienceBorealis – Blogging from Canadian Perspectives*, http://scienceborealis .ca/). Write and submit your blog to be part of their blog list. Chart out a plan on articles you could write for the campus newspaper or online student-run journals during your training. Examples at the University of Toronto include *Hypothesis Journal* and the Department of Immunology's initiative *Immpress Magazine* (*IMMpress Magazine*, http://www.immpressmagazine.com/). Write at every opportunity. Write prolifically for many different audiences, such as scientists, lay people, and children.

Building Your Professional Network

Most graduate students have a narrow professional network, mostly consisting of academic contacts within their own university. This network includes your supervisor and committee members – people who would write your letters of reference. You may also have grown familiar with a few other professors through courses, or perhaps in your role as a teaching assistant. Your network certainly includes other students, peers, friends, family, mentees, colleagues within your community, and student groups. People in this network can give you great advice and support during your graduate program, helping you to transition into a postdoc and on to an academic career. But how do you expand beyond this local network, especially if you are interested in careers outside academia? Here are some tips.

1. *Build on your research circle.* You may have had collaborators that you worked with, possibly located at other universities or even in other countries. These people know you and are part of your network. What about the external examiner for your thesis? Engage them after your defence to thank them for their participation. They can often be called on to write letters of reference. Perhaps they know of job opportunities at their university or elsewhere. Also, reach out to other graduate students working in different fields, but with whom you are linked by a common element, like you are both winners of the same scholarship.

2. *Present your work at scientific meetings.* These meetings provide a great opportunity to build your network. If you have people come by to view your poster, ask them their names and why they are interested in your work. Follow up when you are back home with an email. If you hear a great talk, don't be afraid to meet the speaker afterwards and tell them so. Always identify yourself. "Hi, I'm — from — University. I really liked your talk and am interested in your research. I'm thinking about postdoc opportunities and would like to send you my CV if there are openings in your lab." A detailed

article on tips for conference networking can be found here.[4] And here is a link to a video with additional tips on this topic.[5]

3. *Visit the vendor booths at conferences.* Perhaps you are interested in scientific publishing, technical support, or sales. Drop by various booths at the conference and talk to the people there. Ask them about their jobs and their companies. Perhaps they are looking to recruit. Most of the representatives at these booths are in sales and marketing. However, sometimes the application scientists will also be there and can share insights on those roles. If the company you are interested in does not have any scientist representatives present, ask the sales representative for company publications. Remember, somebody wrote and put together the material handed out by companies. Does this interest you? These publications will contain the author list, and these will be the R&D scientists in the company. Read these publications and reach out to the scientists who wrote the paper, if the work interests you.

4. *Visit the Career Centre at your university.* Try this earlier than the day you graduate. Build contacts there. Let the professionals get to know you. They can help in so many ways, such as with your cover letters and résumés for specific job opportunities. But you need to take the initiative. Attend career development events and get the names and contacts of people who interested you. Most will welcome attention and are happy to help.

5. *Develop alternative connections.* Volunteer, join a club, take a course, be athletic, or play in a band or chorus. It's not all about working hard in the lab. If you are passionate or curious about something, make room for the activities that interest you. There are so many stories of people landing jobs through contacts outside of work. Research is rightfully your focus, but it is okay to take a break. In fact, it is essential for your well-being. See chapter 7, "Integrating Life with Work," and chapter 8, "Wellness." for more on this topic.

6. *Connect with alumni.* They are incredible resources. Get the names of people who graduated from your lab or your department and now have interesting job descriptions. If an alumni list does not exist, take the initiative and build one. Contact these people and set up informational meetings. This could be over a quick coffee or lunch,

---

4 N. Lee, "Essential Networking Tips for Graduate Students," *University Affairs/Career Advice*, 2016, https://www.universityaffairs.ca/career-advice/career-advice-article /essential-networking-tips-for-graduate-students/.

5 Watch this video on networking from Nana Lee (2020): https://www.youtube.com /watch?v=g6kUYW4k444.

or a more formal meeting. Come with a purpose. Be prepared. Go away with information and follow up if you click with them. Don't forget to thank them. Alumni are willing to give back and are often great role models and mentors. They were in your shoes once.

7. *Network virtually.* As we see more jobs going global, virtual interview skills are essential. Indeed, the first round of many job interviews is being done online by video link. Here is a link to some tips on talking to a camera.[6] During the writing of this book in 2020–2, we were in the COVID-19 pandemic and were virtually connecting with students, faculty, and colleagues for several months, so many of us are now comfortable working remotely.

8. *Build relationships with your own students and mentees.* The students that you mentor will become professionals one day. They will have a network as well. Building good relationships with them will open up both of your networks to each other.

> Thinking outside the box when building your network will help you to ensure it is diverse in career paths, location, and experience, which will set you up for success in your career trajectory by having options for who to lean on for support.

Questions to ask yourself about your career path

- Where do I want to be in 5 or 10 years?
- How can I get there?
- Am I on the right path?
- Do I have a Plan B?
- Who do I admire as a role model, and why?

Questions to ask during an informational interview

- What is your typical day like?
- What do you like about your job?
- What key decisions did you make that led you to where you are?
- What steps did you take in your past to gain an edge in your current career?
- What advice would you give someone who wants to be in your position in 10 years?

---

6 N. Lee, "Making Professional Contacts in a Virtual World," *University Affairs/Career Advice* (2020), https://www.universityaffairs.ca/career-advice/career-advice-article/professional-connections-in-a-virtual-world/.

Here is an example of building your network at a conference:

Nana Lee	I attended a career workshop as a mentor, and I met many other professionals who I added to my LinkedIn, and we still keep in touch today. Some of these colleagues and I have helped each other with our own career transitions.

Real examples of the power of networking

1. I played basketball with a group of friends during my stint at MIT. During that time, I made friends with members of the Human Genome Project lab who I probably would not have met otherwise. I kept in touch with some of them through LinkedIn and email. A few years later, I received a note from one of the lab members who had started a biotech company and was in search of a bioinformatician with a certain skillset. He asked through LinkedIn, so I shared his ad with my network. Anyone who was in my network saw the ad first.
2. I wanted to gain experience in a start-up biotech company, but didn't know how to find one. I asked my network of principal investigator friends, and one of them introduced me to a CEO who was hiring for their brand-new start-up. After the interview, I landed the job.
3. I was let go from a company that was running out of funds. I wrote some emails to my network, and one of my connections introduced me to another company that was looking for someone with my skills. After a meeting, I was signed on.
4. One of my clients came to me through word-of-mouth through a music group.

Conclusion

Even after you have landed the job and are established as an early-career scientist, networking will continue with your clients, colleagues, and collaborators. For example, some of the clients that you establish a good relationship with during a job in industry can be helpful in another career down the road. This is especially true if you plan to transition. Establishing good business relationships and attending career workshops as a mentor also helps you build networks outside of your company or firm. Your network continues to evolve. Be sure to review your professional network from time to time; some individuals may have moved on and may not be as important as they once were. You can also give back by introducing others to people in your well-established network. Think of networking as building connections for directions in life. They think of you as the same. We are all connected through some pathways – make yours rich and meaningful.

FURTHER DISCUSSION

1. Describe your current professional network and how you built it.
2. What are some of your challenges with networking? Provide potential solutions for your peers and vice versa.
3. What career professional would you like to meet? Place this title on a sticky note on your shirt or outfit. Walk around your classroom with everyone else, like in a fish bowl. If you can help someone with a contact you know, stop and tell them.

TAKING ACTION

1. Write out the five most important interests in your life – not all job related. Think about who can help you with these things and contact them for a mentorship chat.
2. Through your supervisor or another faculty member, develop a list of three to four alumni who have careers outside academia in areas that may interest you. Contact them to set up informational interviews.
3. Reach out to a colleague in your network to check in with how they are doing.

16 Volunteering, Internships, and Entrepreneurship

Key Messages

- Volunteer to build your network and skillset.
- Seek out internship opportunities to prototype jobs.
- Being an entrepreneur means taking risks.
- Develop your own experiential learning opportunities to expand career options.

In this chapter, we use stories to describe the ways you can create your own experiential learning opportunities. As a graduate student in the sciences you likely have had the experience of working in a lab, applying the knowledge that you accumulated in the classroom, and gaining new skills. But how do you go beyond this learning experience? Meaningful engagement through informational interviews and your professional network can lead to rewarding experiential learning opportunities. Other engagements that provide first-hand experiences include volunteering, internship, or intrapreneurship/entrepreneurship. Canadian national organizations that help graduate students and postdoctoral fellows with experiential learning activities or internship funding include Mitacs[1] and Student Work Placement Program.[2] The experience can also be created by you. There are many learning opportunities that you can take advantage of, even within the limitations of your graduate studies. Every graduate student who is reading this

---

1 See Mitacs website: https://www.mitacs.ca/en.
2 Find wage subsidies to hire post-secondary students at Employment and Social Development Canada: https://www.canada.ca/en/employment-social -development/services/student-work-placements-wage-subsidies.html.

book or receiving career and professional development mentorship is able to achieve their goals by dedicating time to activities outside of research during graduate school. You can do this, too.

> Graduate students can develop skills and use their professional network to create their own experiential learning opportunities.

Volunteering or a Part-Time Job

Volunteering or having a part-time job builds your network, can help you develop skills, and is a way to give back. It's also good for your mental health. These opportunities may be available at your university, in a hospital setting, and in community groups. For example, volunteer to be on a departmental committee or the organizing committee for a meeting. Think about volunteering for your community or working part-time for an organization outside your academic world. The volunteering could even be as simple as a local fundraiser, like a bake sale. If you have an interest in sports, student government, or the arts, do not give up these activities in graduate school. Being a member of a university group or team takes a real commitment, and it can demonstrate your time management skills. Experienced players or artists can also demonstrate their leadership and team building skills as coaches or mentors. Our perspective on volunteering is that if it is for a non-profit organization for a few hours a month, then it is something to consider involving yourself in. We highly recommend that if the activity takes up more than two or three hours a week and it is with a for-profit business, then the experience should be considered an internship with remuneration.

There are many benefits to volunteering.[3] Of course, you will meet new people and expand your network. You can also gain valuable skills and competencies. You will get to know yourself better, especially if your interest in volunteering is based on your values. You will learn to work with others, and you will learn how other organizations operate. You will be part of a new community. Volunteering will also provide a welcome mental break from your graduate studies by allowing you

---

3 J. Fritz, "15 Unexpected Benefits of Volunteering That Will Inspire You," Liveaboutdot-com (2021), https://www.liveabout.com/unexpected-benefits-of-volunteering-4132453.

to focus on another activity. Volunteering can give you a sense of purpose. So, if you want to make a positive difference, volunteer. You never know where it may lead.

Employers look favourably on job applicants who have volunteered or been involved with a meaningful engagement outside of the lab, so be sure to include these activities on your résumé. Indeed, be prepared to talk about them during an interview. These activities tell the prospective employer a lot about your values, interests, skills, and character and can set you apart from other highly qualified applicants. It is duly noted that not all students have the privilege to be able to volunteer. Some students need to use that time to work for extra income. Whether it is time spent on volunteering or on working, as long as the activity reflects your interests and values, employers will find your pursuits to be enhancing experiences for any future career.

> Volunteering or a part-time job can help you gain confidence by giving you the chance to try something new and build a real sense of achievement for the benefit of others or the organization.

Job Shadowing and Internships

Graduate students gain valuable research experience as part of their training and develop a good understanding of life as a professor. What if you decide that being a professor is not a path you would like to follow and you are not sure about other options? A good place to start building your professional network and gaining insights into different career paths is job shadowing. Let's illustrate these activities with a story about Jae who, as a graduate student, was interested in expanding his horizons beyond the academy. Jae attended several career panel sessions, read about career paths, and requested informational interviews with professionals in industry research and development, commercialization, and communications. Through one of the informational interviews, Jae developed a professional rapport with a science communications expert. During the informational interview, the expert sensed Jae's keen interest and invited him to visit him at work. On the day of job shadowing, Jae realized that perhaps the expert might need some help in writing up a certain document. Jae took this as an opportunity to propose writing the introduction based on his knowledge of the subject. In this way, Jae could provide some assistance to a possible mentor while gaining relevant experience. The expert decided that he would hire Jae as an intern for about five hours per week to work on the introduction and other ongoing projects. While working as an intern for several months, Jae also finished up experiments and wrote his thesis. The science communications expert was very pleased with Jae's work and recommended him to a colleague who was expanding his firm. Near the end of his internship Jae was offered full-time employment at this science communications firm through the connection of his mentor who served as an informed reference.

Another story is about Salma. Salma wanted to keep the academic career route open, but was also interested in applying the knowledge and technologies that she had developed during graduate school to the biotech industry. During her senior years as a PhD student, she and a few of her peers created a new online technology that could help in healthcare settings. Salma then visited her campus entrepreneurship resource office where she was guided on entrepreneurship, aspects of small businesses, intellectual property, market analysis, and resources available for funding small start-ups. While she worked on her experiments and publications for her graduate degree, she also developed her biotech start-up idea in the evenings and weekends. She entered a start-up pitch competition and was delighted to receive positive feedback. One of the judges suggested that Salma look for opportunities at start-up companies created by professors at her university. Because of her interest in start-ups and her proven scientific excellence with her several publications, Salma was offered a job in a small biotech company after she completed her thesis work.

Story number three is about Alex. Alex was interested in pursuing academia, and their Plan B was to go into management consulting. During their PhD, Alex published three papers and a review, presented research at conferences, grew their network, experienced mentorship as a teaching assistant and a lab mentor, and led a student council organization on campus. Alex also joined the local Graduate Management Consulting Association[4] where they gained experience in case competitions and grew their network in the consulting industry. Alex pursued an academic postdoctoral fellowship while gaining skills in grant writing, mentorship, people management, and budgeting. Alex also maintained their network of management consulting professionals with regular contacts and updates on their research. After the postdoctoral

---

4 See Graduate Management Consulting Association website: https://www.gmcacanada .com/.

fellowship, Alex applied to academic positions as well as management consulting firms. Alex was thrilled to receive offers from both fields. Alex decided to work with a management consulting company with a focus on developing strategic plans for research intensive universities, combining the best of both worlds. Some people may say that Alex was lucky. We think Alex created their own career options as optimally as possible, so that the job acquisition was really icing on the cake.

The final story is about Abdul. Abdul was a senior postdoctoral fellow in a large and very productive chemistry lab. His supervisor asked Abdul to serve as a lab manager, and he was very good at this job. Abdul was also the go-to person to organize departmental events. Abdul realized that he was not driven by bench work anymore, but that he really liked working with people and helping to organize activities. He also wanted to work in an academic environment. The chemistry department had just created a new position in strategic planning and alumni engagement. Abdul reached out to the Chair, who knew about the leadership role he played in the professor's laboratory, and the Chair encouraged Abdul to apply. Abdul didn't get the job, but the Chair recommended that he look into a summer internship in the university alumni office. Abdul did, was hired, and is now a senior manager there. In each of these stories, the individuals put themselves out there, tried, learned, failed, grew, and eventually succeeded.

Entrepreneurship

Entrepreneurship is usually referred to as the concept of starting a new business or an initiative with other individuals to meet a need and to generate a profit. In the modern era, entrepreneurship can be defined as a new initiative that aims to solve local or even global problems. Many campuses have entrepreneurship resources on-site for students and postdoctoral fellows to help them in cultivating their idea into a potential business. Seek these out. The same resources may also offer entrepreneurship workshops or boot camps.

Some students have said they do not want to become an entrepreneur because it is risky. Other students embrace risk. This depends on your values and personality. A key to success as an entrepreneur is the ability to deal with failure. For example, Walt Disney's proposal was rejected over 300 times by financial institutions before he started his theme park. One would think that Disney is a classic example of a very successful entrepreneur, yet he had to deal with failure.

Being an entrepreneur is not for everyone but some individuals have caught the entrepreneurship bug. Derrick Rossi, the Canadian co-founder of the biotech firm Moderna and four other companies, was keen to move the basic research he was doing in a cell biology lab at Harvard into therapies that would have a direct benefit on patient health. He identified a healthcare need and built technology with experts to meet it. So, if you are interested in translating research from "bench to bedside," becoming an entrepreneur and creating a start-up company is one pathway to success.

Here are some other examples of being entrepreneurial. You decide to bake cupcakes and sell them online with home delivery due to a pandemic. You give music lessons in your home studio through Zoom. You create a new tracking system for labs to manage attendance that is purchased by their department. These are all examples of entrepreneurial thinking. You are creating a solution to a problem in your everyday life. It may not always be a product to sell; sometimes it's a great idea. If you create a collaboration with other scientists based on ideas between your lab and theirs, this collaboration is a creation of entrepreneurial ideas. The ideas generated may result in products or materials that may go towards future innovative scientific thought and perhaps into the creation of future biotechnology. You may even create your own company and become an entrepreneur.

In the traditional sense of business entrepreneurship, a few things should be considered when entering such a venture. Here, we provide a brief overview of what goes into developing a start-up idea:

1. *Build a good team.* You are a leader, but good entrepreneurs build good teams, especially by focusing on bringing in expertise. Your team should comprise individuals who share the same vision and values and can work cooperatively. Your team, however, should also be diverse, with members who have different skillsets and view problems from different perspectives. Your team should be able to bring in a broad range of opinions and perspectives for whatever goods or services you are hoping to create based on a demonstrated need. Your best entrepreneurial idea is something that you think will help with the world's problems. The world has many different people with different backgrounds. Truly innovative ideas and
companies succeed if they include opinions from diverse backgrounds, as we discussed in our previous chapter on equity, diversity, and inclusion.
2. *Market analysis is critical.* What is the need? Who will be your audience/customers/clients? Who are your competitors? How are you going to be different from your competition? What makes your

product or service better or different? Why did you come up with this idea? Market analyses for an idea similar to yours may already exist and be available from various resources on campus. However, if you are venturing into an idea where the market analysis has never been done, you will have to do this yourself. For example, perhaps an idea that you had was providing a smartphone application to enhance engagement level in the classroom. Market research would involve finding other available software and the current number of users they have. If you think that your application has something that none of the competitors offer, then you would have to survey the market that you think may use it. You might send a survey to students asking if they would use such an application based on a description or prototype of your product. Using the results of the survey, and extrapolating to other universities across Canada, you will then have a potential market size.

3. *Find experienced mentors.* Find senior members in your circle who have started a company or have been involved in the start-up process and request informational interviews to answer your pertinent questions. After you've conducted a few of these, you may ask some of these mentors to be on your advisory board. Ventures that are serious about moving forward generally have advisory boards that are at arm's length to their product. Members of your advisory board should not be financially linked to your venture. They ensure good governance and fiduciary oversight and help articulate a clear vision and direction. They are not involved in the day-to-day running of the enterprise but are there to provide advice based on their experience and knowledge.

4. *Find resources.* You may want to consider reading or taking an entrepreneurship workshop series or an entrepreneurial business class. All university campuses have resources on entrepreneurship at the library. In addition, universities will have student entrepreneurship services that can help you find assistance on mentorship, intellectual property issues, market analysis, and courses and workshops on scientific innovation. Here is a link to one example called Design Thinking for Scientists.[5]

5. *Apply for funding.* Many university campuses have accelerators and incubators that provide seed funding for start-ups. They often do this through pitch competitions to attract clients. Try to find all the

---

5 See BCH2200 Design Thinking for Scientists course description (n.d.): http://biochemistry .utoronto.ca/courses/bch2200/.

entrepreneurship offices on your campus so that you can get advice and perhaps receive funding for your venture. After you have some experience in applying for and gaining seed funding, you can then take your pitch to other investors such as individual angel investors, venture capitalists, or small business and innovation funding through government programs or small business bank loans.

6. *Find time.* As a graduate student, you need to devote most of your time to your research. As mentioned above, dedicating a few hours a month to a new activity is an example of multitasking. There are also natural breaks during your research program. Perhaps you can find time after you transfer from Master's to PhD studies or at the end of your program after you submit your thesis or after you complete your degree requirements. Perhaps you can dedicate a summer term to your entrepreneurial activities. There are entrepreneurship programs offered by agencies like Mitacs that provide funding for graduate students and postdoctoral fellows who are interested in partnering with industry.

7. *Be prepared to fail.* Remember Walt Disney? Not everyone will like your ideas. Not everyone will want to join your team. Not everyone will provide you with funding. Not every project will work out. Entrepreneurs are risk takers but they are also problem solvers, team builders, and leaders. Learn from all of your experiences and the experiences of others to stay on the pathway to success. Indeed, science is mostly about failure, as outlined in the book *Failure: Why Science Is So Successful.*[6]

Researchers are entrepreneurial thinkers. Research is, by its nature, risky. We don't know the results we will get or where our research will take us. Taking that entrepreneurial spirit into the business world is something that you can experience as a graduate student or postdoc in many different ways. It may not be for everyone, but we hope that after reading this framework of thinking about your research in an entrepreneurial light, you may consider heading in that direction as a side project. Many start-ups started with ideas from a few friends who were chatting about it in an informal social setting such as during a camping trip, a sporting event, or a shared meal. You are all innovators. We hope some of you can take that innovative thinking and create the next generation of innovative scientific companies.

---

6 S. Firestein, *Failure: Why Science Is So Successful* (Oxford University Press, 2015).

Intrapreneurship

What is the difference between intrapreneurship and entrepreneurship? An intrapreneur is an individual who is like an entrepreneur *within* the organization. An intrapreneur comes up with innovative ideas in a team setting to change or enhance the institution's programming, mission, values, or vision. They may bring new ways of performing tasks or managing people. They may create new subgroups within the organization to bring forth change. We illustrate this with examples about Pam and Sean.

Pam accepted a job as a Director of Research and Administration at a hospital where she was responsible for ensuring that the ongoing research and collaborative work between researchers were aligned with the vision of the institution. After she obtained the job and had worked for a year to be acquainted with the system, she proposed that it was in the research institute's best interest to implement an outreach program for budding scientists in high school. The goal was to connect with the community to attract a more diverse pool of students into research. Such a mandate was not part of her job description, but upon hearing her proposal, her team supported the idea and the program became part of her portfolio.

> An intrapreneur can go beyond their specific responsibilities to bring forth change within the institution regarding something they feel passionate and curious about.

As a graduate student, Sean decided to create a workshop about teaching in higher education for other graduate students. He wanted to bring to his peers what he had learned through his several years of experience as a teaching assistant and from his participation in teaching in higher education. Sean, along with two other senior students, designed a teaching workshop with the guidance of a faculty member, which became an annual event attracting a full class of 30 students.

These two stories of intrapreneurship are different from entrepreneurship in that Sean and Pam did not have to raise funds for their own salary. However, the idea of creating new initiatives, building a team that believes in your vision, and implementing a program with successful feedback are qualities much sought after by employers. Perhaps you have already been an intrapreneur. Perhaps you have also proposed an idea in either school, your community, your volunteering positions, or your part-time work that has made an impact. This is being an intrapreneur, a quality that should be highlighted in your résumé and at interviews when they ask questions about your impact.

Conclusion

Being part of a groups outside of your research through volunteering, part-time jobs, start-ups, or internships can result in very exciting learning experiences. It could also shift the framework in which you see your science and research. Having said that, your number one priority is your thesis work. These extra activities should not take up more than an average of 10 per cent of your time as a graduate student or postdoc. However, if you have completed a project or published a manuscript and you are waiting for your supervisor to read it, you may have some spare time to dedicate to outside projects. There are always moments in a graduate program that provide a break from research. All graduate students and postdocs are at the forefront of new research and science, making them thought leaders. Try to take this leadership thought process "outside" the expected project, whether it is related to your science or not. Expanding your world may provide you the extra experience, knowledge, and network to optimize your future.

FURTHER DISCUSSION

1. Reflect on your values, interests, and skills – how can they bring about actions for meaningful engagement?
2. What are the top three skills required to become a successful entrepreneur?
3. Work in teams to create a new idea for a start-up to address a need and pitch it to the class.

TAKING ACTION

1. Find an alumnus through LinkedIn and take note of the meaningful engagements in their profile as examples. If their career trajectory interests you, perhaps ask for an informational interview.
2. Identify a potential meaningful engagement for yourself, such as an internship, and set up SMART goals to accomplish it.
3. Take a workshop or course in entrepreneurship or attend an industry networking event.

PART VI

Planning: Success beyond Graduate School

17 Getting Ready: Strategic Career Planning

Key Messages

- Strategically plan your career.
- Explore and create opportunities to think outside the box.
- Learn to reframe problems aiming for possible solutions.
- Use informational interviews to explore career options.

This next section of the book deals with career planning. Just because we are talking about this towards the end of the book does not mean that your planning should happen late in your graduate career. Indeed, thinking deeply about where you are and where you want to go should begin before graduate school and will evolve during your training. In this chapter, we outline a framework for strategic career planning. An excellent resource about career planning is *Designing Your Life* (DYL) by Bill Burnett and Dave Evans,[1] in which they highlight how to design five-year career plans of options A, B, and C utilizing the principles of design thinking.

Strategic Career Planning

Strategic career planning does not necessarily mean finding a career title that you hope to aspire to and going for that one goal. Strategic career planning involves knowing the skills that you need to work on for two or three career outcomes. Coming up with three plans (DYL calls them Odyssey plans) is also a feature of the Individual Development Plan (IDP). In brief, Plan A is the career that you hope to achieve in five years if everything goes as you planned and is perhaps the linear career

---

1   B. Burnett and D. Evans, *Designing Your Life: How to Build a Well-Lived, Joyful Life* (Knopf, 2016).

path you are on. Plan B is the path to a career that you would also be happy to achieve, but is a definite change in direction from Plan A. Plan C is a five-year plan based on the premise that you do not have to worry about money or expectations from your parents, the university, or other outside forces. Why a Plan C? Life is short, and we can think about a plan embracing what our heart wants to follow – so that we can incorporate some of it into our plans A and B and perhaps even view it as its own plan.

We have noticed that many students find this exercise helpful as it allows them to break down the grand five-year plan into feasible consecutive one-year plans. For example, in your final year of under graduate studies you were probably unsure about your next steps. Plan A could be becoming a scientific researcher, so you explore graduate school programs and possible careers after that. After some informational interviews, you find the world of science communications and decide that could be a possible Plan B. Plan C could be becoming an entrepreneur with some friends and creating a planning app for high school students. One example of a student's Plan A was to go into biotech, and Plan C was to start a nonprofit teaching organization for the village that she grew up in. She decided to keep Plan C alongside Plan A, so now she is in the biotech industry while she has started her nonprofit. Keep in mind that these plans may fluctuate as you gather more data and stories and as your own life views change.

Do you have a Plan A from your Individual Development Plan? What about a Plan B? A Plan C should be in the delightful category.

Reinhart encountered a highly accomplished MD/PhD student in one of his professional development courses. Every student was asked to prepare an IDP at the beginning of the course, to be revisited at the end of the course as part of an exit interview with the course instructor. This student's three plans were virtually the same: (A) clinician-scientist at a hospital in Toronto, (B) clinician-scientist in Canada, and (C) clinician-scientist in the US or UK. After some design thinking the student came up with (A) become a clinician-scientist, (B) create a company based on their research, and (C) go on the Mars mission. It turned out that the Mars mission needs medical doctors and someone with a science PhD would be a bonus. The student ended up with an academic position in the US, and found investigating the Mars mission through informational interviews with an astronaut "delightful."

Informational Interviews

Strategic career planning requires you to become aware of possible career opportunities. An important component of strategic planning, on top of skills development, is knowing the "inside story." The inside story of any career involves not just reading books and articles about it, but also performing informational interviews with individuals who are already in that particular career. These individuals will tell you the inside story of their career that you will not find on websites and in publications. Examples of questions you might ask someone in academia to gain insider insights are (1) Who are the key players in this field and where is the field going? (2) Who are the key leaders and stakeholders that are moving the direction for that particular research area? (3) Which conferences could you attend to present work and meet these key players? (4) What are the best ways to get a position and set up a successful research program?

Some questions you might ask someone in the biotech industry to get the inside story might include (1) What types of publications could you read to stay abreast of the future of biotech? (2) Who are the influential companies or biotech researchers that are moving the field forward and what are they interested in? (3) What is the current funding status for biotech start-ups in a certain province, state, or country? (4) What trends do they see for the next five years of biotech? (5) How can you create your own company with your ideas? (6) What conferences do industry professionals attend, and where might you gain additional inside stories?

To gain insights into the inside story of government careers, you could ask (1) What is the best way to apply for a government position? (2) When should you start applying? (3) How is the application process different from the private sector? (4) What direction is the government moving towards that you may need to know about when applying in a few years? (5) How is federal science policy affecting potential research opportunities? (6) What is the direction of Canada's research and how does it fit into global biotech research?

Questions to learn about the inside story of a nonprofit organization may include (1) What is their mission? (2) How do they gather public support and funding? (3) How is the organization structured and what kind of talent do they need? (4) What is the future of this nonprofit organization?

Accumulate information and data that you need to make strategic decisions to create meaningful engagements throughout graduate school and your postdoctoral fellowship, and build relationships that will last throughout your career and life.

> Informational interviews are informal conversations with individuals
> working in an area of interest to you – a good example of meaningful
> engagement.

It's More Than Just a Job Title

In our experience, we find that some students tend to work towards
a title, rather than take a more holistic career approach. For example,
graduate students may say "I want to become a professor" or "I want
to become doctor" or "I want to become president of a company." These
are just job titles. If your interest is in teaching, there are many more
career paths beyond becoming a professor. If your interest is in helping
others, there are many career paths beyond becoming a doctor. If your
interest is leadership, there are many career paths beyond president. If
you focus on developing your core competency skills through meaningful engagements, you can more easily transition into any future career that values these skills.

We illustrate this with an example. Instead of saying "I would like to
become a professor," research what common traits professors have and,
among these, which ones you have or need to develop. For example,
traits that are highly sought after in an academic professor are (1) excellent communication skills, (2) an interest in teaching and mentoring
students, and (3) a desire to become a leader in a field of research. Thus,
when in graduate school, you could help with writing a grant for your
supervisor, mentor undergraduate students, and become familiar with
a new field of research. If you develop these skills, you not only have
these ready for a career in academia, but you can also offer these skills
to other places such as in industry where skills in writing, mentorship
of interns and trainees, and leadership are also needed. We will discuss
more about skills related to academic and non-academic careers in the
upcoming chapters.

Conclusion

Strategic career planning involves (1) reflection using the IDP, (2)
seeking out mentors who can help with your IDP skill development
and career exploration, (3) considering your interests, skills, and values to create meaningful engagements that become part of your work

portfolio, and (4) pertinent informational interviews and hopefully some relevant work experiences. It is never too early to start exploring career options. Plan in one-year increments over five years or longer. Try new experiences. Learn from people. Test your ideas with peers. Collect information from those a few years ahead of you in the career path. These are all moments and tools from which you learn and move forward in your career development. Ask the right questions, create opportunities that build upon your existing skillset, and build relationships with people in that field. Incorporate your IDP results into your five-year plan. Remember that these plans are living documents that can change over the course of your professional and career development. Referring back to the time management table in chapter 7, "Integrating Life with Work," these career planning activities are not urgent, but are important; hence, making time for them is essential in driving your career development.

FURTHER DISCUSSION

1. Brainstorm ways to prototype (create a meaningful engagement for) your classmate's trio of skills, interests, and values.
2. Provide constructive feedback for a partner's Plan A, B, or C.
3. Using design thinking brainstorming techniques, post ideas about potential solutions for imposter syndrome in PhDs, vote on the most delightful, and come up with the details of a meaningful engagement.

TAKING ACTION

1. Read *Designing Your Life* by Bill Burnett and Dave Evans.
2. Outline your Plans A, B, and C from your Individual Development Plan and identify immediate action items for all three.
3. Form an accountability partnership with a peer for a meaningful engagement activity, like an informational interview, and update each other every two weeks.

18 A Great Postdoctoral Fellowship

Key Messages

- Consider if your career path would benefit from you gaining experience as a postdoctoral fellow.
- Start early in your search for a postdoctoral fellowship position.
- Use your postdoctoral fellowship to learn management and leadership skills.
- Prepare yourself for an independent career.

The traditional next step in the career path of most PhD graduates in the sciences is to continue their training as a postdoctoral fellow or scholar. A postdoctoral fellowship is where you develop your own project, become an independent researcher, lead a team, initiate collaborations, and develop new knowledge and skills. Postdoctoral fellowships also provide the opportunity to work with a famous scientist or in a prestigious institution. Often, you may move to a different city or country, further enriching your life experience. Many Canadians take advantage of abundant postdoctoral fellowship opportunities in top labs in the US, the UK, or other countries and bring this new experience back to Canada.

Why a Postdoctoral Fellowship?

A postdoc experience remains a rite-of-passage to becoming a professor. Success is measured by publishing consistently in top journals, writing successful grants, and being invited to give research seminars as part of faculty job searches. You hope that your research will be of broad interest so that you will be attractive to the departments to which you apply for professor positions. Also, during your postdoctoral fellowship you may gain expertise in a specialized technique that has broad applicability and demand. But what if you are completing your PhD and are not interested in becoming a professor? What if you want to follow a different path from your supervisor? Do you still need to do a postdoc? Not necessarily. Many PhD students directly enter the workforce upon graduation, having already identified what career path they want to pursue and have developed their transferable skills and professional network. Nonetheless, apart from a career as a professor, there are other paths that value postdoctoral experience.

A postdoctoral fellowship is a great time to develop your research interests and broaden your knowledge in an area outside of your graduate studies. Your postdoctoral fellowship is also a great place to develop your leadership, mentorship, and project management skills. Reinhart did a second postdoctoral fellowship to learn new methods and move into an emerging area of research. Coming with experience from his first postdoctoral fellowship, he was assigned the duties of supervising three technicians, thereby developing his lab management skills. Think carefully about what your goals are during your postdoctoral fellowship(s) – they should certainly include learning new skills and advancing your career. And remember that it is quite common to spend three to five years in a postdoctoral position, so it's important to get the most out of this time.

The main types of careers in STEM disciplines in which a postdoctoral fellowship is required are those that involve leading scientific research. This would be a principal investigator (PI) in an academic setting, such as a professor at a university or a research scientist at a university-affiliated hospital or institute. If you are interested in a teaching position at a college or university, postdoctoral training may not be required. Be on the lookout for contract teaching positions to gain valuable experience and build your reputation. Some senior researcher roles in government and industry also prefer the candidates to have two to three years of postdoctoral experience. If you are interested in working in the private sector there are many postdoctoral fellowships available directly in industry, which can help the transition from school to work.[1] Some industrial postdoctoral fellowship positions can also be sponsored through agencies such as Mitacs.[2] Government postdoctoral

---

1 L. Bonetta, "Industrial Postdocs: The Road Less Traveled," *Science*, Advertising Feature (2008), https://www.sciencemag.org/features/2008/06/industrial-postdocs-road-less-traveled.
2 See Mitacs website: https://www.mitacs.ca/.

research positions also exist at institutions such as the National Institutes of Health in the US and the National Research Council in Canada.

Non-academic postdoc positions are not as common as academic ones, but they do exist and can be found, especially if you find the right network of people. However, some PhD graduates find industry research positions without a postdoctoral fellowship, usually by having had a previous experiential learning experience, such as an internship, or a connection within the company. For example, one of our students, Ming, had a collaborative Mitacs project for her PhD with a local pharmaceutical company for one year during her graduate training. After her graduation, the company hired her full-time based on the quality of her work with them.

Another reason PhD graduates pursue a postdoctoral fellowship, but not an optimal reason, though we see it repeatedly, is as a "convenient" placeholder for a few years to build a career portfolio. For example, when Nana first met Jack, he had just submitted his PhD thesis and was wondering what to do next. He knew he did not want to become a professor. He wanted to become a science writer, so she asked him if he had a writing portfolio, to which his response was "None outside of my scientific publications." Although he had applied to many science writing jobs, he was not receiving any interviews, most likely due to his lack of experience in scientific communications. Jack then decided to take a two-year postdoctoral fellowship while he built his writing portfolio by writing for the departmental magazine and becoming acquainted with members from the Science Writers Association. He also worked hard on his research and published a couple of fine papers. After 18 months, with a new set of meaningful engagements under his belt, Jack applied to communications roles. This time, he landed a job and became a science writer for a communications firm. Learning from this story, if Jack had started his communications portfolio two or three years before his PhD defence, he likely would have been able to bypass the postdoctoral fellowship.

Some people stay in postdoctoral positions too long, often waiting for that elusive faculty position. They may enjoy their research environment and get very comfortable. Indeed, most universities now limit the length of time a person can be a postdoctoral fellow. It's good to think about a postdoc as a transitional training period. A long postdoc may not, however, make you more competitive for a faculty position. Some individuals enjoy being a key member of a successful research group or being in charge of major facilities and are hired on as permanent Research Associates. These individuals typically have highly evolved technical skills and are often involved in the training and supervision of more junior members of the lab. In large research groups they may run whole arms of a research line. Even if postdoc training is not required for a particular job, it might be a good time to reflect, get life experience, and broaden your world view.

> Publications remain the currency of success in the sciences, as a graduate student, as a postdoc, and as a faculty member.

An Ideal Postdoctoral Fellow

From a PI's perspective, the ideal postdoctoral fellow is someone with relevant training who brings needed new skills into the lab. A successful applicant will have a strong track record of publications, as this will make them competitive for external fellowship funding. They must be creative, motivated, and independent. The best postdocs come up with their own ideas and run their research largely independently. The applicant should also have good leadership and interpersonal skills, as PIs often rely on them to help mentor students and impart new technical, data analysis, and troubleshooting skills. They should be ready to supervise others and help their lab mates think about their projects. The applicant's potential is assessed by reference letters, phone conversations with the referees, and the application letter, which must contain specifics about the target lab's research program and what interests the candidate. You need to be able to articulate clearly in your application and in your interview what knowledge and skills you can bring to the lab to help meet its goals.

> The period during which you complete a postdoc is a major transitional point in a science career, positioned between graduate school and a job.

Key Steps to Landing a Great Postdoc Position

How do you land a great postdoctoral fellowship? First, are you ready to move on from your PhD studies and are you competitive for a position in a top lab? Have you developed a record of success as a PhD student, with strong publications? A track record of first-author publications will provide evidence of future productivity – past success is often the best indicator of future success. Are you competitive for postdoctoral fellowship awards and can you write a compelling application that sets you apart from other highly qualified applicants? This can be achieved by completing a major project, publishing a stronger paper, learning a new skill, or setting up a productive collaboration

Second, great reference letters are essential, and you need to choose your referees carefully. Is your current supervisor supportive? Do they think you are ready to move on? Can they write a strong letter of support? Beyond your supervisor, a committee member or a course instructor familiar with your communication, critical thinking, and other skills is ideal. Perhaps this is someone who helped you develop your professional skills. They should know you and your work quite well. Also, when you are asking for a letter of recommendation, ask if the referee will write a *strong* one – "Would you be able to write a positive reference letter, if I included you as a referee?" Although most mentors would only agree to writing a reference letter if they could write a positive one, you should confirm. Talk to them and tell them why you are excited about joining the new lab and your plans.

Third, start early. Good labs fill up quickly. Funds are limited, so apply early. A postdoctoral fellow who brings their own funding is highly prized. So you also need to seek out postdoctoral funding opportunities and be prepared to apply. Your supervisor should advise you here. A year before you defend your thesis is not too early to apply for a postdoctoral position or funding, as long as you have papers out or "in the pipeline." Some high-powered labs might even have two-year waiting lists for postdoc positions. A good start is to connect with potential supervisors at a meeting or conference and follow up after the conference. Developing a solid professional network during graduate school is essential. Who knows about you and your work?

Fourth, aim high. Aim to work in the top labs in the field at the top institutions that have all the resources you need to succeed, including opportunities for collaboration. Be aware that high-profile labs tend to be very competitive, even internally. Is this an environment that suits you? What is the lab culture? Do your research on the topics that interest you and find leading labs in those areas. Go to the lab's website and check out not only the projects and list of publications, but also the people. Talk to your supervisor and others in your network for advice. Often, postdoc fellows will stay in the same area as their PhD topic or use similar techniques applied to a different topic area. It is difficult to switch both areas and techniques. It is possible, but consider your future timelines as well. Do you want to spend another five to six years mastering another topic *and* technique set? Some people do switch to another field and technique set altogether (e.g., from genotyping to X-ray crystallography), but then you must be prepared to take a few extra years to become an expert in your new field.

Fifth, be selective and write a great cover letter (see chapter 14, "Marketing Your Brand: Professional Emails, Cover Letter, Résumé, and Curriculum Vitae"). Do not send out hundreds of nondescript emails hoping that someone will take you. Talk to your supervisor about your plans, and talk to others familiar with the lab(s) that you're applying to. Pick two to three top labs you wish to apply to. The factors that define "top" include the following: (1) excellent track record of publications from most, if not all, lab members; (2) ideal mentorship (this information is usually obtained by an initial information screen of lab members – what is the average time to completion for the PhDs? What career positions are the alumni in?); and (3) an environment with optimal infrastructure and equipment and a collaborative team to work with so you can flourish. Consider all of these factors before you even write to the PI about your interest in their work and why you are suited for a position in their lab.

When you've selected a lab to apply to, be sure to include more than a list of the techniques you're familiar with in your cover letter. Talk about your skillset at large – your excellent communication skills (as illustrated by your compelling letter!) and the fact that you're a team player, highly motivated, independent, and creative, and include any other soft skills you developed in graduate school. First-author papers or papers in which you made a major contribution are a record of your ability to complete a project. Mid-author papers indicate your ability to contribute to a team or to collaborate. In a sentence or two outline a possible project you could work on in their lab – be original. Your project might have three related aims: the first is straightforward continuation of the PI's work and perhaps incremental; the second is more ambitious and will be a major contribution; and the third is risky but tackles a big question in the field and would be transformative. Outline grants that you can apply for to bring in more funding. Present how your technical skills and your other core skills can best help the lab and the professor move forward in their research.

Think about what you can uniquely bring to your future postdoc lab from your experience as a graduate student.

Sixth, evaluate the vibe. Once you get a positive response, visit the lab or at least talk directly with the supervisor. Perhaps you met the supervisor before. Is there an immediate rapport? Can you work with this person? Talk to others in the lab. Are they happy and productive? Are there any issues? Find postdoc alumni from the lab and ask for their opinions on their experiences. Most alumni will be more honest than current lab members as they are not in the lab anymore. Where are the alumni? Were they happy with their experience? How did they obtain their next position? Was the PI helpful in their career development? What type of lab is it – big and impersonal, or small and intimate? Is the supervisor around much? Famous scientists travel a lot! If they're not around, is that an issue for you? Perhaps the supervisor is too hands-on and you like to be left alone to work independently. In other words, the social aspects of the lab are as important, if not more so, than the science. For example, graduate student Aman finished a stellar PhD and found what he thought was a productive, superb lab to do his postdoc in. His interview went well as it seemed that everyone was happy. He moved across the country only to find out very quickly that the supervisor expected everyone to be in the lab seven days a week and had serious communication issues. Although Aman departed to another lab within a year, he could have saved himself some trouble if he had researched the PI further – not only about their science, but also about their human side as well.

Finally, take a break. It's a good idea to have a holiday of at least two weeks before starting in a new lab. This would be a great time to travel and spend quality time with family and friends. Not many opportunities exist in a scientist's life when you can really pause for a break. This is one of them – cherish and take advantage of it. You will arrive refreshed, full of energy, and keen to get back to work and make new discoveries. Reinhart did not take any holidays during his first postdoc but took a six-week break to visit family in Europe before starting his second postdoc. Even during his second postdoc he had to finish off and revise papers from his first. The same is often true when starting your first postdoc. There are typically papers that still need to be written, revised, and published from your PhD after you have graduated. Indeed, some students stay on in the same lab to do a mini-postdoc to get the papers completed and published. In Reinhart's case, work that he had done as an undergraduate summer student in the early 1970s was published in 1983!

Consider what you want to take away from your postdoctoral experience.

Succeeding as a Postdoc

Once you have found a happy place to pursue your science, the goals of a successful postdoctoral fellowship are the following: (1) strong publications; (2) growth as a scientific thought leader; (3) opportunity to spearhead your own research that you will be able to take with you, with permission from your PI, if you choose to start your own lab; and (4) development of skills in teamwork, delegation, mentorship, grant writing, conflict management, budget management, and collaboration building. You should become confident in taking your research to an academic position or your research skills to a non-academic research position. As you progress through your postdoc, continue to focus on expanding your toolbox of techniques and on publishing excellent first-author papers. If you decide to try for an industry position after your postdoc fellowship, make sure you co-author many collaborative publications as well, as these tell companies that you are a team player and can network. Discuss your career plans with your supervisor, and perhaps they will help you find collaborations. Regardless of what you choose to pursue after your postdoctoral fellowship, be prepared to engage in activities that you care about.

During your postdoc you should retain your five-year plans for career options A, B, and C and continue along with your Individual Development Plan. Continue having open discussions about expectations with your PI, writing agendas and follow-up items for each meeting and requesting performance feedback every four to six months so you and your PI can both be on the same page. Some general resources for postdocs can be found at these links.[3]

Use your postdoctoral experience as an opportunity to explore new ways of doing science, to develop new skills, to meet new friends, and to grow as a person.

---

3 See Mitacs website: https://www.mitacs.ca/; and the Resource Library of the National Postdoctoral Association: https://www.nationalpostdoc.org/page/Resource Library.

Conclusion

As a postdoc, you no longer need to take courses or write a thesis, you have yet to deal with full grant writing and teaching responsibilities, and you are free to focus on your research. Your postdoctoral years are a time when you can grow as a scientist and also learn how science is performed in another lab or even at another place in the world. Experience the science and also embrace the different cultures and languages of your lab mates, learn about issues in equity, diversity, and inclusion, and become a better mentor, for you are on your way to becoming a leader in the STEM community for the next generation. Join a postdoctoral organization and if there isn't one, create it. Become a leader in the lab, a leader in science, and a leader in society.

FURTHER DISCUSSION

1. Outline three new skills you would like to develop as a postdoctoral fellow.
2. Discuss the option of an industrial postdoc and how to find it and fund it.
3. If you could live somewhere else for a couple of years, where would it be and why?

TAKING ACTION

1. Talk to a mentor about postdoctoral opportunities.
2. Come up with a list of three potential postdoctoral supervisors and locations.
3. Draft an initial email message to a prospective PI inquiring about a postdoctoral position using the following structure: Why are you contacting them? Who are you? What do you want?

19 Succeeding in Academia

Key Messages

- The pathway in academia remains traditional and linear, with individuals moving from a PhD to a postdoctoral fellowship to a professorship.
- Skills developed in graduate school and your postdoc build a solid foundation to success in academia.
- Ensure that you have the supports and resources necessary for a strong start.
- Mentorship continues to be important throughout your academic career.

You want to be a professor. You have been thinking about this for some time. It was the reason you went to graduate school and did a postdoc in a big lab. You realize that most PhDs do not become professors, but you are sure that you will beat the odds. Some realize that this is not the path for them or that it will not happen for them. You need to think critically about why you want to be a professor. What is it about being a professor that appeals to you? This gets back to closely examining your values and interests. Other kinds of roles that would satisfy your interests might be academic administrative positions, such as working in research offices or in student affairs, or perhaps as a facility director, if you like working at the bench. Again, you need to seek out these opportunities and see if they are a good fit for you. This chapter will examine the traditional pathway to an academic position, a pathway that reinforces the apprenticeship model that continues to grip universities. Whole books have been written about success in academia, for example, *The Professor Is In* by Karen Kelsey[1] and *Planning a Career in Biomedical and Life Sciences* by Avrum Gotlieb.[2] In this chapter we will highlight how you can set yourself up for success starting in graduate school.

Discuss career development plans with your supervisor, preferably early in your graduate training so you can develop options.

Academia Is Still a Linear Pathway

The traditional pathway to a research-intensive academic position starts with completing an undergraduate degree in science, attaining your PhD in a specific discipline like biochemistry, and then following that by completing a postdoctoral fellowship in a top lab where you can refine your future research topic as an independent investigator. To become a professor, you will use the network you have built over your training to explore appropriate job prospects. With a strong curriculum vitae in hand, you will prepare a compelling job application that not only demonstrates your research experience, but also your teaching experience and philosophy. By the time you're ready to apply for jobs, you will have developed a detailed research plan to launch your independent career as a faculty member. Once you're a shortlisted applicant, you will then give a research seminar that is exciting for a broad audience and you will deliver a mock lecture to showcase your teaching abilities. You are ready. Even today, this is still the pathway that almost all newly appointed faculty members in the sciences have followed.

Reinhart's Story

Reinhart obtained his first job as a Professor in the Department of Biochemistry at the University of Alberta in 1980 after two productive postdoctoral fellowships. At the time there were no faculty positions advertised, so Reinhart wrote to a number of departmental chairs to see

---

1 K. Kelsky, *The Professor Is In: The Essential Guide to Turning Your PhD into a Job* (Crown Publisher, 2015).
2 A.I. Gotlieb, *Planning a Career in Biomedical and Life Sciences: Learn to Navigate a Tough Research Culture by Harnessing the Power of Career Building*, 2nd ed. (Academic Press, 2018).

if they would sponsor him for an MRC scholarship that would provide a salary for five years. This is an example of the "hidden" job market. The faculty position did not exist – Reinhart in partnership with the Chair and the department created it. Reinhart wrote a strong application with letters of support from his sponsors, including the Chair of the department, and was successful. Knowing he had five years to prove himself, Reinhart got busy writing grant applications, recruiting students, setting up his lab, and creating research collaborations. He even helped teach a course in his first year to demonstrate his value to the department. It turned out that the department was as keen as he was for him to succeed, so Reinhart had lots of support getting his independent career as a researcher going.[3]

Variations in the Academic Trajectory

Is the pathway to an academic position always straight? Well, no. Especially for explorers. However, re-entry into academia from industry is difficult. Some industrial posts focus on basic research and encourage publications, allowing a smoother transition back to academia. Indeed, many universities are now focused on innovation and translational research. Individuals with experience and connections in the private sectors are valued members of the academy, especially in engineering and the sciences.

Some people may need to take parental leave during graduate school or a postdoctoral fellowship. Familiarize yourself with your institution's policy on parental leave. Know about the grants you qualify for before you re-enter the lab after a leave. Consult the National Postdoctoral Association website[4] or the Canadian Association of Postdoctoral Scholars website[5] for more information.

Taking a break from research, even for a couple of years for personal reasons, creates a gap in your career path, and re-entering the academic stream can be challenging. One reason is that research does not take a break: it keeps advancing. It is very important to keep up with your

---

3 R.A.F. Reithmeier, "How to Become a Successful Scientist: The 2022 CSMB Arthur Wynne Gold Medal Lecture," *Biochemistry and Cell Biology* 100, no. 5 (2022), https://cdnsciencepub.com/doi/full/10.1139/bcb-2022-0206.
4 See National Postdoctoral Association website: http://www.nationalpostdoc.org/.
5 See Canadian Association of Postdoctoral Scholars website: https://www.caps-acsp.ca/en/.

field by reading papers, attending scientific meetings, and keeping in touch with your mentors.

One solution for re-entry into science is to join a research group as a senior postdoctoral fellow with a supervisor who allows you to develop an independent project that you can "take with you." Your supervisor needs to be a strong advocate and mentor. Make sure you agree on which aspects of the project are yours so you do not become their competitor. Future collaborations should benefit both of you as well. Remember that you bring your experience as a graduate student and your demonstrated ability to learn along with your other competencies.

Some positions in the academy, such as a professorship in the teaching stream (Nana's appointment) do not require an extensive scientific research program but do require the demonstration of excellence in pedagogy and educational research. Nana's experience in industry as well as her abilities to innovate educational programs helped her create her unique role in academia.

Re-entry plans

Some organizations are adding career re-entry grants and scholarships for parental leaves as part of their programming: https://www.aai .org/ReentryFellowship (The American Association of Immunologists – Career Reentry Fellowship Program) and https://nserc-crsng.gc.ca /NSERC-CRSNG/Policies-Politiques/Wleave-Fconges_eng.asp (Government of Canada).

A Great Graduate Student

Your success in academia starts in graduate school. Graduate degrees in the biomedical sciences in Canada and the US tend to be long, typically five to seven years for a PhD, although comprehensive data are lacking.[6] Highly productive students will have contributed to three or more papers as first author, most of which will be published in their last

---

6 L. Charbonneau, "PhD Completion Rates and Times to Completion in Canada," *University Affairs/Margin Notes* (2013), https://www.universityaffairs.ca/opinion/margin-notes /phd-completion-rates-and-times-to-completion-in-canada/.

two years of study. These students are essentially working at the post-doctoral level in their last year or so, and are highly prized as incoming postdocs in top labs. They already have their own ideas and work quite independently. They have supervised project students and are seen as leaders in the lab. Make your PhD an innovative one. Find state-of-the-art techniques to propel your project. Near the end of your PhD, you will know more about your thesis topic than anyone else in the world, including your supervisor. Have intellectual and philosophical debates and discussions with your supervisor, committee members, or other students. You do not need to agree on everything – conflicting opinions can offer different perspectives on your problem and stimulate new ideas.

Great graduate students
PhD students are self-motivated with a strong work ethic and are dedicated to:

- Generating significant new knowledge based on independent research using cutting-edge methods
- Developing excellent technical and critical analysis skills
- Understanding their field in depth
- Communicating their findings effectively at conferences and in top peer-reviewed journals
- Gaining teaching experience as a teaching assistant and developing a teaching philosophy

---

A Great Postdoctoral Fellowship Revisited

As described earlier in chapter 18 ("A Great Postdoctoral Fellowship"), a great postdoctoral fellowship allows you to fully develop your research skills and become an independent scientist. Postdoc positions are the bridge between graduate school and an academic position. Aim high. Go to the best labs in the best places. Many Canadian graduate students carry out their postdoctoral fellowships in the US, with some going to Europe or elsewhere, with the goal of returning to Canada. Increasingly, however, there are big labs in Canada that are heavily populated by postdocs, and these labs provide a rich and diverse training environment. Some students decide to stay in Canada to complete their postdoc training, often because of personal circumstances.

Find postdoctoral training funding for yourself, if possible. This can be through government granting agencies such as CIHR, NSERC, NIH, or others. Work hard to develop an independent research program. Challenge your supervisor. Publish as complete a story as possible – avoid a bundle of small papers. Collaborate with others. Top postdocs have a clear record of success in different environments, showing accomplishments in their graduate lab and in their postdoc lab. Note, however, that a single paper in a top journal from a top lab is not a clear indication of future success. A series of excellent papers that develop a theme along a clear line of research is more compelling. A current trend is for postdocs to aim for papers in high-profile journals – a laudable goal, perhaps. But it is the number of citations of the paper, rather than the journal impact factor alone, that is an indication of the true impact of the work. It may take some time for a publication to be cited and more time yet for it to reach a significant number of citations. Timely review articles are often highly cited, and graduate students and especially postdocs should be encouraged to write these.

Supervise others. Teach a bit if you can – offer to give a lecture for your supervisor. Write your own papers and help write grants. Help review papers and grants for your supervisor. Network to get better known. Find grants for yourself. Organize events. Be a leader. Be prepared to go out on your own. Take charge of your own career.

Success in the academic job market correlates with a strong publication record.

Distinguishing Yourself

How do you distinguish yourself from the many other people aiming for the limited faculty positions? First, you must be highly qualified for the position, especially if it is a very defined area of research. Apply for jobs that are good fits and in places you want to live. It is not unusual for trainees to return to their home university, or even department, after completing their postdoctoral fellowship elsewhere. However, they are expected to "bring back something new" to the department and certainly need to be careful not to continue working in the same area as their PhD supervisor. They must be perceived as independent from their former supervisor. An advantage of this approach, perhaps, is that the department already knows them as a successful graduate student and a low-risk hire. Nonetheless, academia is a global marketplace and employment opportunities are more abundant for those willing to look beyond their home university, home town, or home country.

Second, it is important that the right people know about you and your research. Your supervisor can introduce you to key decision makers, including senior scientists and chairs of departments. They can encourage you to present your work at the best meetings. This provides exposure of your work to an informed audience and provides you with critical comments. A poster presentation is a good way to get feedback on your work before publication. Remember, though, that it is a competitive world and you may not want your work "out there" until it is ready to publish. Short oral presentations are good practice for full research seminars. To financially support your attendance at meetings, your supervisor can provide the funds, but you should also apply for travel grants. Meetings build your network. Find meetings based on your interests, as well as the ones suggested by your supervisor. If your supervisor knows which postdoc lab you are entering, they may fund your attendance at conferences related to the new project in the last year of your PhD. Be sure to connect to people while you are there. A good practice is to reach out to potential members of your network ahead of the meeting and meet up while on location. You may even find potential collaborators at meetings where you present your work. After the meeting, be sure to follow up, even just to say thank you and to remain connected.

Third, strong letters of reference are an important part of a strong application for a professorship. Supervisors and other professors who know you well will act as your sponsors. A sponsor is someone who is your mentor and will speak on your behalf even when you are not present in the room. What can they say about you? If it is limited to "Joe Blot is a hard worker and is easy to get along with," that's not very compelling, as all graduate students work hard and most are easy to get along with, especially if they are respectful of their supervisor. A colleague once said, "Writing great letters for great students and postdocs is easy because they write their own letters." Not literally, of course, but they provide enough substance for their supervisor to comment on all aspects of their abilities. Think about what your supervisor could write about you that is not already found in your curriculum vitae. What can they write about your accomplishments and the impact you made? Have you demonstrated initiative? Are you a problem solver? How are your critical analysis skills? How is your technical expertise? Can you supervise and teach? Are you a good team player and can you collaborate? Are you a good writer and speaker? Are you a leader in the lab? Sometimes you are asked to write a draft of a reference letter. Think about what you would say about yourself.

Finally, work on your persuasive communications skills. Can you deliver an exciting research seminar accessible to a broad audience? Is your research proposal easy to read and does it "jump off the page"? Remember to use "grabber" statements in your speaking and writing. Are you a good listener who can engage with other scientists? Are you a team player who has thought about potential collaborations? Have you done your research on the department and its history, faculty members, and future goals? Can you help the department meet its mission in research, teaching, and service? Are you a good fit? Fit is often the turning point for a search committee's decision. Basically, do the faculty members want you as their colleague in the lab next door or as a partner in teaching? A caution here is that people do have intrinsic biases and tend to connect with people like themselves. On the other hand, departments are keen to diversify and be inclusive and more equitable. What will you bring that is new and exciting, other than a new face? If you know where a field is going and can plan to get there first, you will be a success.

A Wide Search May Be Necessary

When you are ready to apply for faculty positions, there may not be openings in your first choice of university or city. Be flexible. A partner or spouse that can, and will, move with you allows more choice of location. Some universities consider hiring a couple together, especially at larger institutions. Apply only to positions that you would take. The success rate of getting interviews is very low, but don't waste your time or that of others by doing "practice" interviews for jobs you would not take. With that in mind, keep your options open since successful scientists can move from one institution to another early in their career (within five to ten years) if positions are available. This may involve moving from a smaller institution to a larger one or relocating to a city of choice. After that, it becomes more difficult to relocate unless you are a "superstar" or willing to take on a challenging, but rewarding, administrative position such as departmental chair.

The Job Interview

The job interview is where strong candidates shine. This is where they bring their curriculum vitae and research to life. The interview can include a formal research seminar, a sample lecture, chalk talks, meetings with the search committee, students and administrators, and one-on-one meetings with faculty members – your future colleagues. The research seminar is an important part of the interview process. This is where you get to tell a compelling story that is of interest to a wide audience. This is where you get to lay out your future research direction and to convince potential colleagues that they have much in common. This is where your effective communication skills are demonstrated and where the fundability of the projects is assessed. A sample lecture demonstrates your ability to organize material and communicate concepts effectively with students. Chalk talks illustrate your ability to think on your feet without the benefit of prepared slides.

The formal meeting with the search committee usually involves a series of set questions posed to all candidates. It is certainly a good idea to go through a mock interview. Answers should be short, to the point, and focused. You will have an opportunity to introduce yourself and to ask questions. Avoid long rambling answers. Start with short focused answers and then elaborate. You will always be asked about your strengths and weaknesses and how you managed a challenging situation. Be prepared.

> As a graduate student or postdoc, be sure to attend recruitment seminars at your institution and meet with candidates. You can even volunteer to be on the search committee – a golden opportunity to learn the "inside ropes."

Meetings with graduate students tend to be informal but the students have input into the process, so be engaging and respectful. Be well prepared for the one-on-one interviews. Know to whom you will be talking to and what interests them. Go to their websites. Read their papers ahead of time. Develop a rapport and cultivate potential future collaborations and partnerships. Ask questions. Show an interest in their research. The research landscape is flattening and barriers between disciplines are breaking down. So seek out those who can help you achieve your goals and those who you can help to achieve their goals. Be a willing collaborator.

> Throughout the interview process always be professional, respectful, courteous, and thankful.

Remember the interview is not over just because you are sitting down to enjoy a drink or meal together. Some questions that faculty members consider include: How will the candidate interact with others in the department? Are there opportunities for collaboration? Could they teach a course together with another faculty member? Will the candidate bring in a new area of research or new methodology? Are they personable, confident, interactive, and interesting? Will they be a valued colleague? Are they a team player? Do they bring unique qualities to diversify the department?

It is important that you get a sense of excitement about the opportunity – this is a place where I'd love to work and where I can succeed. These are people who would become my colleagues and friends. There are lots of opportunities to recruit graduate students. I can count on the support of my Chair. I will have adequate space and the financial resources to set up my own lab. Teaching and administrative assignments are light at the beginning so I can focus on getting my lab up and running. I will have mentorship and the support I need to write successful grant applications and papers. There are no barriers to my success.

Your Offer

In negotiating any offer, draw up a couple of lists – one is must-have, the second is nice-to-have. The first list contains deal-breakers and the second is a list of perks. Think about what you need to make a good start in your new position as a new faculty member. It is important that you negotiate your starting salary, although there is usually a range with an upper limit. Are there salary awards that I can apply for? The benefits packages are typically standard, but may have options with regard to family benefits. However, it is not only about salary and benefits. If your partner is also looking for a position, you should make this clear to the hiring committee if an offer is being made. Many universities have programs for spousal hires, although the second position is often a contract appointment. The institution should cover your moving expenses and can often help with housing costs. Is there faculty housing? What about day care? Are there any subsidies for housing or day care? No harm in asking.

In terms of your research activities will you have the infrastructure, equipment, space, and administrative assistance to optimize your work? What funds are available to fund your research for the first three years? Is there funding for graduate students? Is start-up funding available to equip your lab and is there funding and room for any specialized equipment? Is the space renovated to suit your needs? In which building will you be located? You may wish to be located next to a potential collaborator. Do you get a private office with a desk, chair, and computer? What is your teaching load? Is there teaching relief for the first year? What agencies should you apply to for funding? What if you don't get funded right away? Is there bridge funding? Many of these items should be discussed in person with the Chair, but you will receive a formal offer in writing. It is important to remember that once you sign on the dotted line, your leverage has gone. Also, are you willing to decline an offer, or is this position the only one available to you? Do you have a competitive offer from another institution? If so, you need to weigh the pros and cons of both offers. If you are serious enough about the position to have applied for it and are fortunate enough to have been selected, both you and your employer have a common interest in your future success.

Your Own Lab

Once you arrive at the university, you will be presented with an empty, or near empty, lab space that you will quickly need to make your own. You will have some start-up funds available to set up the lab and a pile of application forms to apply for more funding. You will also be the main resource in the lab and should spend as much time as possible at the bench. Very few researchers are trained in lab management, although this is changing with some programs offered at the postdoc and new faculty level.

Recruit wisely. Don't rush, especially in taking on students. Recruit undergraduate project or summer students to work in teams – the best may continue on as your graduate students. Wait until you have solid external grant support to hire technicians. Technicians will eventually become the main resource in the lab, providing continuity and training to new students. Postdocs should be recruited to bring high-level expertise to the lab. They are expensive to hire and are often looking forward to academic appointments. Is your lab a good launching pad?

You are the CEO of your lab with managing hires, expectations, the working environment and, undoubtedly, conflict. Attend workshops and develop skills on setting expectations for your lab members, cross-cultural mentorship, effective team management, emotional intelligence, wellness, leadership, and ways to train your team to provide each other with effective peer performance feedback. Your core competency skills will continue to develop and will be strengthened as you gain experience in being the leader of your own lab, a committee member of the department, and perhaps a leader in various administrative roles. HHMI has useful resources for new faculty at this link.[7]

Multitasking Is an Essential Skill

As mentioned before, multitasking is a skill that needs to be developed, particularly for a career as a professor. It would be useful to shadow a professor early on to get an idea of a typical day in their life. You will find out why your supervisor is not in the lab every minute of the day and learn about the many duties that a university professor has.

A day in the life of a professor	
Reinhart Reithmeier	*Up early, work on a manuscript, make tea, breakfast with the family, check weather, walk to work, greet people in lab, answer emails, go out to have a coffee and talk to someone, review a paper, prepare for an undergraduate lecture, give the lecture, skip lunch with a colleague and eat at desk, meet with a graduate student to review their latest findings, attend an unimportant meeting, meet with a colleague to discuss common research interests, walk around the lab and talk to everyone ("Anything new? Any problems?"), check email, go home, buy fresh food, talk with partner, have dinner and a nice glass of wine, play with the kids, read them a story, watch a favourite TV show, in the quiet of the evening read a couple of papers or a thesis, edit a manuscript, answer emails, make tea, read a book or a poem or a magazine, sleep well.*
A day in the life of a professor, teaching stream	
Nana Lee	*Up early, yoga, write for 10 minutes, breakfast and help make lunches for the family, walk child to school and take subway to work, greet people in the building, answer emails, bring post-its and markers for class, post a conversation starter on the board and turn on music for students to discuss as they enter, deliver an interactive class, lunch with a colleague or students, attend committee meetings, plan for conferences, consult with students, try to go home to pick up child from school, Zoom meetings, go for a run, cook and eat dinner with family talking about what we did and how we felt that day, compose music and play piano, walk, personal calls, read, write what I am grateful for, plan for the next day, try to go to sleep on time.*

7 *Making the Right Moves: A Practical Guide to Scientific Management for Post-docs and New Faculty*, 2nd ed. (Howard Hughes Medical Institute and Burroughs Wellcome Fund, 2006), https://www.hhmi.org/sites/default/files/Educational per cent20Materials /Lab per cent20Management/Making per cent20the per cent20Right per cent20Moves /moves2.pdf.

You may have a plan for the day, but often the unexpected happens – expect it! Try to leave some open time in your calendar every week. Try to fit in some physical activity every week. Don't take your work on vacation – leave your laptop at the office (but do keep in touch!). Take a serious break from your routine. You will return refreshed and keen to get back to work.

Your First Grant

It is vital to apply and get grants in order to get a strong start in your independent research career and to sustain and grow your research enterprise. Writing a great grant is hard work. You may have had experience in writing scholarship applications, so you have developed some persuasive writing skills. You may also have helped write your supervisors' grants or been asked to help review grant applications during your graduate student and postdoc years – a great experience. Before you start writing, talk to mentors who have been successful in getting funded. Everyone has a different writing style. But do start early, write daily, get your ideas down, and then put your grant aside and have a fresh look at it later. Remember, you are writing for non-experts. Early in your drafting stages, present your grant as a three-minute pitch to a group of colleagues to gauge their level of excitement. If you can't get the people in your own department excited about your work, how do you expect to excite a distant group of reviewers? Have your grant reviewed internally by three people: a content expert, someone with grant panel experience, and a great writer. Meet with all three, together if possible. Accept critical comments. Make your grant easy to read. Don't cram the pages with details – leave some white space and use lists. What is the knowledge gap that you are trying to fill? Make sure that you are addressing the goals and aims of the purpose of the grant set by the granting agency. Are you asking the important questions in your field? Write several grants. Start with a highly focused, small grant to an agency, perhaps one with a focus on a particular disease. In Canada it is easier to get a small NSERC grant than a larger CIHR grant. You may not get your grant the first time you apply, but most new investigators are eventually successful in getting funding based on a strong track record as a graduate student and postdoctoral fellow.

> The average age of an applicant for a successful NIH R-01 research grant in the US is now over 40!

Here is a strategy for writing grants – use the W5H: what, why, who, where, when, and how? Start with *what* – what do you want to do? Next, *why* is it important? Is it new and exciting? Why is it important to the agency and is the project a good fit with its mission? You need to generate excitement by this point. *Who* will do the work? Describe your team. Do you have a track record in the area? Are you an expert? If not, have you recruited expert collaborators? Link specific projects to specific people. *Where* will you do all of the experiments that you suggest? In your lab? Describe the facilities available to you. *When* will the work be done? Specify the timeline. *How* will the work be done? What are the methods you will use? Are they the most appropriate and modern? The best ones? Avoid being too ambitious. Remember, you are no longer in a big lab with seemingly unlimited resources. Write aims that will appear as publications. Some aims should be straightforward, and should be supported by the literature and substantial preliminary results. Others can be longer term and more ambitious, showing your ability to anticipate future directions. Do not highlight potential problems; instead, provide alternative strategies. Try to be visionary and aim to be a leader in the field by asking the big questions.

A useful guideline to drafting your grant application is to propose an overarching goal to your research, then to propose three aims (two are too few, four are too many):

Aim 1. Incremental, easy to achieve, and has a short timeline; is a
   direct continuation of (your) previous studies; good for an MSc
   student or a new PhD student.
Aim 2. More ambitious, achievable over the five-year term of a grant
   and great for a talented PhD student.
Aim 3. Aspirational and high risk, but would be a major breakthrough
   in the field if completed successfully; perfect for launching your
   career in the big leagues and great for an experienced postdoc.

The box below shows an example of how you might apply this three-aim strategy, in brief.

Understanding talin: An essential partner in wound healing
Our goal is to understand the role of talin, a key cytoskeletal protein in cell adhesion and wound healing, and a potential drug target. This goal will be achieved with three aims:

Aim 1: To create a panel of talin mutants and determine their expression
   levels and effects on cell growth and morphology in transfected HEK cells.

Aim 2: To create transgenic mouse lines harbouring talin mutations and determine the effect of the mutations on the cell morphology and mobility of mouse embryonic fibroblasts.

Aim 3: To screen a drug library for compounds that either enhance or interfere with talin protein interactions and determine their effect on wound healing in tissue and mouse models.

Introduction: Mutations that disrupt the cytoskeletal protein talin delay wound healing; however, the mechanism by which this occurs is poorly understood. Using mouse embryonic fibroblasts from transgenic animals that harbour talin mutations in combination with cell sorting and high-resolution imaging, we will determine the effect of the mutations on cell size, shape, and mobility.

Great Teachers Are Made

Teaching methods at the university level are varied and evolving, but the formal lecture remains central. Not everyone can be a great lecturer, but everyone can be a good lecturer. Effective teaching can be learned. First, respect your students. Assume they are smarter than you are – many are! Everyone can learn something from everyone. Next, be very well prepared, well organized, and clear. Less is more. Do not overwhelm your students with details that are readily available to them. Go slow, even slower than you think appropriate, as it is the first time students are being introduced to the material, but make it interesting. Modulate your voice. Engage your audience. Make eye contact. Pause at moments to ask "Any questions?" Pause for group activities. Encourage critical thinking, especially in assignments and tests. Allow the students to use information they have or can obtain to solve a problem. It is never too early to expose undergraduate students to primary scientific literature, classic and modern. You can even use one of your own papers to great effect. The style and delivery of lectures vary according to the size of the class. An ideal size is 30 students or less, like a high school class. This promotes interaction and dialogue. A class of six is great for discussion. One-on-one is a good size for mentoring. Classes of 1,000 require performance art. You need to connect with the audience and be the focus of their attention. Attend lectures by top teachers and have them attend your lectures to give you feedback. Ask for advice. Attend teaching symposiums and workshops to learn about flipped classrooms, engagement tools, group activities, and how to incorporate experiential learning or community partners. Patience, practice, and dedication can make you a great teacher too.

Mentors Are Still Important

You will have had a number of mentors during your graduate training, but mentors continue to be important throughout your career. An essential ingredient to success as a university professor is to establish a close relationship with a mentor after you land your academic position. This could be a more senior member of the department or someone in a similar research area in a related department. A good choice for a mentor is someone who is 5 to 10 years more advanced than you in their career path. They have just gone through the processes that you will go through, such as setting up a lab, getting funded, teaching, and preparing for tenure review. The best mentors form a close bond with their mentees. The meetings can be as casual as a quick coffee to discuss a small issue, or as intense as a thorough review of your grant proposal. A Chair should certainly serve as a role model and mentor for faculty members in their department. They are, however, in a position of authority and often must make difficult decisions, making them less than ideal as a mentor sometimes due to their conflict of interest.

Tenure reviews come quickly at Canadian universities – typically within five to seven years of starting an academic position. Your main day-to-day focus, however, should be on the work to be done rather than the upcoming review. Taking care of your lab will in and of itself take care of your research, leading to good papers and grants, and this is what will earn you tenure. An assistant professor's daily activities include setting up a lab, obtaining funding, recruiting graduate students, publishing papers in excellent-quality journals, teaching at the undergraduate and graduate levels, and joining important committees at the local and national levels. But don't take on too many administrative duties early on. An external salary award is a powerful indicator of a competitive candidate, although many new investigator awards are based on the training track record. Your future research potential needs to be clearly demonstrated with an active lab supported by grants – in this early part of your career you need to be on an upward trajectory. Make yourself indispensable to the department, not only in your research but also in your teaching and committee work.

Tenured – Now to Relax?

Tenured professors do not have the luxury of putting their feet up on their desks drinking coffee while their labs tick along nicely. "Publish or perish." Research is increasingly competitive – both research funding and publications. There is no silver medal in research. Do you know the second group to discover insulin after Canadians Frederick Banting and Charles Best? Though publishing and obtaining funding remain difficult at all stages of the career, full professors do have the benefit of a long track record, a high level of expertise, a leadership position in their field, and the wisdom that comes with experience.

A tenured professor is responsible for keeping the wheels turning by putting energy into ideas, people, and funding. This continues for an entire career. Important papers published over a number of years attract citations that can now be easily monitored. Are you really only as good as your last paper? Not necessarily. A steady stream of a few highly cited papers is clearly better than a flurry of short papers that are only self-cited. Publications remain the currency of success in research. They are part of the virtuous (or sometimes vicious) cycle that leads to grant renewals, further research, and papers. The wheel turns, at times slowly, but turn it must. Great graduate students and postdocs are essential to the success of any lab and become a part of this cycle, often trapping them in a lab. Make sure this life is for you. If not, get off the merry-go-round, but step carefully.

Administration Lies Ahead

Many professors develop superb organizational and leadership skills and are often called upon to assume important and rewarding administrative positions. Academic leaders are often highly respected researchers. But great researchers don't always make the best administrators. Managing a department is very different from leading your own research group where you may be considered "the boss." Administration is not about "herding cats." It's about being a role model and a leader and setting a high standard. As Chair of a department you remain a peer faculty member, but with additional responsibilities. Your role will include supporting, empowering, and inspiring faculty members. It's about building consensus within the department around a common vision and direction. It's about never doubting the capabilities of others. It's about treating everyone as individuals and with empathy and respect. It's about removing barriers to success. It's also about being realistic and decisive. Most importantly, it's about trust. Many professors have the biggest impact of their career while in senior administrative positions as Chairs, Deans, and Presidents. Working on your leadership skills in graduate school will allow you to reap the many rewards of leadership positions throughout your career. It's a great way to give back and have a positive impact on the careers of others.

	Reinhart as Chair
Reinhart Reithmeier	*Being Chair of Biochemistry at the University of Toronto was the best job I ever had. It was also the hardest, especially in my first year. Professors are not trained to be administrators, although this is changing. I learned quickly that running a department is not like running your own lab. Not everyone will think your ideas are great. Other, more senior Chairs served as mentors for me and provided great advice and support. Early on in my tenure as Chair, I met with all faculty members and asked each one what they expected of me as Chair. The best suggestion I got was to "be a booster for the department." I also learned to be an active listener, hard for a professor who can talk for 50 minutes straight in a lecture!*

Conclusion

Being a professor is a rewarding career, and if it's the right fit for you, you should definitely pursue it, even though it can be challenging. You are at the cusp of research. You can be creative, collaborate, and mentor the future generation of scientists. You can inspire others in the classroom, in your lab, or at a student or community event. You have flexibility with your time and who you work with. You can create new programs and even become an academic leader. But there are plenty of enjoyable and rewarding careers outside of this prototypical academic track, which we will go into in more detail in the next chapter.

FURTHER DISCUSSION

1. What words or phrases would your supervisor use to describe you in a reference letter?
2. Give a three-minute pitch of your proposed research as an independent scientist to the class.
3. Discuss your teaching style and philosophy.

TAKING ACTION

1. Read *Planning a Career in Biomedical and Life Sciences*, 2nd ed., by Avrum Gotlieb (Academic Press, 2018).
2. Conduct an informational interview with a new faculty member to understand their challenges.
3. Research a department where you may be interested in a faculty position and write a mock letter to the Chair expressing your interest and what you could contribute to make the department more successful.

20 Succeeding beyond Academia

Key Messages

- Developing core competencies will position you for success no matter which career path you choose to pursue.
- Explore career options in different sectors of the economy, including in emerging areas.
- Networking will provide connections to diverse career opportunities.
- Be prepared to take advantage of job openings, including in the hidden job market.

The key ingredients in achieving a successful career outside academia are similar to those for inside academia. They include demonstrating excellence in scientific research, especially with collaborations, and having a strong set of core competency skills as described in chapter 9, "Developing Core Competency Skills." Depending on the sector, employers will care about your particular research expertise just as much as your communication skills and your role in a research team. If the non-academic job is a research position in a company or government, then your technical skills are certainly relevant experience. Other key competencies include interpersonal, teamwork, and leadership skills, an ability to effectively multitask within a budget and time constraints, a familiarity with innovative technologies, the ability to adapt, and being a personable, effective communicator with people of diverse educational and cultural backgrounds. The professional network you build should include both the academic and non-academic parts of your world. Your network can open doors to accruing pertinent experiences through collaborations, internships, or contract employment.

Your career trajectory may diverge from your original intention after graduation or during a postdoctoral fellowship, but remember your skills are transferable.

Before the Job: Accrue Pertinent Experiences

As outlined in the previous chapters, the successful acquisition of any job, whether academic or not, depends on thoroughly reflecting on your personal values, skills, and interests, setting SMART goals (see chapter 9, "Developing Core Competency Skills") using an Individual Development Plan (IDP), strengthening competency skills, and creating meaningful engagements *during* your graduate education. Try to find opportunities to "talk the job, walk the job" for your intended career, as described in part V, "Networking: Meaningful Engagement with Others." If you are interested in a career in science communication, then accrue writing opportunities through student-run publications and your own professional blog. If you are aiming to be in science policy, then be involved with a student cause, volunteer for local political campaigns, or attend national science policy meetings.[1]

Charlie's Story

From our experience, many students think that they should keep *every* career option open. Such a concept may work in the first or second year of graduate school, when you are still exploring career pathways and deciding what would be a good fit for you. However, after exploring with research, informational interviews, and a network, it is best to focus on two or three different career pathways, as pursuing and applying for everything at once is overwhelming.

We illustrate this with Charlie's story. Charlie was in the third year of her PhD. Charlie entered Nana's office in a general state of confusion and anxiety. Charlie had many questions:

1. How do I plan for my career in the midst of uncertain times like the COVID-19 pandemic?

---

1 See Canadian Science Policy Centre website: https://www.sciencepolicy.ca/.

2. How do I build an effective timeline to completion if I am uncertain about my research output due to challenges with completing my experiments?
3. Should I go for a postdoctoral fellowship if I know I do not want to become a professor?
4. What is job availability going to be like after I finish my PhD?
5. Where could I search for jobs – Canada, the US, or Europe?

All or some of these questions may have crossed your mind at some point, too. Nana told Charlie to take a deep breath. Nana then explained that these questions would be overwhelming for anyone and that they would tackle them one at a time. The first concept that they addressed was the impact of the COVID-19 pandemic on the research and future career of a PhD student. University Deans, department Chairs, and professors acknowledge the fact that some students may not have the same research output as they would have had if their experiments were not delayed or halted for several months. For some, graduation was delayed. Other students shifted their projects from bench work to computational studies. Indeed, some worked on COVID-19, since interest was high and new funding was available. If Charlie's supervisor and their previous students took about five to six years for a PhD, Charlie's timeline would probably stay the same. That would mean that Charlie has two to three years left of her PhD, which would give her a good timeline for career planning. Apart from a pandemic, other personal circumstances could have a similar negative impact on your productivity. Such situations cannot be predicted, and committee members will take this into consideration when assessing the body of work by the PhD candidate.

A postdoctoral fellowship is always an option even if becoming a professor is no longer on the table. A postdoc can serve as a transitional period to a career path outside academia, especially if working in industry is an option. When speaking to Charlie, Nana reinforced the notion that this choice should not be just to fill time, but rather it is a time to develop new skills and build a network.

Nana then asked Charlie not about what job would make her happy, but what type of work she would be happy doing. Charlie replied, "I want to be working with people, bringing science projects to the people. I am not sure how to do that." It is less stressful to think about the *type* of work than the target job *title*. Your job title may not even be invented yet. So don't focus on the jobs that may or may not be available. Charlie's answer made her realize that she wanted to cultivate the knowledge of jobs that revolve around this concept and the skills needed to work with the public, such as emotional intelligence and equity, diversity, and inclusion.

Nana and Charlie then discussed goals for Charlie for this year: exploring possible careers at nonprofit organizations, science centres, outreach programs, and clinical trial programs and conducting informational interviews. Next year, Charlie is to find a job to shadow and potentially make that into an internship, working in one of the sectors she explored.

As for location, Charlie wanted to stay in Canada close to her family, but she was open to exploring other cities. In that case, Nana recommended that Charlie build her network in a few, but not too many, other cities and perhaps spend a vacation in one of the cities that interested her, to see if she liked the city and to conduct in-person informational interviews with folks that live and work there. Setting boundaries on the location of your career alleviates anxiety, since it could be overwhelming to think that the whole world is an option. For example, if you have a partner who has to stay in a certain city, then you will only cultivate your network within that city. Such a focus will help you build your community and network within that area, which will increase your chances of obtaining a job in that area. Instead of sifting through hundreds of jobs in many places, your job search approach can be targeted and specific. Also, a lot of work is global and can be done remotely.

At least one, or better, two years before finishing your graduate training or postdoctoral fellowship, start assessing yourself and where you want to be. Where do you want to live? What kind of a job would you be happy with? What kind of work do you like to do and are good at? Do you have to consider your partner or other close family members or friends? Are you going to apply for jobs in government, industry, or a nonprofit organization? If you do not know these answers, try to intern, job shadow, attend a life sciences job fair, and talk to people who are in these fields already. Once you have assessed your needs and wants, it is time to see what is out in the world that fulfills your passion or curiosity. If your dream job does not exist, you can create the one you want. Often people reinvent a position to make it their own.

Again, try not to limit your search to a job title when you are ready to move on to a career. For example, perhaps your goal is to become a medical doctor but your real interest is helping others, which opens up many more job options. Try to figure out what type of work you would like to do, who would you like to help, and what you would like to be engaged in. If you start by reflecting and build upon that, you will find stepping stones to that dream career that will make you happy.

Applying for a Career outside Academia

If you are applying for an industry position, then hopefully you have a network of individuals who can give you information about relevant companies, have had some experiences that strengthen your core competency skills and, at the very least, have read up on everything about that company, ensuring that this company is potentially a good fit for you and that you are prepared for an interview. If you're applying for a management consulting position you should have hit all the stepping stones towards a consulting portfolio, and therefore have examples of initiative, teamwork, and problem-solving from your student consulting group or other community organization. If you are applying for a communications or outreach role, you will have completed the stepping stones of conducting informational interviews with people in this field and found relevant and meaningful engagements and experiences.

The actual application, including the cover letter and résumé, should set the stage for what you can offer the company. During the interview, you will then show that you have been preparing for this job over a number of years with all of your pertinent experiences. Remember that if you get an interview, you have already demonstrated that you are qualified for the job.

> Your job application will demonstrate that you have already "walked the walk" of the job through your meaningful engagements.

You may enter a career and, in a few years, you may want to transition into something else. It will be the same recipe then as now: you will hit many stepping stones as you transition through various experiences and careers throughout your life. If you decide to go from an industry position into a nonprofit, it would be best if you had some nonprofit experience while you were in industry. If you want to transition back into academia from an industry setting, then try to have an academic mentor to help you find ways to effectively manage that transition as well. Applying for a career outside of academia from your PhD or your Master's degree is just the first of many such transitions that you will have throughout your life.

The Hidden Job Market

How do you find a hidden job? If the job is hidden, it is a position that is not advertised widely enough for just anyone to apply. A job may be hidden if the employer must recruit internally first before broadening the search, such as is done at some universities. To find out about hidden jobs, your network becomes a powerful tool. Here is a real example. A colleague was looking for a bioinformatics programmer who also had bench experience in a specific area of biochemistry, so he sent a message to all of his biotech contacts through LinkedIn, knowing that if one of his contacts referred somebody, the candidate will have already passed the first screen of "personality." Another example is a company that is looking for a certain individual with leadership qualities who also has experience in microarray assay development to lead a development team. The CEO has lunch with an affiliate company's CEO, and when she brings up that they are looking for such a person, the other CEO recommends a few scientists.

How do you become aware of these inside hidden jobs when your experience is limited to working hard in your own lab to publish in top journals? How do you find these jobs when you have only been inside of academia? This is where all those years of networking while being a graduate student and postdoc pay off. All the contacts you made then will now be in your LinkedIn network and you can see where everyone is in their career pathway. Email your contacts individually, not in a massive, nondescript group email. Tell them where your interests lie, and ask if they know of anyone who would be able to use your services.

You may also choose to work with a recruiter, as some know of hidden jobs. A recruiter is an individual who helps companies find the best candidates. Indeed, many companies use third-party recruiting agencies to find candidates, especially for leadership positions. Recruiting companies keep highly qualified individuals on their roster and will bring them forward as candidates for highly competitive positions. Be sure to update your online profile. Many companies will check your public profile. The recruiting company has prescreened the applicant pool to find highly qualified candidates. Once the recruiting firm picks a short list, these individuals are brought in to interview with the company's key players.

Even if the job is advertised, research the institution you want to work for. For biotech companies, research their research. What are they working on? Who is their lead scientist? What is their major product? Most importantly, do you believe in their product? Many leading pharmaceutical companies publish as well. The authors are all part of the company. How are they funded? Publications by the company disclose their funding, and this may be how they might find funding for you. If the company or nonprofit organization or government lab inspires you, write to them and tell them how you can help their company with your scientific expertise and teamworking abilities. Market yourself in a great cover letter and résumé.

> The knowledge of hidden jobs travels through word-of-mouth, from colleague to colleague through verbal discussions or on media such as LinkedIn.

	Nana applies for hidden jobs
Nana Lee	*After my two-year postdoc, I applied for three jobs, none of which were advertised. One was through my network and two were to places that I researched, and I wrote in my cover letter what I could do for them. I was offered all three jobs. Have a careful plan so that your job application is so specific for the employer, it is difficult to turn you down.*

If the job is advertised, as many are, you have to consider if the job description was written with a candidate already in mind. What does this mean? If an institution or a company already has someone they would like to hire, some of the larger companies legally must still advertise and make a short list of candidates after interviews. They may already have a candidate who they know will fit, but they are required to list the ad. For example, if the job listing is open for a short time, say a week, that is a good indication they have a candidate in mind. If the job posting seems very specific, it is probably written with a person in mind. Having said this, it is almost impossible to know if the ad was written for someone, so if you think you can beat the other candidate, then go for it! The "internal" candidate doesn't *always* get the job! And if you don't get the job, but stand out enough, you may even create an opportunity for yourself to do a student internship or part-time work. Some websites with job postings in the life sciences include LinkedIn, Biospace,[2] and Biotalent.[3]

At the end of the day, it is not about you taking a job, it is about you helping the company. CEOs want to hire people based on what they can offer the company. The company's job is not to train somebody who is a novice, but to bring in someone who will strengthen the

---

2 See BioSpace website: https://www.biospace.com/.
3 See BioTalent Canada website: https://www.biotalent.ca/.

company. Sure, you will have to be trained in their style and the team's methods, but you must possess something they think can benefit the growth of their company. Why else would they pay you a generous starting salary?

The Interview

Once you send in your great cover letter and résumé (see chapter 14, "Marketing Your Brand, Professional Emails, Cover Letter, Résumé, and Curriculum Vitae"), the next step is an initial phone, virtual, or face-to-face interview. This initial interview is usually prescheduled and is about 20 minutes in length. Most questions are not very scientific, as the recruiting personnel, sometimes from the HR department, are looking for qualified individuals who are great communicators and team players. It's about fit. Again, remember that if you receive an interview, you are qualified for the job. But can you work with the other employees and can they work with you? Some of the questions you may be asked during an initial interview are listed below.

Case examples of first-round interview questions

---

1. Could you describe a scenario at the workplace in which you resolved a conflict?
2. How would you describe yourself?
3. What sets you apart from all the other candidates for this job?
4. What are your strengths/weaknesses?
5. Could you describe a situation when you had to communicate your work to people of different disciplines?
6. What would you do if you were in charge of a project and some other team members were falling behind in meeting the deadline?

Use the STAR (situation, task, action, results) method in answering interview questions. Tell the stories of the impact you have made. Once you pass the phone or virtual interview, you are on to the in-person interview. This interview may be with just one decision-making group or person for one hour, or you may go for a half-day interview with many people on the team. For all of these interviews, you must be personable, have a great handshake or appropriate greeting, be enthusiastic, and know the company. Be familiar with their mission statement and think carefully about how you could help them achieve their goals.

Nana comes prepared	
Nana Lee	*For one of my interviews, I brought along a few papers published by the company and asked the scientists questions about the methods, to which they said,"Wow, I feel like I am at my PhD defense. You really know the work here."*

While the company is scrutinizing you, you scrutinize the company's work. If you are going to work there, you should understand and believe in their science, so ask them questions! Pretend you are the external committee member at a defence and ask questions without being too pushy.

Remember that at the face-to-face interview, it is also a time for you to ask questions to get to know the team, just as they asked questions to learn more about you. Ask about company culture and how everyone got there, details you do not see on their website. Chances are, you will know somebody who knows somebody who knows them. Find this common link and, if possible, mention genuine relevant contacts in the interview as well – "Oh yes, I did work with Maya a few years back." Ask them if they have opportunities for independent work and career development. Is there room to grow in the position you are applying for? Ask them, "What would you expect from me that is not written on the job description? How do you want me to help you? How do you assess performance?" Some other questions to ask are summarized on the Ladders website.[4]

During your interview, turn your cell phone off. Dress neatly and professionally. Give yourself plenty of time to get there as you will be navigating new directions, walkways, and buildings before the interview. Smile. Be pleasant and engaging. Be interested and be interesting. You may want to bring your laptop to show them a slide or two about your current work, if it is pertinent. Always have a clean copy of your cover letter and résumé on hand. You've got this!

Suggestions for virtual interviews

- Ensure you have ample lighting so people can see you; the best lighting is from a side profile.
- Make sure the background is uncluttered; a blank wall or a bookshelf works.

---

4 S. Ginsberg, "Questions to Ask Interviewers in an Interview," Ladders (2017), http://www.theladders.com/career-advice/interview-questions-stump-employers-job-interview.

- Check that all tech connections (such as sound, camera, and internet connection) are working at least a day prior to the interview.
- Prepare to have your résumé on hand so you can drop it into the chat box, if someone does not have it handy.
- Do not have beverages near your laptop.
- Wear a solid-coloured collared shirt or dress – grey or blue is best for video; it's good to avoid white or green.
- Mute your phone, but keep it handy as a back-up with telephone contact numbers of your interviewers.
- Make sure your housemates or family in the same space are aware of your interview so as not to disturb you.
- Practice talking to a camera to ensure your whole face is showing.
- Smile and remember to use pauses when necessary.
- Take note of the participants' names so you can write to them all afterwards to thank them.
- Practice with a friend.

Negotiating the Offer

Whew! You did it! You have a letter of offer delivered to you by courier or email. Often a telephone call comes first. The letter is thick and has many pages to sign dealing with salary, vacation, benefits, confidentiality, and intellectual property. Take your time and read it over carefully. If necessary, discuss it with your partner or spouse. Almost everything is negotiable, so only sign on the dotted line when you are truly happy with the whole package. Use your negotiation skills. Remember to think about common interests, not fixed positions. It is not all about salary. But if the offer is lower than you expected, state that, and back it up with facts from www.salary.com or www.glassdoor. com, which tells you the industry standard salary based on location. Salary is conditional upon experience, your publication record, out-of-school work experience, what you are bringing to the company, and location. Most great companies hire the best, not the cheapest. Other factors you should consider are vacation days, sick days, wellness days, family days, working from home options (although this may become available after you spend a few months on-site), intellectual freedom (can you consult for another company on the side?), daycare, daycare reimbursements, career development (it constantly continues!), stock options, pensions, and FedEx Days.[5] FedEx Days are days that you can spend working on anything you want that you think would benefit the company's product or efficiency. At the end of the FedEx Day, employees present their ideas over food and beverages. Ask the company if they have these, and if not, could they implement such days? Many great ideas come from these days.

As a part of your negotiation, make sure you have everything you need to function well and succeed in your new position, whether it is an ergonomic keyboard or chair, private office, assistant, or lab space. Do they have mentors you can be paired with? Depending on the company, some of these items should be negotiated before you accept the job. It is up to you and your own preferences as to when you want to ask for certain items, either during negotiations or during the first year. Having said that, have everything in writing with dates so each party is well informed. After you accept the offer it is difficult to ask for more. Also, remember that not all jobs start out as permanent ones. Most start out as probationary, a time for both you and the company to figure out if you are a good fit for each other. Consider contract positions as well. One-year contract positions are great entry-level positions, as most of them end up as permanent ones after a fulfilling year for both sides. Be well prepared for your negotiations and take time to consider the offer.

> Almost everything is negotiable.

Continual Success during the First Job

Congratulations! You are now in your first job after your graduate degree or postdoctoral fellowship. You are now sitting at your new desk, with a corporate email account, you've signed all the confidentiality and intellectual property ownership forms, and it is your first workday. Well done! How do you keep continuing to be successful? How do you maintain your growth as a professional? How do you continue to excel as a problem solver and scientific thought leader? Continue strengthening the core competencies you started working on in graduate school. Find mentors. Always. This is just the beginning. Among other things,

---

5 Watch this video on FedEx Days by Rob van Lanen (n.d.): https://www.youtube.com/watch?v=rtj713dntUw.

you will be managing grants, people, experiments, sales and marketing, pitching the project to investors, and assuring client satisfaction. These responsibilities are all about interacting with people and building strong relationships – the most important part of the job and your scientific career. Strengthen skills in giving, taking, and implementing feedback with action items. Strengthen emotional intelligence, conflict management, and cultural humility. A firm handshake, having a beverage over a deal, or knowing when to bow are all examples of cultural etiquette that may work in one world, but not in others.

Advice from Nana	
Nana Lee	*Be bold. Make a difference. Empathize with those around you. That could be your success.*

Conclusion

A few years down the road, you will experience things that may affect your career development, whether it be finding a partner to share a life with, children, aging parents, relocation, or wanting to grow in other directions. Constant self-reflection and assessment are necessary every few years to make sure you are happy with your career and life and to make sure you are not just "coasting." If you are continually promoted until you are President of Worldwide Sales, that's great! But is that what you want? You have climbed the corporate ladder, but is it the right ladder for you? You should be constantly growing and reinventing yourself as companies change due to public and scientific demands. Keep looking for opportunities to develop professionally. Expand your network. Keep learning even if it might be slightly uncomfortable. Invest in yourself by taking courses, attending workshops, and getting certificates to continue your personal growth, and obtaining qualifications for your next job. Have a five-year plan and a ten-year outlook. A common question during interviews is "Where do you want to be in ten years?" What are your goals and aspirations? Few jobs have security for life, and you will likely have many career transitions. As a PhD graduate, you are likely to have a creative drive that propels you into different and new pathways. Embrace the uncertainty with excitement and some plans. You can do it!

FURTHER DISCUSSION

1. Come up with a list of careers outside academia and discuss why they interest you.
2. Discuss a challenging situation you faced in your work or professional life and how you resolved it.
3. Interview a classmate about an outside interest they may include on their résumé.

TAKING ACTION

1. Research a company and prepare a list of questions to determine whether you are a good fit.
2. Connect with an alumnus through LinkedIn working in an area of interest outside academia and request an informational interview.
3. Do a remote mock interview with a colleague for a position outside academia.

21 Creating Your Science Career

Key Messages

- Career exploration beyond the traditional pathway to professor is a key to success.
- There are many positions within academia other than professor that are occupied by people with PhD degrees.
- Individuals with PhDs bring high-level skills to their work and have advanced opportunities.
- Be prepared to create your own career path to success.

As we covered in the last two chapters, diverse career pathways both inside and outside academia are available to Master's and PhD graduates. Indeed, new types of jobs – jobs that never existed before – are continually emerging. The pathways to some of these jobs have been covered in this guidebook. If, however, you are unsure of career options, seek help from professionals in career centres, look them up on Science Careers MyIDP,[1] and/or find a mentor or alumni who can answer your questions regarding these pathways. It's never too early to start your career exploration.

Explore Another Path

You have considered your values, interests, skills, and personality and are now ready to explore career options. To assist you, below is a list of non-academic career choices listed in categories by field. We recommend that you use these lists to start your career exploration. After you

---

1 See Science Careers MyIDP: https://myidp.sciencecareers.org/.

have explored the careers, perhaps by reading about them, select a few for a deeper dive and then conduct informational interviews. You may then go on to the other meaningful engagements that we discussed in the previous chapters. Your career should stem from your values, your interests, your skills, and what you care about as a person. Your career may not even exist yet, as you venture into graduate school. Your career may be something that you create. You may be an intrapreneur. You may be an entrepreneur. At the very least, we hope that with the tools gained from this book you can create your own pathway no matter where it leads. Do not feel as if you have to remain in a preconceived box, or stay within the lines, or even be inside the confines of the professions in these lists. Your graduate degree does not define you. You are not an MSc or a PhD, but a person with an MSc or a PhD, a credential that very few people hold.

> With your graduate degree, your professional network, and your ability to explore, you can create a job at a place where you are happy to work.

Careers outside the Professoriate

Business

Management consultant
Innovations officer
Market analyst
Recruiter
Venture capitalist
Founder and CEO of your own company
Research analyst at financial institution

Communications

Writer/editor for scientific journals
General science writer/editor for newspapers, newsletters, or hospitals
Writer for a grant writing service (e.g., at the University Health Network)
Science consultant for the entertainment industry
Patent officer/tech transfer officer/patent agent
Founder and CEO of your own company
Science/medical liaison
Science translator

Government

Research and development officer
Grant and research administration
Office of innovations
Policy advisor
Intelligence analyst
Forensic scientist
Biodefence researcher
Regulatory affairs officer
Educator

Science Industry

Pharmaceutical field scientist
Biotechnology application scientist
Artificial intelligence data researcher/analyst
Pharma or biotech sales representative
Medical affairs specialist (regulatory affairs, medical science liaison, reimbursement, medical information, market access)
Forensics analyst
Cosmetic industry scientist
Food supplement industry representative
Medicinal plant R&D scientist
Data analyst

Education

Lecturer/lab course coordinator or director
Learning strategist
High school teacher/head of science department
Tutor
Science outreach program leader
Graduate professional development program officer
Educational writer
Think tank moderator
Job coach

Nonprofit Sector

Independent science research foundation advocate
Social program coordinator

Public/global health organization volunteer
Environmental policy and research advisor
Health/hospital research scientist
Clinical trial manager
Food science/nutrition scientist in hospitals

Professional

Physician
Pharmacist
Dentist
Veterinarian
Lawyer
Health professional (nurse, physician assistant)
CPA

University/Hospital Research Institutes

Grant administrator
Graduate administrator
Undergraduate administrator
Career centre advisor
Research facilities manager
Animal care director
Health and safety officer
Trainer
Planner

The last category is a sector that few graduate students explore. Many PhDs continue to work in the academic sector – not as professors or lecturers, but often in high-level administrative positions in research offices or in managing large projects. Explore careers in this sector with which you are not very familiar but where you have an inside track. This is especially true for administrative and support positions within universities and hospital research institutes. Reach out to people working in the research office, in communications, and even in the Offices of the Vice Dean and Dean, right up to Vice President and President.

Useful career exploration websites for graduate students

- Canadian Association of Postdoctoral Scholars: https://www.caps -acsp.ca/en/
- Cheeky Scientist: https://cheekyscientist.com/
- Inside Higher Ed: https://www.insidehighered.com/
- National Postdoctoral Association: https://www.nationalpostdoc .org/
- Nature Careers: https://www.nature.com/careers
- PhD Career Guide: https://www.phdcareerguide.com/
- PhD to Life/Beyond the Professoriate: https://beyondprof.com/
- The Muse: https://www.themuse.com/
- The PhD Hub: https://thephdhub.com/20-amazing-websites-and -or-resources-for-phd-students/
- The Versatile PhD: https://versatilephd.com/
- University Affairs: https://www.universityaffairs.ca/

Nana's Story

Nana's current career did not exist before she created it. How did she do that? Here is her story.

Even as a PhD student, I was interested in mentorship and helping my peers explore their careers, as part of the student council. Throughout my postdoctoral fellowship and industry career, I was active in providing guidance and being part of career panel discussions for those junior to me. Thus, it was a natural career transition for me out of industry to more of a mentorship or teaching role in a university and to bring back the skills I had developed during my years in biotech. It was through my collaboration with key individuals, including Reinhart, that we created a pilot course in 2012 about graduate professional development (GPD). It was the first ever curriculum-embedded GPD course to be created in the Faculty of Medicine at the University of Toronto with a structured format for credit and a final grade. I did not start my career journey during my PhD thinking I would be "Director of Graduate Professional Development" one day. In fact, this position did not even exist at the time. However, I did know that I would be somehow involved with communications, science, and educating the next generation of scientists about core competencies and gaining skills through meaningful engagements. Hence, when the opportunity arose with Reinhart, our pilot course became multiple courses that became a full-time faculty position in 2017. If anyone wants to know more about how I created my own career, please feel free to contact me for an informational interview or a fireside chat with a group of students. As part of my current role, I have also been an intrapreneur, as I have created new programs and have advised on existing programs, such as the Graduate and Life Sciences Education PhD Leaders Program (https://glse.utoronto .ca/glse-and-dr-nana-lee-announce-innovative-phd-leaders-program), a higher education teaching workshop series, and new peer student initiatives around mentorship, wellness, and start-ups.

Outside of the academy, I also owned a small business running a music school with piano lessons. Nana Lee Studios started with teaching my own children, and when their friends visited, they became interested in piano, too. One friend learning piano grew into many kids learning piano, as other parents heard about my lessons and requested them too. I did not have a website or flyers. It was all through the network of the neighbourhood and word of mouth. By the end of one year, I had acquired 11 students and was thoroughly enjoying the experience. Apart from teaching music, I strengthened my skills in financial management and maintained positive relations with the children and their parents. My lifetime interest in music also led me to take song-writing courses at Berklee Online School of Music, start YouTube and Sound-Cloud channels with my compositions, and attend song-writing conferences, which further led me to making connections within the music industry. Time will tell where this will lead. I also recently reconnected with my first scientific love of space biology by attending my first space biology conference and connecting with researchers and education colleagues, and I found an education committee to stay involved. Discovering new communities of what you love to do and care about is a constant, lifelong meaningful engagement. Life is full. Have flexibility, imagination, and resilience. Follow your curiosity. If I can do it, you can do it, too.

Alumni Career Profiles

Zayna Khayat, PhD Biochemistry
It all started with a game of Ultimate Frisbee. Zayna's friends invited her to join in a Friday night sporting event. Being a dedicated PhD student, she hesitated because she had experiments to finish off as she neared the end

of her studies. Zayna decided to postpone the experiments for a day and instead participated in the Frisbee game. At the game, she met someone who worked for Boston Consulting Group (BCG). Zayna found out that BCG hires PhD graduates for their strong work ethic and problem-solving skills. She followed up with the BCG employee and requested a meeting with them for the following week to find out more about the company and their work. Zayna was now on BCG's radar through this new connection and she stayed connected on LinkedIn. Shortly afterward, her new contact told her about an opening at BCG, she was encouraged to apply, got an interview, and landed the job. Zayna often wonders what her career path would have been had she stayed in the lab that Friday night.

Tonny Chao Huang, MSc Medical Biophysics
Tonny started searching for careers halfway through his three-year Master's degree in Medical Biophysics. He was looking for opportunities in fast-paced environments where he could gain exposure to a diverse range of experiences at the outset of his post-academic career. He began his exploration by attending networking events hosted by local life sciences groups, which gave him a sense of the great variety of career paths available after graduate school. Through these events, he also found opportunities to volunteer and work part-time for local start-ups throughout the remainder of his studies. These experiences confirmed Tonny's desire for dynamic work with close-knit teams, but he wanted to expand his horizons even further. His curiosity eventually led him to management consulting, and after enjoying his experience in a few case competitions, he decided to pursue the industry during the last year of his studies by doing informational interviews with people from different companies. Shortly after his graduation, Tonny became a consultant with Kearney, a global strategy and operations consulting firm. He is now a senior manager with the company, where he focuses on building strategic partnerships and new business models for global consumer health and life sciences companies.

Masha Cemma, PhD Molecular Genetics
When Masha was finishing her PhD in Molecular Genetics at the University of Toronto, she already knew she would not follow the traditional path of a postdoctoral fellowship leading to a faculty position. Late in her PhD studies, Masha spent a term at the World Health Organization (WHO) in Geneva as a Global Health Fellow working on policy to combat anti-microbial resistance. Her PhD background in microbiology and

WHO experience positioned her for success during her Mitacs Canadian Science Policy Fellowship where she supported a newly created international network of high-containment laboratories. She then built her professional network by volunteering at the annual Canadian Science Policy Conference where a diverse range of stakeholders from academia, government, and industry gather to discuss emerging issues in science, innovation, and technology. Masha's experiences in science policy and her networking, together with a successful application to a Recruitment of Policy Leaders program, positioned her for her current job in the Office of the Chief Science Advisor of Canada. A solid publication record, networking, fellowships, and application to a formal recruitment program allowed Masha to realize her dreams of working in policy and having an impact on science beyond the lab bench.

Jamil Shariff, PhD Astrophysics

Aside from a deeper understanding of the origins of the universe, how does one benefit from spending six years building a state-of-the-art telescope and launching it on a helium balloon flying over Antarctica? Jamil, who completed his Astrophysics PhD at the University of Toronto on just such an experiment, found the answer to be surprising. Although the project's goal was to learn about cosmology, his work required him to understand every system onboard a craft flying in near-space, which engaged him in numerous engineering disciplines.

An aerospace colleague in Jamil's lab had contacts at MDA, the Canadian company famous for building the robotic "Canadarm" on the International Space Station. MDA was curious about the university's research on high-altitude ballooning. They invited Jamil to give a presentation at MDA and were surprised by the broad skillset afforded to graduates from his lab. This meeting led to an invitation to attend an annual MDA robotics conference. Jamil applied to present the next year, and had a five-minute conversation with a manager, who asked him to return for an interview. Jamil was offered and accepted a position at MDA as systems engineering staff on the "Canadarm3" robotic project for the upcoming Lunar Gateway: a new space station in lunar orbit.

Bruce Seet, PhD Microbiology and Immunology, MBA

Though he was once advised by an undergraduate professor to focus on a single area of study if he wanted to succeed, Bruce's career path has defied this advice. After his BSc in Human Physiology, he pursued a PhD in Microbiology and Immunology and a postdoctoral fellowship in Molecular Biology and Cancer in Toronto. During his time as a student, he began collaborating with a Swedish bio-instrumentation company that encouraged him to share his research at conferences and meetings around the world. These early experiences allowed him to gain industry exposure, refine his communication style, and expand his network inside and outside academia. Following his postdoctoral fellowship, he landed a contract role at GlaxoSmithKline (GSK) in their R&D Alliances team. After gaining a year of experience at the company and having established a reputation for delivering high-quality work, Bruce transitioned to GSK's Medical Affairs division as a Medical Product Manager (later called Scientific Advisor) to support the launch of their human papillomavirus (HPV) vaccine. In addition to the HPV vaccine launch, he subsequently supported the launch of GSK's H1N1 influenza vaccine for the 2009 pandemic, a massive effort by the company and a significant learning experience that would later serve him for the COVID-19 pandemic. Simultaneously, Bruce started a part-time MBA program at the University of Toronto, funded through a full scholarship, the Science to Business Fellowship, awarded by the Canadian Institutes for Health Research. Three years later, armed now with an MBA, Bruce took on a series of roles in other functional areas at the company, including marketing, policy, and market access and reimbursement, where he contributed his diverse knowledge towards different therapeutic disease areas including infectious diseases, cancer, rare diseases, and other specialty care areas. After eight years at GSK, Bruce joined Sanofi Pasteur as a Director of Medical Affairs, refocusing on vaccines. Over the next eight years, he expanded his responsibilities, helped grow the Canadian medical affairs team, capabilities and strategic impact, and established a new team of medical science liaisons. In 2022, Bruce embraced a new challenge as Head of Medical Affairs (Canada) at Novavax Inc., a relatively small but ambitious biotech company, where he's applying lessons gained throughout his career to build the company's profile and footprint in Canada. Bruce credits his success to diverse early experiences, an open mind, a passion for learning, exceptional mentors, and a strong work ethic, allowing him to capitalize on various opportunities throughout his career journey. He also acknowledges the value of his volunteer and community building activities outside of work, particularly through the efforts with his team at the Science to Business Network (S2BN), a nonprofit organization he founded in 2011. Reflecting on his path, Bruce quotes Louis Pasteur, a pioneer of germ theory: "le hazard ne favorise que les esprits préparés" (Chance only favours prepared minds).

Becky Chapman, PhD Chemistry
Becky Chapman decided that she would not be following an academic path halfway through her PhD in Physical Chemistry at the University of Ottawa. While she enjoyed her research and recognized its importance, Becky hoped to pivot towards the application of science to real-world issues through policy. She knew her curriculum vitae demonstrated interests beyond academia, as she had participated in governance societies throughout her studies. While writing her thesis, Becky regularly checked job postings and applied for any of interest. Her focus was almost entirely on the federal government, but by chance, she came across an ad for a position at a science policy not-for-profit called the Council of Canadian Academies (CCA). The job sounded interesting but called for non-academic work experience she did not have. Becky applied anyway and secured an interview. While the hiring committee was concerned about the absence of the desired work experience, they were impressed with her application and interview, and offered her an internship. The six-month internship gave Becky the opportunity to learn the art of non-academic writing and communication, and she was able to demonstrate she had the skills and aptitudes to be successful at CCA. She parlayed the internship into a permanent position at CCA, where she enjoys researching and writing on a wide range of science topics to support decision-making in Canada.

Alena Rudolph, PhD Organic Chemistry
During her BSc in Chemistry in the University of Waterloo co-op program, Alena gained valuable work experience at several companies and discovered her passion for organic chemistry. Prior to starting

her PhD in Organic Chemistry with Mark Lautens at the University of Toronto, she worked as a medicinal chemist at a pharmaceutical company near Boston. After her PhD, Alena became a postdoctoral fellow in the Netherlands in the laboratory of a Nobel Prize winner and an inventor of molecular motors, Prof. Ben Feringa. Alena then moved back to Canada to an R&D position at a Canadian contract development and manufacturing organization (CDMO) where she started at the lab bench and eventually moved to her present role as a supervisor and a technical leader. Her career in a CDMO has proven to be one of the more technically demanding, fast-paced, and multidisciplinary environments that she could have aspired to work in. Alena works on challenging projects, including synthesizing one of the most complex active pharmaceutical ingredients on the market. Alena would advise that a graduate degree is just as much about personal growth as it is professional growth. Learn from your peers and mentors, by what they do and don't do well. Move around the world and learn to judge things from different perspectives. Take risks; some of the most exciting opportunities lie in unlikely places.

Conclusion

Exploring career options should begin early in your graduate studies. It is important to make informed decisions, so gathering information is vital. Some of these decisions include: Should I complete a Master's degree or go on to a PhD? Should I do a postdoc? Do I really want to be a professor? How can I make career transitions? What are my options? Who can help me? If you are contemplating academy versus industry or to postdoc or not, Nana's article may help guide you in your decision.[2] The stories discussed in this chapter illustrate the different career paths of successful graduate students. It's time to take action and write your own story.

---

2 N. Lee, "Developing Your Thought Leadership for Any Career," *Inside Higher Ed* (2021), https://www.insidehighered.com/advice/2021/05/17/advice-grad-students-determining-whether-they-should-pursue-career-academe-or.

FURTHER DISCUSSION

1. Work in groups to create a list of different positions in industry or government.
2. Discuss how your values, interests, skills, and personality are a good fit for a position of interest to you.
3. Discuss the challenges you foresee in moving into this career option.

TAKING ACTION

1. Find a job ad in a sector that you are interested in pursuing and determine how well you meet the qualifications.
2. Invite alumni working in your area of interest to an in-class career panel.
3. Visit your university career centre for a tailored career exploration consultation.

PART VII

Conclusion

22 Personal Reflections

Key Messages

- The realization that most PhDs do not become professors motivated Nana and Reinhart to create professional development courses and write this book.
- A PhD can prepare you for a successful career in academia and beyond if you make the most of it.
- Success has many meanings based on your values, interests, skills, and personality.
- Life is for living.

Writing this book during the COVID-19 pandemic has been a time of deep reflection for Nana and Reinhart. We decided that the experiences we have accumulated in teaching graduate professional development courses and what we have learned from the stories of our students should be documented for the benefit of others. Our hope is that this book will help guide you on your own path to success.

Nana Lee

Succeeding in graduate school and beyond is in your hands, with support from your mentors, network, and peers. Success "metrics" in academia typically include a high grade-point average, strong letters of recommendation, awards, scholarships, publications, grants, citations, and invitations to speaking engagements. These types of metrics are measurements created by a very long tradition of the academy, from the University of Bologna in Italy, founded in 1088 to promote learning in monasteries, to modern universities created to train individuals and be places where research is conducted in fields such as medicine, mathematics, and government. Along with this historical background, we have created quantitative metrics such as grades and citations to measure scholars as successful. But this is too narrow a view.

In the modern era, many PhD and MSc graduates pursue careers outside academia and government. Employers in the twenty-first century, particularly those outside the academy, may look at different metrics for success. The impact of technology – in the era of "information at your fingertips" – has changed even the measurements in the classroom. Youth today are probably more likely to remember *where* to find information, as opposed to knowing *what* the information is. For example, knowing all of the structures for the amino acid sidechains would be helpful, as usually measured on traditional class tests. However, with this information easily available on your personal phone, the potential employer would want the student to be aware of the different sidechains, but they would likely be more interested in whether the student knows how these different types of amino acids would change the structural properties of the protein – metrics that address problem-solving and critical-thinking skills rather than recall ability.

Success in the career world outside of academia does not only include all of the metrics we use for scholarship and research productivity, but it also includes the impact of how your research and engagements relate to the potential employer's own vision. Success will have a different definition for you, especially after you have completed the metrics of success in academia. What is beyond those metrics? Success is defined by you with your views of the world, community, family, and work. Success to some people is knowing that they have tried their best and learning from failures. Knowing your true self through reflection, participating in impactful activities throughout your life, achieving your goals by overcoming challenges, and always striving to grow every step of the way – doing all of this while acquiring a career that could help you achieve your fullest potential as a professional and a mentor – perhaps this is what we can call success.

As for me, perhaps I could have stayed in a traditional research academic role. Perhaps I could have majored in piano composition or performance, like my music teacher had recommended. Perhaps I could have accepted the postdoctoral fellowship at the Ames Research Center. Perhaps I could have stayed in the biotech industry. Perhaps I could have stayed in the United States or worked in South Korea. I know that during every step of my career and professional journey, I made decisions based on the information that I had at that time, while taking into consideration my personal and family life, which are all important to me. We all go through hardships. We all have dreams. I believe that life success cannot be measured by a diploma or a report card or a high-paying job. I believe success is being able to utilize all the tools that you have; with your interests, skills, and motivations while empathizing with others, you can create or be part of something positive and fulfilling.

Success can be learning how to read on your own, overcoming financial challenges for you and your family, being the first person in your family to attend university, or implementing what you have discovered for scientific and societal growth. Success can be starting new in another country. Success can be taking little steps in shifting how a community views your ethnicity, culture, or gender so that you are safe, welcomed, celebrated, and cherished. Success can be incorporating your professional career with the needs of your family, your parents, your partner, your children, and yourself. Success can be overcoming your own fears and living your own truth.

Success is trying our best, learning from mistakes, and helping others – living a fulfilling life. Why do we keep going to school? Why do we keep on learning? Because one day you're going to take all of that knowledge – your past, your present, your network, and everything you've ever done – to help somebody just by being you and extending your hand. I believe that it is every hand that you have helped along your way, including yourself in a time of crisis or doubt, that is a true measure of success. Considering that the readers of this book are graduate students and postdoctoral fellows, we have all been lucky to have attained our positions in academia. I hope you can continue your journey, carry forth your luck, be your version of success, and help others for now and for the future.

On a personal note, my mother was a life mentor for me. She taught me to strive to be my best and to face challenges with grace. She advised me to find my dreams and career first in my twenties before I started a family, if I wanted one. Sadly, she passed away from cancer during my PhD work. She did tell me that if she were to visit Earth in spirit, she would fly back as a butterfly. The illustrations of the butterflies in chapters 19 and 20 are in memory of how her mentorship and values helped me in my careers in and out of academia. May my experiences and my words, which were all possible due to her, help you as well. She still continues to visit me in my dreams, telling me to listen to my heart and that everything will be okay. I try to live with her zen-like calmness in my own life. I hope some of the words in this book provide you with her gift as well. In addition, my own success, especially during the last few years of writing this book, was the continued development of emerging to speak with my authentic voice – professionally and personally. I continually develop my skills in EQ, listening, and setting healthy boundaries – all the while feeling uncomfortable at times and learning from my mistakes along the way. Perhaps my Asian culture affected my willingness to truly embrace failure and the ability to speak up, but I have strengthened these skills and continue to do so as I write this. Just like you, I am continuing a life-long development of myself. And I embrace all of it! I hope you discover and embrace your successes and failures, which wait for you beyond the horizon with just as much zest and fortitude.

Reinhart Reithmeier

There has been a transformative change in graduate education in the new millennium. The traditional role of professors has been to train the next generation of professors using an apprenticeship model. This model worked well when universities were expanding and professors were retiring at age 65. Professors liked this model. Students could become knowledgeable enough in their discipline to teach at the university level through extensive course study taught by professors, typically in the first two years of graduate school. Students learned the craft of research at the hands of a master with years of experience in the field. Many professors were leaders in their field and viewed as mentors and successful role models. Students were keen to follow in their footsteps. This was my career path as described in this article.[1]

There is a growing recognition that not all PhD graduates become professors. This was always the case, but the situation became more acute with the increased investment in postgraduate education and an increase in the number of PhD graduates. This caused a serious misalignment, where PhDs continued to be trained for work in an academy that was already at capacity. Graduate students were the first to notice this change. There emerged many articles in popular magazines about how a PhD was a waste of time,[2] and even books like the highly

---

1 R.A.F. Reithmeier, "Lessons from a Red Squirrel, Mentors, and the Pathway to Success," *Biochemistry and Cell Biology* 92, no. 6 (2014), https://doi.org/10.1139/bcb-2014-005.
2 See "Why Doing a PhD Is Often a Waste of Time," *The Economist* (2016), https://medium.economist.com/why-doing-a-phd-is-often-a-waste-of-time-349206f9addb; M. Fisher, "Is Getting a PhD a Waste of Time?" *The Atlantic* (2011), https://www.theatlantic.com/culture/archive/2011/01/is-getting-a-phd-a-waste-of-time/339261/.

rated novel *A Degree of Futility*,[3] by PhD graduate and journalist M.P. Fedunkiw, that tells the story of three history PhDs trying to survive as they enter a tough academic market in the year 2000. While most students entered PhD programs with the intention of becoming a professor, many realized as they moved through their graduate program that it would not happen for them or that it is not for them.

The term Alternative Academic Careers (Alt-Ac) crept into the parlance, reinforcing the view that success was landing a coveted faculty position and that others had to make do with an alternative career that was definitely a Plan B. In the Humanities it was common for PhD graduates to take on part-time work as sessional lecturers just to stay in the academy, hoping for that elusive tenure-track position at their home university or at another prestigious institution. Some took jobs at smaller schools or left their home country to find meaningful employment. It was "Professor or nothing." PhDs in science were trapped in endless postdoc positions, desperately applying for any faculty position in sight. Many PhD graduates clung to the notion, reinforced by their professors, that success was landing a job as a professor and that anything else was a failure. Many students were at a loss for what to do after graduation and anxiety levels about career paths were at an all-time high, although this is slowly changing.

Universities began to get the message that not all of their PhD graduates would end up as professors. Students were struggling to find a rewarding career path. Professors were not equipped to advise on diverse careers. "Just do a great postdoc in a great lab and everything will work out" was a common refrain. But things are finally changing. Career centres traditionally set up to advise undergraduates began to open their doors to graduate students. Schools of Graduate Studies and departments began to set up courses and workshops not only to assist graduate students in their current studies, but also to better prepare them for work outside the academy.

Where do all of these new graduates go if the professoriate market is limited? Career outcome data were lacking for recent PhD graduates. This gap was addressed early on in the US by groups like the NIH and the Council of Graduate Schools, and in Canada with initiatives like the 10,000 PhDs Project at the University of Toronto and at other universities like University of British Columbia and University of Alberta. Now, almost all universities track their Master's and PhD graduates

---

3 M.P. Fedunkiw, *A Degree in Futility* (Friesen Press, 2014).

and make the data publicly available on their websites. The career outcome data show that about one quarter of recent PhD graduates end up as tenure-track professors. In the sciences this number is lower, at ~15 per cent. So this career pathway is still open but remains highly competitive.

The reality that the majority of PhD graduates do not become university professors led Nana and I to create a professional development course in the Department of Biochemistry at the University of Toronto with the goal to better prepare our PhD graduates for diverse careers in the academy and beyond. We worked on helping students build their transferable skillset, with a focus on communication, and their professional network. We provided students with the tools to do so – tools like résumé-writing workshops and informational interviews. We also introduced concepts like mindfulness, strategic planning, and design thinking. We quickly realized that developing these skills was not only important for success after graduate school, but also in graduate school. That realization was the reason to write this book.

Appendix: Sample Syllabus

BCH2024H Graduate Professional Development (GPD)

Course instructor: Nana Lee, nana.lee@utoronto.ca
Credit: 0.25

Welcome to GPD!

You are about to embark on an adventure. GPD empowers learners to optimize their graduate experience to prepare for any career path. The primary goals of this course are to (1) reflect on your skills, interests, and values; (2) explore options; (3) learn how to set a professional development plan during your studies and effectively market yourself during and after graduate school. Being part of the GPD team also grants you lifetime office hours.

Reading

Success after Graduate School: A Guidebook for Biomedical Graduate Students to Optimize Their Graduate Experience by Nana Lee and Reinhart Reithmeier (2016). You may pick it up from the U of Toronto bookstore in the Medical Books reference section or have it mailed to you. *IDP* refers to the individual development plans from Science Careers: https://myidp.sciencecareers.org/.

Course Outline

(Meets for two hours every two weeks in a classroom where tables and chairs are set in groups of four, with tables in a circular pattern to promote collaboration)

Class	Prework	Topics to discuss	To bring	Deliverables
Class 1	Start reading the book, update IDP, view videos 1–3, 5 (10 min. each)	Individual Development Plans: Options	Updated SMART goals	
Class 2	Videos 6–7	Brainstorming Your Meaningful Engagement Informational Interviews Reading a Job Description Script Feedback	Your job description Your three-minute script	
Class 3	Videos 8–9 Videos 10–12	Q & A on Networking Group Activity on CARs	Job application with CARs	Job description, cover letter, résumé for peer feedback
Class 4	Video 13 Video 14	Mock Interviews Presenting Impromptu Peer Feedback on Slide	One static slide	Job description, cover letter, résumé to instructor
Class 5	Videos 15, 17–20	Q & A on videos 3MT Practice	Revised static slide	
Class 6	Video 21	3MT Final Presentation, Networking	Final slide	3MT presentation, IDP & book reflection, informational interview presentation (if applicable)

Breakdown of Marks (deliverables + presentations + attendance/ participation)

1 Written Assignments (50 per cent)
   Job application: Write a one-page cover letter and a résumé for a job description or proposal. Include the job description as well. **Prepare for class three discussion.** Electronic copies due by **class four** as word documents. **(25 per cent)**

IDP and book reflection: Write a 700–900 word reflection (not a summary or review) on *Success after Graduate School* and how it changed your views, if any, on designing your own graduate experience and/or career path. Also include a reflection on your IDP with three specific SMART goals by **last class. (25 per cent)**

2 **Presentations (25 per cent)**

Three-Minute Thesis (3MT) final: Present your research in three minutes with one static slide to the general public, describing why it is significant to today's society. (12.5 per cent)

Guests: Present your informational interview summary or bring in a guest for last class. (12.5 per cent)

3 **Attendance and Participation (25 per cent)**

Rubrics and Suggestions

Deliverable #1. Job Application: Cover Letter/Résumé (10 points each, 20 points in total)

Criteria – Cover Letter	Points
Company header and date	1
Opening paragraph	2
Middle section (WHY that company, what are you offering)	4
Last paragraph/closing	1
Signature	1
Your contact info	1

Criteria – Résumé	Points
Overall appearance	2
Experience – CAR statements	6
Education	1
Skills if applicable, selected awards/publications	1

Deliverable #2. Book Reflection (20 points in total)

Criteria	Points
Insightful new ideas regarding your own career development and reasonable SMART goals with specific next steps	10
Clarity, grammar, professionalism	10

Presentation #1. Three-Minute Thesis (20 points in total)

Criteria	Points
Clarity	5
Time (between 2.5 minutes and 3 minutes)	5
Helpful illustration	5
Engagement	5

PRESENTATION #1. 3MT TIPS AND TOOLS

1. Start with a story or a question. Here is a good example: "Do you know that our own immune cells fight cancer? Some of us may be walking around with cancer cells (pause) but are perfectly healthy because our own immune cells can overcome them. (Pause) Let me tell you a war story happening in our own bodies."
2. Avoid filler words such as "like, so, uhm, ok, right, uh." If you feel compelled to use them, just leave a slightly longer pause.
3. End with a pause and then "Thank you."
4. Slide has a title on top, your name on the top right hand corner without PIs, institutions, degrees.
5. Every word and picture are placed in the slide if essential to the story. Try to refer to your slide within the first 20 seconds, if not earlier, and continue on with the illustrations as visual aids. Minimize text.
6. Show your confidence, own the room with your story and your presence. You are the expert.
7. Best way to practice is to draw the slide as you tell the story like a chalk talk.
8. Abandon the notes and use cue words on the slide. A good series of illustrations will bring forth the story.

Presentation #2. Networking Event

All students are to contact a professional who has a career you would perhaps explore after graduate school. Guest should be somebody who has been through the job application and interview process, landed their job, and is now a working professional who is being remunerated for their work. Sources of potential guests: LinkedIn with keywords of your alumni department, network of your labmates, 10,000 Coffees, LSO, LSCDS.

You (not a friend) are to invite them to this networking event. If they do not respond in two weeks, ask with a gentle reminder; if they do not write back, do not contact them again. Try to find someone else. Please email me your confirmed guest's name, degrees, job title, and affiliation for the networking event.

If your guest cannot make it for this date, request an informational interview. Please prepare a two-minute presentation to summarize your informational interview experience during Class #6. Topics to include are how you contacted them, how they made their career transition, and what you thought of the whole experience. Enjoy the process!

Individual Development Plan Consults

As part of GPD, we offer a 30-minute, one-on-one consult to discuss anything you like regarding your own GPD and to go over an IDP.

I will be sending out a Doodle to book everyone's meetings – please only check ONE timeslot indicating when you can make it, and make sure nobody else has signed up for that time.

Policies

Communications

Instructors will use the course's Quercus site and UToronto email addresses when communicating with students. As a matter of professionalism, students are expected to use their UToronto email addresses as well.

Academic Accommodations

Students with diverse learning styles and needs are welcome in this course. In particular, if you have a disability or health consideration that may require accommodations, please feel free to approach the Course Coordinator and/or the accessibility services office (http://www.accessibility.utoronto.ca) as soon as possible. The accessibility services staff are available by appointment to assess specific needs, provide referrals, and arrange appropriate accommodations. The sooner you let us know your needs, the quicker we can assist you in achieving your learning goals for this course.

Coursework

Re-marking requests should be made directly to the Course Coordinator within two weeks of the return of the marked work. Re-grading requests may result in an increase, no change, or decrease in the grade assigned. There are no makeup assessments and no grades will be redistributed to other assessments. Late reports are not accepted unless for medical reasons. Email directly to the Course Coordinator for consideration of assignment extensions.

Academic Integrity

Please refer to the SGS calendar for the definition of plagiarism and how not to plagiarize.

Resources

Video links listed on the course website: http://biochemistry.utoronto
.ca/courses/bch2024h-professional-development/
Simon Sinek's "Start with WHY": https://www.youtube.com/watch?v
=sioZd3AxmnE
Adam Leipzeg's "How to Know Your Life Purpose in 5 Minutes": https://
www.youtube.com/watch?v=vVsXO9brK7M
France A. Córdova's "Embrace Uncertainty": http://science.sciencemag
.org/content/351/6276/994
Résumé CARs: http://careerrocketeer.com/2012/06/what-does-a-car-have-to
-do-with-your-resume.html
Résumé Action Verbs: https://gecd.mit.edu/sites/default/files/jobs/files
/resume-action-verbs.pdf
Core Competencies: http://www.workforce.com/2002/09/03/31-core
-competencies-explained/

Updated syllabus © 2023 by Nana Lee. Instructors are welcome to use the syllabus in whole or in part with permission by Nana Lee.

Glossary

Allyship: a sustained effort by a trusted individual to engage with a disadvantaged group to bring about meaningful change.

Competencies: skills and abilities that you are able to demonstrate.

Cover letter: a one-page introduction expressing your interest in a job, submitted along with your résumé.

CRAVE: a mnemonic for assessing your activities to ensure they are Clear, Realistic, Achievable, Validated, Expectations.

Curriculum vitae: a written summary of your academic career, education, awards, activities, and publications.

Emotional intelligence: the ability to understand and control your own emotions and to recognize and manage the emotions of others.

Entrepreneur: an individual who creates and runs a business and is willing to take risks to do so.

Equity, diversity, and inclusion (EDI): Equity involves creating equal opportunities for all by eliminating systemic barriers like discrimination and bias. Diversity recognizes the value of individual, societal, and cultural differences. Inclusion is creating an environment where all are welcome and celebrated.

Gantt chart: a graph that displays various activities along a time scale, commonly used in project management.

Graduate professional development: a series of activities, including courses, workshops and career panels, designed to build the skillset and network of graduate students and better prepare them for careers in academia and beyond.

Growth mindset: the ability to take on challenges and learn from them.

Impact: the positive and measurable effect of activities on others or on an organization.

Individual Development Plan (IDP): a living planning document that outlines your career goals and the skills needed to achieve them.

Informational interview: a short, private conversation with someone working in an area of potential interest to you.

Interests: what you like to do.

Internship: a paid period of training designed to build skills and experience.

Intrapreneur: a person within an organization who develops innovative solutions and products.

Leader: a strong communicator with a vision who inspires others to work together to achieve a common mission.

Meaningful engagement: to work purposefully with others or within your organization.

Mentor: an experienced and trusted advisor who influences the growth and development of another more junior individual.

Multitasking: the ability to organize multiple tasks to complete them in a timely fashion.

Network: an interactive collection of people with whom you share a common interest.

Personality: individual traits affecting thinking, feeling, and behaviour.

Principal investigator: typically a professor who leads a research team and obtains the resources through grant applications.

Résumé: a short (two-page) competency-based summary of your qualifications and experience relevant for a particular position.

Role model: a person whom you admire and hope to emulate.

Skills: expertise you have developed to perform an activity or task.

SMART: a tool to organize and achieve goals (Specific, Measurable, Achievable, Relevant, and Time-Bound).

Sponsor: an individual of authority who supports another more junior individual, such as a graduate student or postdoc, through mentoring, providing letters of reference, and building connections.

Stipend: a salary provided to a trainee, such as a scholarship or fellowship.

Supervisor: in scientific research, a professor who guides your research.

Transferable skills: abilities that can be applied to various tasks and professions, such as communication, critical thinking, teamwork, and leadership.

Values: things that are important to you that guide your decisions and interactions with others.

Wellness: developing habits through diet, sleep, and activities to promote physical and mental health.

Work-life integration: the ability to successfully blend career and personal activities and priorities.

Further Reading

Barker, K. *At the Helm: Leading Your Laboratory*, 2nd ed. Cold Spring Harbor Press, 2010.

Burnett, B., and D. Evans. *Designing Your Life*. Knopf, 2016.

Cohen, C.M., and S.L. Cohen. *Lab Dynamics: Management and Leadership Skills for Scientists*, 3rd ed. Cold Spring Harbor Press, 2018.

Fisher, R., W. Ury, and B. Patton. *Getting to Yes: Negotiating Agreement without Giving In*. Penguin Books, 2011.

Gottlieb, A.I. *Planning for a Career in Biomedical and Life Sciences*, 2nd ed. Academic Press, 2018.

Haggerty, K.D., and S. Doyle. *57 Ways to Screw Up in Grad School: Perverse Professional Lessons for Graduate Students*. University of Chicago Press, 2015.

Humphrey, J. *Speaking as a Leader*. Jossey-Bass, 2012.

Iconomopoulos, F. *Say Less, Get More: Unconventional Negotiation Techniques to Get What You Want*. Collins, 2022.

Kelsky, K. *The Professor Is In*. Crown, 2015.

Peggs, H.M. *Supervising Conflict: A Guide for Faculty*. University of Toronto Press, 2023.

Sinche, M.V. *Next Gen PhD: A Guide to Career Paths in Science*. Harvard University Press, 2018.

Sinek, S. *Start with Why: How Great Leaders Inspire Everyone to Take Action*. Portfolio, 2009.

Index

Page numbers in **bold** indicate glossary definitions. Page numbers in *italics* indicate figures.

Printed and bound by CPI Group (UK) Ltd, Croydon, CR0 4YY

09/06/2025

14685781-0001